Teachers
Make a Difference

TEACHERS MAKE A DIFFERENCE

Thomas L. Good
University of Missouri

Bruce J. Biddle
University of Missouri

Jere E. Brophy
University of Texas, Austin

UNIVERSITY
PRESS OF
AMERICA

LANHAM • NEW YORK • LONDON

University Press of America,™ Inc.

4720 Boston Way
Lanham, MD 20706

3 Henrietta Street
London WC2E 8LU England

Library of Congress Cataloging in Publication Data

Good, Thomas L., 1943-
 Teachers make a difference.

 Reprint. Originally published: New York: Holt,
Rinehart, and Winston, c1975.
 Bibliography: p.
 Includes index.
 1. Teaching. 2. Educational tests and measurements.
3. Educational research. 4. Educational innovations.
I. Biddle, Bruce J. (Bruce Jesse), 1928-
II. Brophy, Jere E. III. Title.
[LB1025.2.G623 1982] 379.1'54 82-11007
ISBN 0-8191-2157-6 (pbk.)

All University Press of America books are produced on acid-free
paper which exceeds the minimum standards set by the National
Historical Publications and Records Commission.

Preface

A major purpose of this book is to document the fact that teachers and schools *can* and *do* make a difference in the educational progress of students. Unfortunately, it has become a kind of national sport to criticize American education, and persons who have limited contact with schools often develop and promulgate exaggerated and negative views (such as, schools are stultifying environments for students) about the quality of schooling. These views often turn out to be more myth than fact when reports from classroom studies and classroom students are examined. Nevertheless, the cumulative impact of popular articles, news stories, and specious or incomplete research reports has helped to erode public enthusiasm for paying educational bills.

Critics of education pose countless questions, but perhaps those most pressingly in need of answers include the following: Why spend more money for public education if increased expenditures do not improve student progress? Why spend vast amounts of money training teachers if teachers make no difference (that is, behave the same way in the class or have the same effects on students)? Why spend money for research when definitive prescriptions for classroom life have not been found?

It is our intention to take up such questions and to show that teachers and schools *do* make a difference. Furthermore, we believe that in the past decade classroom research has "paid off," and that subsequent funding of appropriate research will provide even richer dividends.

However, our intention is not to whitewash teachers and schools. Much of what goes on in *some* schools is undesirable, but much of life in other schools is acceptable, interesting, and occasionally inspiring. Our goal is to put criticism and arguments in proper perspective. Schools have a full range of effects on students. This is true for programs and innovations as well. For example, there are both effective and dreadful open classrooms, and there are both exciting and dull self-contained classrooms. We will discuss such differences and identify some of the ways in which teachers and schools make a difference.

A second purpose of this book is to illustrate the appropriate use of research data in the attempt to improve educational practice. The book consistently argues against fadism by illustrating that "attractive" ideas offering simple solutions for solving complex educational problems turn out to be more fiction than fact when research data are collected and examined. Research, we argue, should *precede* and guide educational innovations, especially when such innovations involve vast sums of money. Unfortunately, as we shall see, educational research typically *follows* innovation and hence has little constructive effect on educational practice.

Despite this criticism, the tone of the book is positive and we review recent findings that appear to have application value for the classroom. But here too we argue for a more sophisticated view, rather than for research *per se*. Specific features that need to be included in research studies—if they are to have value for the classroom teacher—are spelled out in nontechnical terms. We feel that teachers need to know why research has not given them immediate answers and, more importantly, to recognize the type of research that is likely to pay off in usable theory and insight in the future. Such information complements the teacher's professional training, and also provides an opportunity for the reader to achieve a personal way of responding to the complex literature on school and teacher effectiveness.

A third and equally important purpose of the book is to provide comprehensive coverage of a few important topics that are widely discussed in education today. These substantive topics were selected for coverage because they are important areas of interest and value to teachers. In addition, chapter topics included in the book were chosen because they help facilitate the realization of the two objectives discussed above: (1) to demonstrate that teachers are a critical factor in the success of any educational practice; and (2) to illustrate the role and/or integration of research findings into educational practice.

The third goal is to provide in-depth treatment of important topics that normally do not receive expanded treatment in regular textbooks. Expanded and accurate coverage is provided in a nontechnical, down-to-earth fashion. We feel that these discussions will help teachers to comprehend and deal more effectively with certain aspects of their classroom roles. Topics covered in the book include: a discussion of major studies that have examined school effectiveness; implications for teaching practice that are drawn from recent comprehensive studies of teacher and student behavior in real classrooms; discussion of open and individualized classrooms and information about how well they work; the use of behavioral objectives and criterion-referenced testing in the classroom; the forms and efficacy of accountability; measurement and promotion of affective development in the classroom; identification of educational goals and suggestions for improving educational research.

Reviews of these substantive areas emphasize recent findings and are written generally for the classroom teacher. However, much of the material would be of interest to anyone interested in educational practice, including parents, researchers, policy makers, and foundation officials.

We hope the book will enjoy a wide reading audience including the group of persons mentioned above. But the book has been written with an eye toward its usage in courses for pre- and inservice teachers. To facilitate that intent, chapters are descriptive and reasonably open-ended, allowing readers to react directly to data, information, and concepts without the interference of heavy personal advocacy from the authors for a particular form of educational practice.

The book is especially applicable in psychology and method courses in which students are encouraged to consider the teacher's role in the educative process. But given the emphasis placed upon several topics relevant to measurement theory and practice (e.g., criterion-referenced testing, measuring affective growth, accountability, etc.) the book could be used profitably in introductory measurement courses by instructors who want students to integrate practice and theory.

In summary, this book is written for teachers, teachers in training, parents, researchers, policy makers, and others who want information about the effects of schools and teachers on students, and who want to know more about the research process and how it can be used to improve educational practice. It draws its major facts and general message from research findings, but it is written in straightforward English without a heavy reliance upon a statistical vocabulary. Despite the general reliance upon research, the authors will offer their own clinical judgments from time to time. Where these appear, they will be noted as personal judgments or hypotheses, not facts.

Columbia, Missouri   *T. L. G.*
Columbia, Missouri   *B. J. B.*
Austin, Texas   *J. E. B.*
February 1975

Acknowledgments

The authors are especially grateful to Dr. Philip Jackson and Dr. Myron Dembo for reviewing and offering useful suggestions for improving a rough draft copy of the manuscript. Richard Owen, the Education Editor at Holt, Rinehart and Winston, was especially helpful in his support and assistance throughout the preparation of this manuscript.

The bulk of the manuscript was typed at the Center for Research in Social Behavior at the University of Missouri and we are grateful to the Center for secretarial assistance and general support. The rest of the manuscript was typed at the University of Texas at Austin. Drs. Good and Biddle would like to acknowledge the general administrative support for educational research extended by several administrators at the University of Missouri, including most notably Herbert Schooling, Chancellor of the University; Lloyd Berry, Dean of the Graduate School; and Bob G. Woods, Dean of the College of Education. Dr. Brophy would like to acknowledge the helpful criticism and general support he received from Dr. Carolyn Evertson and other colleagues and staff at the Research and Development Center for Teacher Education.

Throughout our professional careers, the three of us have been fortunate enough to have had the help of some truly outstanding secretaries. We wish to acknowledge their valuable role by dedicating this book to them. They have been essential, not only in preparing manuscripts, but in assisting us in most aspects of our professional lives. We especially acknowledge those secretaries who worked on various aspects of this book: Beatrice Mladenka Fowler; Julie Fray; Paula Gee; Sue Gunn; Fran Head; Peggy Henry; Janet Honea; and Sherry Kilgore.

Contents

Teachers
Make a Difference

Chapter 1 Schools, Teachers, and the Effects of Education

"I hope you get Mrs. Erskine next term for civics. She's a great teacher. You'll learn a lot." "There's only one good teacher in high school and he's leaving at the end of the year." "I don't care how competent a teacher is, unless they break up the age-graded curriculum no teacher can make a difference." "If it hadn't been for two or three of my teachers who really cared I'd be a bum today!" "He's boring in speech class, but his debate team is the best in the state year after year."

Schools and teachers often provoke intense feelings in their present and former students. Furthermore, since everyone has been in school, everyone has strong feelings about how to make school better. "The teachers are okay." "They need to get rid of that stupid, uptight principal." "Kids don't get enough homework." "Those teachers don't emphasize grammar the way they used to . . . " "Why, my son in the fifth grade don't write good at all!"

Despite general and personal interest in education and despite the important role the school fills, not a great deal is known about the effects of schools on students. How many *good* teachers are there in the neighborhood school? Is it better than the school across town? Do teachers as depicted in *To Sir with Love, Up the Down Staircase*, or the venerable *Mr. Chips* really exist in the inner city schools or even in academies? How could we find out? The purpose of this book is to answer this and related questions.

Do Schools Make a Difference?

Most would agree that schools make a difference in the broadest sense. Students enrolled in a school do better than students not attending any school. This is not to argue that parents or some other agency could not outperform schools in some areas if they spent a great deal of time educating children. However, school enrollment helps children to develop important skills that they usually do not develop naturalistically without special instruction.

Indeed, in Chapter 4 a couple of studies will be reviewed to show that when students are denied schooling for a long time, or even a relatively short period of time, they fall behind children attending school. More importantly, however, it will be argued that because of important *differences* among schools, some have very little influence on learners while others have a much greater impact.

Recently analyzed data suggest that time spent in school is associated in a positive way with student achievement gains (Wiley and Harnischfeger, 1974). Thus, time in "instruction" appears to be an important variable and the number of instructional days varies by law from state to state as well as with the health and whim of individual students. Other differences between schools will be explored later in the book.

It is strange and unfortunate that there is little agreement on how schooling can be most effective. And, as we shall see below, there are some who would challenge even the assertion that school enrollment *per se* makes a difference. But, if we assume that school enrollment does benefit a child, we might ask additional questions. Does enrollment in Miss Kanes' fifth grade class instead of Mrs. Johnson's make any differences for the classes of children or for a few individual students? Does it matter if a child attends Longfellow Elementary School rather than Wilson Elementary School?

Let's talk about a particular situation. Does attendance at Harvard Business School make any difference? The sensitive reader might ask, "make any difference in what and compared to what?" Our refined question might be, "After ten years, do Harvard Business School graduates earn more money and have positions of power more frequently than graduates of other top business schools (in Chicago or Indiana)?" This is an interesting conjecture, because there are some data to suggest that graduates of some business schools do "out-earn" graduates from other business schools, but one can question whether this is a legitimate measure of school effects. To begin with, many of the characteristics that make Harvard graduates attractive to employers are present *before* the students enter Harvard. For example, Harvard does not give them their high aptitude or social sophistication. What a Harvard background may provide the graduate is a large number of important alumni who are business executives and who, for a variety of sentimental and practical reasons, are predisposed to give Harvard graduates serious employment consideration.

General questions are raised any time one wants to measure school effectiveness.

1. What is a legitimate measure of the effect of schooling? If money earned is an inappropriate criterion, but is the only one available, then the question of school effectiveness remains unanswered.
2. Did students have a skill *prior* to instruction, so that immediate and subsequent differential performance is better attributed to other factors (aptitude, home, background) than to schooling?
3. If schooling is effective in some way for raising threshold performance on variables of interest, then what mechanisms or what *processes* are used in effective schools that are not used in ineffective schools (what goes on in an effective classroom or school)? Are the resources better or utilized to greater advantage? Are learning assignments more challenging? Are teachers better equipped or prepared? Do teachers do their jobs more effectively? And so forth.

Seldom have researchers collected data in such a way that would allow a clear answer to the question, "Do schools or teachers make a difference?" No definite answer exists because little research has been directed on the question in a comprehensive way.

In general, research resources (e.g., money and personnel) in this country have never been applied to education with a serious and systematic approach. The resources are partly historical; it was assumed that schools were doing the job that they were created to do. Only in the early 1960s were educators in this country given an explicit *charge* to improve the intellectual functioning of disadvantaged children. Even this task proved to be impossible to fulfill, a least to the degree and with the speed that was envisioned. Successful short-run results were not possible, mainly because the research base for specifying program needs (how money might profitably be allocated) had not been established.

Ironically, in the late sixties and early seventies, when research had begun to provide some successful program prescriptions, funds were cut back drastically, so that the majority of preschool curricula for disadvantaged children continue to be developed and applied without a research base that answers the question, "Does this particular program make any difference?" This rapid retrenchment of research funds in the preschool area was part of a general ebb of educational and social science research funds.

Public and congressional expectations for American education was at an all-time high in the early 1960s, when the decision was made to infuse vast amounts of money into preschool education. The failure to produce instant solutions to the debilitating effects of poverty on school achievement led many concerned Americans to question the value of schools. "We can send a rocket to the moon but we can't help a child read!"

Such general dissatisfaction was given specific focus by the Coleman Report (Coleman, *et al.,* 1966) that blatantly dispelled many assumptions that Americans held about their schools. (These results will be viewed fully in Chapter 2.) Perhaps the most serious question raised by the Coleman data was that of the relationship between money expenditures and the quality of education. Educators had long assumed that fancy laboratory facilities and other plant improvements would facilitate student learning (as always in American education, ideas and application precede *research*).[1] That is, it was assumed that the more books, the more staff and, generally, the more resources, the higher student achievement would be.

Coleman's data suggest that extra expenditures do not make any difference in school outcome measures within a socioeconomic group. However, some have overracted to these data and concluded that school expenditures *ipso facto* make no difference and that schools have no important differential effects on children. Both of these conclusions are erroneous.[2] Coleman concluded that school expenditures are unrelated to school achievement because their sample of schools was *selective* in a way that left no room for any other conclusion. At the time these data were collected, the neighborhood school pattern and the financing of schools principally through local property taxes guaranteed that socioeconomic status (SES) and money spent in school districts would be highly correlated. Note that in Table 1 the normal pattern

TABLE 1

Possible Patterns of Relationship between School District
SES and Per Pupil School Expenditures

	High Expenditure	Medium Expenditure	Low Expenditure
High SES	1	2	3
Middle SES	4	5	6
Low SES	7	8	9

[1] *Indeed, even a recent evaluation report from the U.S. General Accounting Office fails to make this distinction, and it implicitly assumes that research should be responsible for establishing the efficiency of programs that were initiated without research. The most useful research takes place before, not after, innovation.*

[2] *We would not hypothesize that relatively small increments of money for a relatively short period of time would influence student achievement in any major way (that more money does not automatically transfer into changed classroom practice or altered teacher behavior has been demonstrated by Fox, 1967). Needed are articulate and comprehensive program designs to systematically guide spending efforts.*

would be for *most* schools to fall into either cells 1, 5, or 9. Some schools fall at points 2, 8, 4, and 6, but rarely are school types *3* or *7* found.

Of course, the real question is, "When extra money *is* spent on low SES schools, does it have positive effects on children?" Are school types 7 and 8 outperforming school type 9? Few 7 and 8 type schools were included in the Coleman sample, because the sampling represented the existing distribution of schools. Thus a carefully selected sample would have been necessary to answer the question, "Does extra money spent in low SES districts make a difference?" Atypical schools were needed to be identified to see if student achievement was higher in those rare cases where as much money was spent (for a number of years) on schools serving children from low SES levels as was spent in schools serving high SES levels.

In summary, the Coleman design only *suggests* that extra money (spent within a narrow SES range of schools) does not make a great deal of difference. For example, within the class of schools serving children from high SES districts (generally these schools vastly outspend middle and low SES schools), an extra budget of perhaps 5 percent does not make a difference. Clearly this limited statement is considerably different than the common but inappropriate claim that school funding does not affect educational outcomes. Even here, though, we do not know that large extra spending (say 30 percent) would not make a difference even within SES.

Furthermore, there are data to suggest that schools within high, middle, and low SES classifications show varying effects on school achievement. That is, there is reason to believe that some schools (no matter what their SES) are more effective than others of comparable SES levels promoting high student achievement (Brookover, 1973). Even if expenditure *per se* is not the controlling variable, and even if at present it is not possible to explain why some schools are more effective than others, such data show that schools have different impacts on learners (that cannot be explained by the characteristics children bring to school).

But what about other effects of school? Most available data concerning school effects is related to subject matter achievement or post graduation income. Thus, the answer to the question, "Do schools make a difference?" is sharply limited to just a few variables. And, of course, the same set of data does not answer the question to everyone's satisfaction. The core point, "For what does the school exist?" is sometimes answered in unrelated, if not incompatible, ways. To some, the chief goal for schools that are to prepare students for a world with limited resources is to prepare students with increased compassion, empathy, and ability to cooperate with others. Others, concerned with the same lethal problems of shrinking resources, see the need for schools to prepare students who possess greater technical competence.

In general the goals of American schools have been amorphous and elusive.

Teachers and schools are vaguely responsible for everything but held explicitly accountable for nothing except possibly student subject matter achievement.

But surely schools exist for more reasons than mastery of academic content. Are not students in the eleventh grade expected to demonstrate more political sophistication and general competence in voting than eighth graders? And is it not presumed that this increased sophistication is due to course work in civics and American history in addition to maturational factors? Similarly, many would assume that generally "more" school experience is associated with less vulnerability to specious advertising claims and improved ability to ask productive questions in confusing situations (questions that provide sufficient information for making decisions). Some educators would argue that school provides children with wide experiences in working with classmates of varying ethnic backgrounds and aptitudes, so that genuine respect for individual differences emerges. Still others would argue that schools can, should, or do affect moral behavior.

Indeed, some critics state that schools vary considerably and importantly in these dimensions, and that here school differences really count. However, questions involving the effects of school on non-subject matter achievement or on affective or moral behavior cannot be answered, because such behaviors have seldom been studied. But enough data do exist to suggest that *particular* schools (and *particular* teachers) make a difference on some of these variables. Students' affective reactions are found to vary from school to school and within each school, from room to room. Teachers, as we shall argue below, have considerable and differential impact on the extent to which students find classroom life a pleasant, acceptable, or uncomfortable experience.

This is not to suggest that situations in which students daily go through humiliation and frustration do not exist. The writings by Kozol (1967), Silberman (1970), and others no doubt accurately represent the barren process of schooling that unfolds in *some* schools. But there is no reason to presume that joylessness is the only or even the prevailing condition of schools. For example, we have personally witnessed school situations where children and adolescents work in obvious satisfaction and in the absence of coercion. Indeed, as we shall see from several independent studies, there are data to suggest that many students find school a satisfactory place to be.

Even in an era when it is popular to criticize schools, there are examples where teachers or schools have been cited as newsworthy examples of competency. For example, see the description of Bayside, a traditional high school in New York City, as reported by an educational writer of the *New York Times* (Maeroff, 1973).

The point here is simple: A full range of schools operates in the country, and some are more satisfying for their students than others. By selective orientation to some schools, one can document *any* point of view. Some schools are bad, some are mediocre, and some are good. But the situation is more complex than this. For example, some schools are bad for reasons that the community cannot control; whereas, other schools are bad for reasons that can be altered. Such distinctions have seldom been made by school critics of the past decade who have systematically pointed to schools and school personnel as inept and inane, if not immoral. But such distinctions *must* be made if schools are to be understood, especially if schools are to be held accountable or to be improved.

Do Teachers Make a Difference?

A major purpose of this book is to show that teachers and schools *do* make a difference. Our particular focus is on the classroom teacher and we will review a body of literature showing that teachers vary in their influence on students. As noted previously, so far data have not been collected in such a way as to answer this question in a direct way, but the bulk of the literature indirectly suggests a teacher effect (see, for example, the first grade reading studies reviewed by Chall, 1967). In several instances it will be possible to cite some data collected recently where teachers were teaching under similar circumstances, some with better results than others. Such data *directly* show that teachers make a difference.

Our reasons for focusing upon the *teacher* are straightforward: (1) First, as noted above, teachers *do* make a difference, and given the sharp criticisms directed at schools and teachers, we believe this message merits dissemination. (2) Much of the popular controversy in recent years (the Coleman, *et al.* Report, the Jencks, *et al.* reanalysis) has centered on *schools*, and such data have nothing to say about *teachers*. Even if schools do not make a difference (and we do not grant this assumption), some teachers within schools could regularly be of great benefit to students but find that their impact is washed out by the relative ineffectiveness of other teachers in the school. This is especially possible if teachers tend to be randomly assigned to schools within SES level. In our opinion, this effect is typical; individual teachers are more likely to show "effectiveness" than are individual schools. (3) It is impossible to deal with all schooling variables that might make a difference in student progress in a brief book, but a focus on the teacher seems both useful and manageable. This does not mean that the teacher is the only important variable, or even the most important one, although the teacher clearly is and will continue to be a vital influence. Several other variables of interest will also be discussed (individualized learning plans, open classrooms, etc.). However, such topics will be shown to be related to teacher influence and tied to the general discussion of teacher effects. That is, teachers in individualized learning situations or open classrooms contribute variance of their own to the situation (some open classrooms are better than others).

How Can We Find the Answer?

How much difference teachers as a group or as individuals make is a complex, elusive question. The technical difficulties of associating student progress with the efforts of individual teachers are compounded by the way in which data are reported. Typically, schools, not teachers, are used as the unit of analysis and when teachers are used, variance estimates are frequently missing. Given the present status of the literature, it is impossible to calculate, with accuracy, the magnitude of teacher effects. However, a recent study of teacher effects on student achievement indicates that teacher influence in some cases is considerable (Acland, 1974). Estimating the precise degree of difference that teachers make is beyond the scope of this book: the case that teachers vary in their effects on students will be made here. In subsequent chapters, it will be shown that further funding of research on teaching and continued support for teacher training is both desirable and necessary. Clearly, if schools and teachers did not make any difference such continued study would be useless and attention to reallocating or reducing the distribution of money given to schools might be in order.

We believe that research on teaching will pay off eventually in the identification of teacher behavior and learning arrangements that help students to achieve important objectives. However our call is not an indiscriminate plea for more research. Ill-designed research is of no value. Throughout the book we will attempt to identify those conditions necessary for the collection of data that will help educators to make decisions more effectively. Since we believe that research is vital to the effective functioning of schools, we will be careful to point out from time to time the ways in which research and evaluation data can be misused in the zeal to support educational claims.

In addition to suggesting that teachers do make a difference, we would like to suggest how teachers make a difference. A few recent studies have attempted to isolate those teaching behaviors that differentiate relatively effective from relatively ineffective teachers. Unfortunately, research has not yet linked teacher behavior and student achievement in a direct causative way. Thus it is impossible to say that teaching behaviors x, y, and z are associated with distinct areas of student achievement. But several patterns of teaching behavior have been found to co-occur with higher levels of student achievement. Furthermore, several of these findings have been replicated in separate studies. We will provide information about these promising teacher behaviors in Chapter 4. Such information, in addition to being interesting in its own right, will also be a useful source for targeting classroom behaviors and sequences that teachers may want to monitor in assessing their own classrooms (systematic strategies for assessing classroom life are presented in Chapter 10).

Furthermore, since it has become popular to argue that research on teaching should include a full range of dependent measures (how school affects students), a chapter has been included on measuring affective behavior. The chapter is written primarily for the classroom teacher and attempts to provide useful suggestions for collecting, analyzing, and using affective data from students. The goal is to provide skills for working with noncognitive classroom goals.

What Difference Does This Knowledge Make?

In general, the latter part of the book is an attempt to deal with topics of concern to educators. Affective measurement already was mentioned above. Accountability is another issue that will be discussed and legislation from the states with accountability laws will be summarized briefly. In part, accountability is an outgrowth of the nation's disappointment with educators' inability to match high expectations (expectations that the educators helped to flame, however). Disappointed expectations have even resulted in court cases. The San Francisco school district has been sued for one million dollars by the parents of a high school graduate who cannot read, but was awarded his high school diploma.

Discussion here will help the reader to gain perspective on accountability issues. How teachers are being held accountable will be described, as well as the difficulties of using existing accountability systems. Efforts will also be made to show how a conscientious teacher (or school) could hold himself (itself) responsible for his (their) instructional effects.

The practice of accountability provides an excellent example of the need for the careful collection of data over a period of several years to obtain the necessary information for appropriate decision making. However in the haste to provide useful information *now*, without an adequate base, some educational systems will apply irrelevant and/or undependable data. Both the promise and dangers of accountability will be discussed in full.

Finally, open classrooms, individualized learning environments, and criterion-referenced measurement will be discussed as attempts to break the debilitating effects of the age-graded curriculum that forces too many students to learn either too quickly or too slowly, and the school grading "game" which guarantees that some students will always be rated poor in comparison to other students who learn more quickly. The question here, of course, is, "Do changes (as *operationalized*) make a difference?" It is becoming clear that such arrangements offer considerable promise (backed by some data), but that the data are too "thin" to allow a complete view at present. Nevertheless, the available data suggest that curriculum organization is affected by the teacher who implements it, and that hidden or vague curriculum assumptions which adversely affected practice in traditional classrooms are not automatically solved by new structures.

Earlier we mentioned our interest in communicating the ways in which research can be used and misused as well as providing substantive information about the fact that schools and teachers do make a difference and to provide tentative suggestions about how teachers make a difference. The chapters on criterion referenced measurement and open classrooms are included (aside from their considerable substantive value) because they provide the opportunity to discuss the use (and often the misuse) of educational research. Furthermore, these chapters and the chapter on affective development provide a basis for illustrating how the collection of useful data not only helps to qualify and illuminate the effects of educational programs but also helps to identify new questions for subsequent research. For example, data from several individualized programs suggest that student personality variables are critical factors in determining the speed with which a student moves through the curriculum (in graded curriculums student aptitude has been the dominant factor).

Finally, suggestions for measuring teacher and student behavior in open and individualized classrooms will be provided for the interested reader. In review, then, the latter part of the book deals with the pressures that are being placed on the school by disgruntled critics and legislators (accountability), and it reviews strategies that schools are using to respond to such pressures (individualization, open classrooms, humanism, and so on).

The book critically evaluates the core of the educational process. In summary, the focus might best be stated as a series of questions that the book deals with. What differences do schools and teachers make in lives of children? What data do we have and what do these data mean? Why hasn't educational research on important questions been supported? How might we collect more viable data? Given that schools and teachers have different effects on students, how do these effects come about? What is accountability? Can teachers realistically be held accountable? How can affective measures be collected in the classroom? Should the age-graded curriculum be abolished? How effective are open classrooms? Should criterion-referenced measures be utilized? How can viable data be collected in individualized and/or open classrooms?

We now begin the process of trying to answer some of these questions. Chapter 2 deals with the criticism that has been raised at schools and with the critics who suggest that schools haven't done their job. Much of the criticism directed at schools has been misdirected or is inappropriate, but some has been relevant, and schools must respond to it. Chapter 2 attempts to place over-reactive criticism in proper perspective.

Chapter 2 Schools and the Critics

The most obvious thing about education must surely be that it works, at least in some minimal sense. Once upon a time there were but few literate citizens. Throughout history the vast majority of human beings lived in relative ignorance of letters, numbers, and a broad understanding of their societies and themselves. Today these conditions are no longer true. Among western countries, literacy rates are seldom less than 90 percent of the population. Books and newspapers are everywhere, and the average person can compute the balance for a checking account. These enormous changes in the lives of citizens are the fruits of mass public education, and in this sense the rise of such educational systems has been one of the revolutionary forces which has produced our modern world.

But does our education system work *well*? The past decade has seen the appearance of numerous critics who have claimed that our schools, teachers, and educational systems are failing to produce the effects for which we have presumably created them. Some critics merely reflect their own opinions or a particular ideology. This would appear to be the case, for example, with authors such as Hyman Rickover (1963), John Holt (1964), Jonathan Kozol (1967), and Ivan Illich (1970). These critics ask us to look carefully at the structure of our educational efforts and to reexamine our intentions and their relationships to our present schools. However, such criticisms are not based on research. They are opinions, and their assumptions about education and about its impact on pupils and society may be fallacious. Gage

(1972) has neatly demonstrated that even the most strongly held beliefs about education often turn out to be in error once they have been subjected to research.

Other critics, however, *have* conducted research, and some have concluded that our schools or our teachers are doing a poor job. Worse, yet, if we are to believe the reports of their studies which have appeared in the popular press, "evidence" is now available to "prove" our schools to be failures, our teachers to be ineffective, some of our pupils to be ineducable, and our expensive system of mass public education to be a waste of tax dollars. Nor have these criticisms gone unheeded. Well-intentioned schoolmen and school board members have used such reports as reasons for radical shifts in their programs. State legislators have used these same studies as reasons for cutting support for schools or for instituting programs of radical "reform." Citizens in general have cited them in arguing the advisability of ceasing programs that might heretofore have been thought to improve our educational effort.

Most readers will have heard of one or more of these studies. Since our major thesis is that teachers make a difference, we must first clear the air concerning studies which appear to say that education *does not* make a difference. As we shall see, the research designs use in these studies have been weak and relatively inapplicable to questions about whether teachers make a difference in the lives of pupils. Moreover, these studies do not really provide definitive answers even to questions about whether schools or schooling make a difference.

The Presumptive Ineffectiveness of Teaching

For years some teachers have wondered whether *anything* they might do will seriously affect their pupils. Some gifted and motivated pupils seem to survive even the poorest school conditions and achieve national prominence. Such would be true, for example, of Abraham Lincoln or George Washington Carver. Conversely, some pupils appear so uninspired or perverse that they manage to fail despite massive infusions of expensive education. This can happen even with members of the same family. Some siblings of famous persons, although presented with all manner of educational advantages, managed to spend their lives as bums or drunks. Indeed, some pupils appear "destined" to succeed or fail, so that teachers do not see much that they can do to affect the processes whereby these dramas are played out.

Among scholars, perhaps the leading proponent of this view of education is Stephens (1967). Stephens' pessimistic argument is based on the fact that research on teacher effectiveness so far has managed to produce remarkably little knowledge which is helpful to educators. It may surprise readers to learn that more than 10,000 studies have been conducted on the topic of teacher effectiveness. As Gage (1960) has noted, the literature on this subject is overwhelming, and even bibliographies have become unmanageable. In general, this research has provoked poor reviews. Most studies report only weak relationships between independent variables such as teacher-training programs and effectiveness criteria such as ratings given teachers by their principals or pupil test scores. In numerous cases, the findings of one or more studies have been contradicted by other studies. As The Committee on Teacher Effectiveness of the American Education Research Association commented two decades ago:

> The simple fact of the matter is that, after 40 years of research on teacher effectiveness during which a vast number of studies have been carried out, one can point to few outcomes that a superintendent of schools can safely employ in hiring a teacher or granting him tenure, that an agency can employ in certifying teachers, or that a teacher-education faculty can employ in planning or improving teacher-education programs. (Committee, 1953, p. 657)

Stephens views this research effort as destined to fail from the start. In general, he argues that the reason why so little has been found concerning the effectiveness of teachers is that teachers simply *aren't* effective. In short, the major forces that cause a pupil to succeed or fail in school lie within the pupil (be they the product of native ability or of family and community), and the best the teacher can do is provide pupils with a pleasant environment in which they can proceed towards their eventual destinies of success or failure.

Is Stephens right? Finding out requires a complex program of research that has yet to be conducted. However, most other reviewers attributed the lack of secure findings to poor research designs, and not to an intrinsic lack of teacher effects. Most of this research has exhibited at least four major design faults: failure to observe teaching activities; theoretical impoverishment; use of inadequate criteria of effectiveness; and lack of concern for contextual effects. (For an expanded discussion of these points see Chapter 3 of this text or Dunkin and Biddle, 1974.) Let us see what each of these criticisms means.

Probably the most significant weakness of teacher effectiveness research has been its failure to observe teachers in the process of teaching. Instead of seeking the causes of pupil growth in the interactions of teachers and pupils, investigators have been content to study the effects of variables such as curricular innovations, teacher background experiences, or programs of teacher education. Variables like these can only affect pupils *if* they result in substantial changes in the classroom activities of teachers and pupils. Without process information (descriptions of teacher and classroom behavior) about these activities, we cannot be sure what such changes might be if indeed there are any at all. Yet, few researchers to date have examined the processual effects of such variables, and those that have done so usually reported few changes (see Dunkin and Biddle, 1974, Chapter XI). Apparently, the customs of the classroom are resistant to change.

A second difficulty has been the lack of a theory of teaching in most of the teacher effectiveness studies. In fact, much of this effort may be characterized as "dust-bowl empiricism." Studies have been conducted on a wonderous array of teacher characteristics including, among others, teachers' eye color, voice quality, clothing style, musical ability, and even strength of grip! Why anyone would expect any of these to relate to teacher effectiveness is a mystery.

A third difficulty has concerned the peculiar criteria which often have been employed to assess effectiveness. Most studies have used *ratings* of teachers rather than measures of pupil learning. Principals, pupils, supervisors, or others rated teachers' effectiveness, and these ratings often constituted the sole criterion used. Such ratings have several difficulties. For one, raters often were provided with few cues as to what might constitute "effectiveness" in teachers, so that they may have used a variety of standards in making their ratings. For another, single ratings are known to be unreliable for assessing even observable characteristics of teachers. Moreover, in those few cases where pupil growth was measured, investigators generally chose a standardized test of achievement or intelligence. As we shall see later in this chapter, this too is a weak criterion when used alone.

Finally, most studies of teacher effectiveness have sought "universal" characteristics of teachers that would work in *any* context and with *all* pupils. Thus, various teacher characteristics or curricula were supposed to work equally well with pupils in middle and lower class schools, or with third graders and eleventh graders. This seems unlikely. For example, "warmth" might be important for kindergarten or first grade, but the ability to handle "discipline" might be more important in high school. A few teacher characteristics may prove to be universal determiners of effectiveness, regardless of context or pupil population, but we suspect that the majority will be context-dependent.

In short, then, it is difficult to take Stephens' argument seriously. Indeed, studies of the *processes* of teaching appear to have begun to produce useful information concerning the effectiveness of teachers (see Chapter 4 of this book and Dunkin and Biddle, 1974; or Brophy and Good, 1974). We suspect that the reason for lack of success in early teacher effectiveness research was poor design features rather than any inherent ineffectiveness of the teaching process. However, this is our opinion, not fact. The data we have used to form our opinion that teachers do make a difference will be shared in subsequent chapters. To find out *how* teachers make a difference and how much difference they make, it will be necessary to conduct the research we shall discuss later in the book.

The Inheritability of Intelligence

A second major controversy has arisen over the issue of whether intelligence is determined by native ability or by social experience, and, if by the latter, whether teachers can do anything to increase pupils' intelligence. Intelligence tests were originally developed in France as a means of predicting the ability of pupils to perform on "later academic tasks." They were presumed to measure some sort of relatively stable pupil ability however, for it was found that pupils who had "advanced" test scores one year were likely to be "advanced" in later years, while those who were "retarded" also tended to remain so on subsequent administrations of the test. This observation led to the IQ or intelligence quotient, originally obtained by dividing the "mental age" of the pupil by his chronological age. Pupil IQ is used by most teachers as an index of fitness for school work.

Now we come to the controversy. First, does an IQ score represent a single ability, or is it an index of a number of different abilities that are only partly correlated? Not all pupils are equally gifted in everything. One pupil may be a fine athlete, another be strikingly musical, another have an eidetic memory for the feats of baseball players, and still another be a whiz at arithmetic. Not all of these types of talents are related. Most studies have concluded that musical ability, for example, is relatively unrelated to that bundle of traits that are measured by the typical IQ test. Indeed, certain psychologists such as Cattell (1941) have spent years on the problem of trying to disentangle the various abilities a person may be said to possess. Moreover, those abilities that make for success in performing "later academic tasks" are likely to be somewhat arbitrary, since they will reflect the values and artifacts of the society that set the school curriculum.

Nevertheless, it also appears true that the various subtests of most IQ tests have positive correlations with one another, which leads most psychologists to conclude that there is a general factor ("g") which is common to all of them. Unfortunately, most educators tend to think about "g" to the exclusion of other factors that might make for success in the future lives of pupils. Thus pupils with low IQ scores are often streamed into less-talented subgroups of the pupil population and denied access to certain experiences of educational enrichment, although they may have talents that would enable them to benefit from such experiences. (One of the authors knows a teenager who has considerable talent as a cartoonist but is presently denied access to art classes because he is not in the "appropriate" stream in his junior high school.)

Second, to what extent is IQ inherited and to what extent does it reflect social experiences? European psychologists generally have believed that IQ is primarily a matter of native ability, and they have built social institutions on this belief. As an example, various European countries administer early intelligence or achievement tests to pupils and then separate those with high and low scores for quite different secondary school experiences. Those who go to the "gymnasium" or "grammar" school are trained for university entrance; those who attend other high school types are trained for mechanical, clerical, or other supportive occupations. Within the context of American values, such procedures seem harsh and unfair. But *if* IQ should actually reflect native ability in the main, it would be humane and sensible to separate those who "have it" from those who do not and to provide educational opportunities that maximize the abilities of both groups.

In contrast, most American psychologists have tended to stress the influence of social factors in determining the score one achieves on an IQ test. While not totally denying the influence of native ability, Americans tend to point out that pupils from poor home environments tend to drop in subsequent IQ testing, while those raised in better home environments improve. Also, noting that items on any IQ test presuppose a knowledge of the culture, they stress that those whose native language is not that in which the test is given tend to do more poorly than if they are tested in their native language. If American psychologists are correct, it makes more sense to keep all pupils in an academically rich school environment, so that all pupils will have maximal opportunity to improve their performances and raise their measured IQ's.

The problem is particularly poignant because of the known correlation of IQ with ethnicity and race in the United States. Black Americans and, in particular, individuals from lower class ethnic minorities (especially those of recent migration to the country) are known to have lower measured IQ's (on the average) than middle and upper class Americans of white, Anglo-Saxon origin. If we take the typical American interpretation of these differences, the reason why blacks, for example, score lower is that they are handicapped in taking the IQ test not only because they come from culturally impoverished homes but also because they are raised within a black subculture that is not represented in the middle class oriented questions on the IQ test. To segregate blacks because of lower measured intelligence, then, would be to impose inferior schooling upon those who are already unfairly handicapped because of their backgrounds.

This optimistic interpretation of the inheritability of IQ recently has been challenged by several critics, particularly Jensen (1969, 1973), Schockley (1971), and Eysenck (1971). Of these, the best known is probably Jensen, whose views have received wide publicity in the United States and who has been accused of "immorality" and "racism." Quite apart from the controversy, let us examine Jensen's argument.

Much of Jensen's work is based on secondary analyses of data from other investigators, particularly data from Sir Cyrill Burt (1966) which concerned the measured intelligence of a group of British identical twins that had been reared separately. In theory, identical twins have the same native ability, and thus the same inherited intelligence. Most twins, of course, are reared in the same home, which means that they receive roughly the same social advantages that might relate to IQ. No wonder, then, that nearly all studies of intelligence have found that identical twins have similar IQ's. However, if one looks at the measured IQ's of identical twins who are reared in separate homes, it ought to be possible to estimate the degree to which native ability determines measured IQ in contrast with the degree to which IQ is influenced by social experience.

Jensen did just this, and concluded that native ability was by far the largest factor influencing measured IQ (accounting for perhaps 80 percent of the variance). Moreover, Jensen went beyond this conclusion to suggest that if his estimate is correct, differences in measured IQ's as sizable as those between black and white Americans (for example) are difficult to explain by social factors alone. This implies that black Americans are less intelligent (have less native ability) on the average than white Americans, and also that compensatory programs designed to provide academic enrichment for blacks may be a waste of educational time and money. Needless to say, Jensen's arguments have appealed to racists, who have seized upon his conclusions as an excuse for attempting not only to delay programs for the improvement of black schools but also as a rationale for arguing against school integration, busing, and the like.

Such arguments are clearly shocking. But are they based on a reasonable interpretation of data? In short, can we believe Jensen? Unfortunately, available data do not allow definitive answers to these questions. As might be imagined, the sample of twins reported on by Burt is by no means representative of the ethnically diverse American population to which Jensen would like to apply his interpretation, nor are the other samples upon which he based his analysis. In particular, these samples do not exhibit the extremes of social conditions that exist in different segments of American society today.

Even if it should turn out that native ability does account for the large amount of variance in the samples analyzed by Jensen, such may not be the case at all for Americans, some of whom are reared in affluent suburbs, while others have spent their youths in crowded, one-room shacks in the rural South or in drug-ridden urban ghettos. If conclusions are to be drawn from survey data, the study sample must be representative of the population to which the investigator wishes to generalize. Unfortunately, Jensen's data do not meet this requirement, nor has any study yet produced.

Needless to say, others have come to different conclusions than Jensen. In a carefully reasoned work we shall shortly review in another context, Jencks, et al. (1972) concludes that native ability accounts for perhaps 45 percent of the variance of measured IQ, social background another 35 percent, and the tendency for these two factors to co-occur for the remaining

20 percent. If Jencks, *et al.* are correct, *both* native ability and social background are important in determining measured IQ. This interpretation still leaves unresolved the question of whether black-white differences in average measured IQ are due to heredity or social experience. In the long run, however, the question is futile anyway. Even Jensen is willing to point out that talented persons appear among *all* ethnic and racial groups, and IQ differences within each group are far larger than the average differences among groups. Given this, it seems obvious that educational policy should be based on individual pupils' abilities, *not* on their race or social class. It is probably our American racial preoccupation that causes continuing interest in the question of whether black-white differences are induced by nature or nurture. We have long known that persons of Jewish background tend to score more highly than native-born white Protestants on IQ tests, but we do not often interpret these latter differences in terms of native ability!

In the meantime, where does this leave the teacher? What are the educational implications of our present knowledge concerning the intelligence test controversy? *First,* far too much credence is usually placed on the measurement of a single intelligence factor. Pupils have many abilities that are not measured by the typical IQ test, abilities that schools can use to help pupils prepare themselves for useful and rewarding lives. Curricula should be planned with the idea that pupils vary in numerous abilities, and teachers should remain aware that pupils who lack ability in one or more fields will have talents elsewhere.

Second, too much attention is also paid to isolated measurements of intelligence. For years we have known that pupils' measured intelligence may vary by 20 or more IQ points when the equivalent tests are administered on separate occasions. In part, this results from the unreliability of the testing situation. However, recent research suggests that long-term changes in measured intelligence may also take place (see McCall, *et al.,* 1973). It should also be remembered that an IQ is merely a ratio between "mental age" and "chronological age," and hence a measure of the rate at which a child is acquiring knowledge. It does not measure the child's ability to stick with a problem until it is solved. Dependence on single measures of ability seem particularly tragic when the school uses them to stream pupils into separate and unequal curricula. Moreover, belief in the immutability of intelligence also affects teachers in subtle ways by creating in them expectations for pupils' abilities which may be quite unjustified.

Third, because IQ tests measure factors associated with social background, educators should be particularly careful when using them to plan for those whose backgrounds are atypical. Blacks, Spanish speakers, Indians who come from reservations, recent migrants, those whose native language is not English —all earn somewhat lower scores on IQ tests than do native-born, middle and upper class Americans. It is tragic and immoral to use these scores as excuse for denying access to educational advantages to these pupils, instead of planning compensatory programs to help pupils with talent towards the realization of their potential.

Fourth, at the same time, let us recognize that intelligence tests *are* designed to measure pupils' ability to accomplish later academic tasks. Pupils who consistently score poorly on IQ tests (for whatever reason) are not likely to do well on academic tasks. For this reason it is neither kind nor educationally effective to place pupils of low ability in competition with others without giving them compensatory help. To illustrate, many universities today are admitting minority students with poorer records and lower IQ scores than are required of majority students. Given the students' poor background experiences this seems fair, but if the universities do not provide them with compensatory experiences either they will fail, or the universities will have to lower their academic standards. The provision of compensatory education that brings ill-prepared candidates to the point where they can compete with others on an equal footing seems much more preferable to the alternative.

Finally, *fifth,* let us recognize that a substantial component of measured intelligence *is* due to native ability. Pupils who consistently score lower than their fellows on IQ tests, and who have managed to resist attempts to provide them with compensatory experiences, probably *are* less able to cope with educational demands than their peers. By the same token, those consistently scoring high are probably more able to cope with the rigors of scholarship and should be encouraged towards higher education and a professional career. To this limited extent, then, measures of intelligence may be used to help provide pupils with appropriate educative experiences.

In summary, many American educators have believed that intelligence test scores are affected by social experiences, and therefore that they can be improved through appropriate educational experiences. Jensen and other recent critics have suggested that such scores are mostly dependent on native ability, and have questioned the advisability of compensatory education programs. The truth appears to lie somewhere between these extremes. What is needed now is for educators to recognize the limited validity of IQ scores and to plan educational experiences that will capitalize on whatever interests and abilities their pupils may have.

The Effects of Schools

We now turn to a series of studies which have questioned American beliefs concerning education and have suggested that our schools, if not our teachers, are basically ineffective. To put these studies in context, let us consider some cherished beliefs concerning the purposes of education that most Americans hold.

The United States is a land of vast disparities in wealth. Some of the richest people in the world live in our country, but also some of the poorest. Although our standard of living is high, on the average, we still tolerate more abject poverty and more extremes of wealth than are tolerated in most other Western countries. How is wealth redistributed elsewhere? Mostly through the use of income and inheritance taxes which are used to supplement the incomes of the less affluent and to provide various social services that American citizens must buy with their salaries.

Why do we tolerate such extremes of wealth and poverty? There are many reasons, but one of the most central seems to be our belief in individual initiative. In America, the Land of Opportunity, it is presumed that the rich and poor both have gotten what they deserve, that there will always be an opportunity to succeed for the man with talent and motivation. Given this belief, education is often viewed in economic terms—as providing the individual with greater opportunity for financial success. Thus, public education should be provided equally to all, because then it will be possible for persons of talent (whatever their background) to "make it big." For years we have *believed* that such mobility was likely, and that a good education was the key to economic success, even though there is little more vertical mobility in the United States than in other Western countries (see Blau and Duncan, 1967, p. 6). If we practiced what we preached, persons who were handicapped for competition in the economic race would be provided *better* schools to enable them to be more likely to "get ahead."

This belief is closely tied to another, the idea that education is also the way to eliminate intolerance, injustice, and racial prejudice. America is blessed with citizens of many different backgrounds. Since its inception, the public school system has been viewed as a means for bringing these diverse groups together and providing common education in citizenship for the populace. In particular, it has been stressed that one of the reasons why impoverished minorities fare so poorly is that they have attended inferior, segregated schools. "If only" these groups were provided equal opportunities for education, it is argued, they would soon achieve equally with other Americans. Once again, then, schools are viewed as an effective mechanism for producing social change, in this case the provision of equal opportunity to minority persons.

For some years, social scientists have doubted the validity of these beliefs. It seems unlikely that schools alone can provide both equalization of income and amelioration of injustice in America. This position is supported in several recent studies which purport to show that schools are accomplishing neither task to any great extent. We refer, of course, to the famous survey, *Equality of Educational Opportunity*, commonly termed "The Coleman Report"

(Coleman, *et al.*, 1966) and to the more recent interpretations of these (and other) data by Mosteller and Moynihan (1972) and Jencks, *et al.* (1972).

These studies have been interpreted by some to indicate that our schools accomplish very little, that additional expenditures in education are unwarranted, and indeed that the teacher's role is limited to providing pupils a pleasant classroom experience while they are being held out of the job market for economic reasons. These studies pose a major challenge to American education, and it is useful to review their methods, findings, and shortcomings.

The Coleman Report constituted a massive survey of some 4,000 public schools, chosen from across the country. Data were gathered from teachers, principals, school district superintendents, and pupils at various grade levels. Altogether some 645,000 pupils were involved in the study, and their achievement levels on several standardized tests constituted the major data. In addition, statistics were also gathered concerning characteristics of the schools and the neighborhoods in which they were located, characteristics of teachers, and background information concerning pupils and their aspirations and attitudes towards school. The primary purpose of the study was to establish whether schools were or were not providing pupils with equal opportunities for achievement. Data concerning community, teachers, and pupil backgrounds were used primarily as "controls" for extraneous influences that might otherwise have confused the findings concerning the main issue of the study.

The study produced three major findings concerning schools and achievement. *First*, minority pupils were found to perform at substantially lower levels than white pupils. Moreover, differences in performance were greater at the upper grades. *Second*, the average quality of available school services varied widely both within and among regions of the country. Substantial variation in school quality *was* found within each region, and, in addition, schools in the South were found to be of lower average quality than schools elsewhere in the country. Neither of these findings appears too surprising. However, *third*, school characteristics appeared to exert little influence upon achievement, which instead was highly dependent upon the pupil's social background! Indices of school quality, per-pupil expenditure, size of the school library, and the like, appeared to have little relationship to pupil achievement once the investigators had taken into account background characteristics of the pupils.

It is this last finding that has fueled much of the controversy surrounding the Coleman Report. Critics of American education have taken it to say that it is useless to spend additional funds to upgrade schools, since this will do little to improve the achievement of our children. However, the matter is not quite as simple as the critics would have us believe. For one thing, the Coleman Report also went on to say that school quality makes *more* of a difference for minority pupils than it does for white pupils. (To put this another way, pupils from advantaged homes seem able to withstand exposure to a poor school, whereas for pupils from a poor home, attending an excellent school may be of crucial importance in achievement.)

Moreover, pupil achievement was also related to the backgrounds and educational aspirations of other pupils in the school. Thus, a pupil from a disadvantaged home would be expected to do substantially better in a school where the other pupils were achieving highly. Finally, the average quality of teachers in schools also was related to pupil achievement, and again this relationship was stronger for minority pupils than for white pupils and stronger at the upper grade levels. This suggests a "cumulative impact of the qualities of teachers in a school on the pupils' achievements" (Coleman, *et al.*, 1966, p. 22, *see also* the review by Bargen and Walberg, 1974). In sum, those who had assumed that they could increase the achievements of pupils simply by spending more money on schools were shocked by the Coleman Report. However, those who believed that achievement varied as a function of pupil aspiration and *teacher ability* received detailed support for their views.

The Coleman Report has received criticism, and some of its major findings have been challenged on statistical or methodological grounds. Let us see what has bothered some of the critics. For one thing, some of the statistical techniques used have been questioned. However, when other, presumably better, analytic procedures were used, they led to only very minor modifications of the major findings of the study (Mosteller and Moynihan, 1972). Criticisms that have questioned the relationship between the sample used by the investigators and the cause-and-effect interpretation they have chosen to give their findings have been more crucial. It is unfortunately true in America that rich schools are found in affluent suburbs, while poor schools appear in impoverished rural counties and deteriorating city centers. In fact, the United States may be the last Western country where equality in per-pupil expenditure among schools is not a national policy. Given the high correlation between school expenditures and community affluence (hence also pupil social class), when one controls for the latter one may also wash out any influence the former has on pupil achievement.

To put this another way, the Coleman Report *did* find raw relationships between school quality and pupil achievement. These tended to disappear when controls were imposed for community and pupil characteristics, a finding which the authors interpreted as indicating that pupil achievement was controlled by pupil characteristics rather than by the school. But the same findings might also be taken to indicate that school quality does affect pupil achievement, but that school quality is so tied up with community and pupil characteristics that an independent measure of it cannot be obtained. *The only way* in which these two interpretations can be resolved is by studying rich schools that happen to be located in poor communities and poor schools that are located in affluent suburbs. Unfortunately (for science) such schools are almost nonexistent in the United States. A field experiment which provides massive infusions of funds, equipment, and trained teachers in a poor school district to see whether a quality education can truly overcome poor home background is needed.

However, as we have noted in Chapter 1, the call is not for spending money *per se*. Needed is the selective expenditure of money to find the necessary antecedant conditions of student achievement and then the implementation of such features on a broad scale. We need to use existing research (some of it quite good) selectively, expand the existing research base, and apply such results to the improvement of suburban schools (many of which serve poor communities, contrary to the popular stereotype) and inner city schools.

Another criticism concerns the measurement of pupil achievement. For various reasons, the investigators chose to concentrate on a standardized test of verbal ability, "a vocabulary test measuring verbal skills" (Coleman, *et al.*, 1966, p. 292). To say the least, this measure did not represent more than a fraction of the goals toward which most teachers strive in their classroom instruction. Indeed, it may be questioned whether such a criterion relates to *any* subsequent experience in life, and thus whether any of the findings concerning achievement in the Coleman Report are valid. We will return to this problem below. Like teacher effectiveness research, the Coleman Report may also be faulted because it deals with input and outcome variables concerned with schools but not with the *processes* by which education is accomplished in those schools. However, for our purposes, perhaps the most crucial criticism is that the report considers pupil achievement to be a matter of *school* differences, rather than *teacher* differences. Although the authors did report findings supporting the notion that teachers make a difference, these findings were based on the average of teacher qualities for a given school and not on the differences among teachers within that school.

Surely good and poor teachers may be found in most schools. If teachers make a difference, and if pupils are to be exposed to both good and poor teaching as they progress through a given school, then small wonder if it turns out that there are only minor differences among schools in the average levels of achievement they produce! This does not mean that the determinants of pupil achievement are unknowable, however. If they vary with the individual teacher and are observable only within the classroom where pupils and teachers interact, then the data of the Coleman Report missed them completely!

Given these criticisms, it would appear that the case for the ineffectiveness of education is far from established by the Coleman Report, despite its scope. Are schools effective or ineffective? It will take additional studies to answer the question. Are teachers effective or ineffective? The study appears to suggest that they are ineffective, but most of the data presented are irrelevant to the question. But what about the criterion of pupil achievement? Are there ways to tell whether this is an appropriate variable for predicting pupils' chances for life success? Indeed there are, and the even more controversial study of Jencks and his associates (1972) is devoted to this problem.

This latter work set as its task the study of what makes for "success" in the pupil's adult life. Among the indicators of success examined were: cognitive skill, educational attainment, occupational status, and subsequent income. Among the potential determinants of success examined were: pupil intelligence, pupil social background, school quality, segregation in the school, and academic tracking. The volume examines data from the Coleman Report and other studies and uses a variety of complex statistical techniques.

As was reported earlier in the chapter, Jencks, *et al.* provide a carefully reasoned estimate of the relative influences of heredity and environment on pupil IQ scores. Among other findings, the following are particularly noteworthy. *First*, inequality—indeed shocking differences in status, income, and opportunities for education—is endemic in American society. Moreover, those who have the most of any one of these tend to have the best access to the others. *Second*, among those factors determining life success (measured in terms of income), native intelligence and social background are clearly the major determinants. However, other factors for which the authors do not have data (for which they have coined the unfortunate term, luck—but for which a large component must surely be persistence by the pupil) determine a large part of the differences. *Third*, school factors appear to have relatively little to do with life success. Jencks, *et al.* argue that schooling in America does more to reinforce differences in social status than to equalize opportunities, and that even if educational opportunities were actually equalized, relatively little difference in pupils patterns of life success would result. Rather, desegregation of schools will not help equalize the incomes of blacks and whites much. But, *fourth*, does this mean we should abandon the attempt to improve schools, for example by desegregating them? Not so, say the authors. Pupils spend about a fifth of their years in formal education, and it is up to us to make these experiences as humane as possible. Besides, if we want a racially integrated society, it is up to the schools to provide such experience for the next generation. Finally, *fifth*, how do we achieve equality, if not through the schools? By redistributing the income, they argue. Thus the recommendations of Jencks, *et al.* are addressed not so much to American educators as to American society at large.

So much for findings and arguments. Despite their startling character and the fact that they challenged cherished beliefs concerning American education, some of Jencks, *et al.*'s findings are worthy of careful thought. Their documentation of the unequal character of American schools is particularly noteworthy. They are presumably also right when they assert that schools today serve to reinforce differences rather than to equalize them. On the other hand, since most of their conclusions are based on data drawn from the Coleman Report, many of the criticisms that we considered earlier also apply to their findings.

As an example, rich schools tend to be found in rich communities, and poor schools in poor communities. For all their statistics, Jencks, *et al.* do not know (nor do we) what would happen if serious attempts were made to equalize expenditures in schools or, better yet, to provide compensatory education for a substantial community of disadvantaged pupils. Again, their analysis says very little about the effects of individual teachers and almost nothing about the *processes* of education. Their study is also handicapped in the range of variables examined as indicators of the effects of education. Indicators of the proximal effects of schooling on pupils are confined to pupil achievement scores for the most part, while distal effects are assessed in terms of income, occupational status, or educational attainment. To coin a phrase, there is more to life than is dreamed of in this narrow philosophy.

In summary, then, America is a land of great inequalities. Despite this fact, we believe in the ideal of equality and hold a set of beliefs concerning the functions of education in leading us towards that ideal. One belief is that schools ought to and can provide experiences that will enable pupils to make up for poor home environments through equal, if not compensatory, educational experiences. Another is that schools ought to and can be used to solve the problems of racial prejudice and injustice. Both beliefs are challenged by the research we have reviewed. The Coleman Report advances data to show the relative ineffectiveness of excellent schools for producing pupil achievement (when controls are imposed for community characteristics and pupil backgrounds). The Jencks study goes further and suggests that life success is generated primarily by pupil ability and social background, that schools tend to have little influence on the matter, and to the extent they have an effect at all it is to reinforce inequality rather than to induce equality. Both studies may be faulted for their assumptions and methods. Neither study has much to say at all about the effectiveness of teachers, although the Coleman Report asserts that teachers make a difference in the overall effects of the school.

Can Schools Make a Difference?

We have now reviewed three quite different research efforts that have recently appeared to challenge our conventional notions concerning the effectiveness of education. Stephens concludes that the reason why we know so little about teacher effectiveness, despite much research on the topic, is that pupil growth depends on pupil characteristics and not on teachers' efforts. Jensen and company argue that much of the potential for pupil achievement is fixed by native pupil ability, and that programs of educational enrichment are essentially a waste of time. Coleman and Jencks and their colleagues point out that our schools are not presently producing the effects on pupils that we had hoped they would produce. Indeed, their effects are, if anything, opposite to those embodied in our beliefs concerning equality of educational opportunity.

To say the least, each of these research traditions has generated controversy. Each may be faulted on a number of grounds, and at least some of the conclusions they have advanced are either questionable or probably in substantial error. Nevertheless, each has generated furor among educators. Each has been used as an excuse for concluding that our educational efforts are presently ineffective, that support for schools should be reduced, and that programs should be abandoned or curtailed.

What, then, are the facts of the matter? Can *schools* make a difference? On balance, we suggest that these studies have *not* shown our educational system to be ineffective but rather that some of its effects are homogeneously distributed in America. This point appears not only in the studies we have reviewed in this chapter, but also in the recent IEA Studies of Achievement in mathematics and other subjects. To quote Featherstone (1973), "One point that keeps getting blurred in American (educational) debates is that the research that has been done does not show that schools make no difference. What it does show is that by certain crude measures schools are very similar to one another." To reinforce this point, Wiley and Harnischfeger (1974) have recently shown that time spent in instruction is positively correlated with school achievement. The Coleman and Jencks research also shows that American education simply does not (and probably cannot) accomplish some of the tasks we have given it in trying to alleviate the problems of persons who are disadvantaged. On this question we stand with Jencks; education alone cannot be expected to "make up" for poverty, prejudice, and broken homes. To expect it to do so is naive and distracts our attention from the need to restructure other social institutions in our society.

But quite apart from these conclusions, what do these studies say concerning the effectiveness of teachers? Can *teachers* make a difference? In general, these studies say remarkably little concerning teacher effectiveness. Only Stephens addresses the issue directly and he analyses weak data, so that his conclusions may be questioned on several grounds. Jensen and company ignore teachers for the most part, while the Coleman and Jencks studies consider teachers only *en masse*, as just another component that would make for a better or poorer school. To answer the question, then, requires other kinds of studies than those we have reviewed here. Have such studies been conducted? Indeed, such studies are not only well underway (as we shall see in the next two chapters), but some at least have begun to produce significant information concerning the effectiveness of teachers. But for the moment let us note simply that whatever the implications for school policy of the critical research we have reviewed, these studies have provided us with remarkable little information concerning teaching and the effectiveness of the individual teacher.

In the following chapter, we will discuss some of the factors involved in studying teacher effectiveness, pointing out research designs that will be needed if solid information is to be accumulated in this area. Then, in Chapter 4 we will review studies which have produced such information.

Chapter 3 Problems in Previous Research on Teachers and Schools

Several studies which suggested that teachers and schools don't have a significant impact on students were discussed in Chapter 2. In the present chapter, we will further review these studies and others relating to the effects of teachers and schools on students. To begin, we will review and critique the research done to date, pointing out some inherent problems that make it difficult to draw clear-cut conclusions. Finally, we will present suggestions for improved research designs that seem likely to produce more useful information about effective teaching.

Problems with Available Research

Almost all of the available studies of teacher or school effects have defects which prevent us from drawing clear conclusions from their results. For example, several large studies which used schools or school systems as their unit of analysis were discussed in Chapter 2. Conclusions about teaching effectiveness could not be drawn from such studies because they did not measure the teaching process. Although the individual teacher is the appropriate unit of analysis in a study of teaching effectiveness, no separate records were kept on the performance of individual teachers and actual classroom behavior of the teachers was not investigated. In short, such studies cannot tell us anything about teaching because teaching was not measured.

More specific and smaller-scaled studies will now be discussed. Many of these involve significant design improvements over those previously named, but most still fail to measure effective teaching.

Curriculum-Oriented Studies

Many studies of new curricula have been made; usually these are designed to show improvement over existing forms or to work to better advantage on an experimental group as compared to a control group taught in a more traditional method. There have been a large number of such curriculum evaluation studies, but they have produced mixed and mostly negative results.

Perhaps this should not be surprising, because investigators interested in curricula usually ignore individual differences in teachers. In fact, in most such studies achievement data were simply collected from classrooms that used the new curricula and comparisons were made with other classrooms. The behavior or attitudes of the teachers were never measured at all. However, investigators who did observe teachers to see whether or not they were teaching the new curriculum correctly, often found that many of the teachers were not. In some instances, willing teachers were trying to instruct in the new curriculum but were doing it wrong because of inadequate training. In other cases, teachers were simply unwilling to change their behavior and, since no one was checking on them, they continued in their old, accustomed ways. With experience, all teachers develop habitual styles and teaching patterns that they do not quickly and easily change unless motivated to do so. Consequently, it is typical to find that teachers involved in a curriculum evaluation study differ considerably in the degree to which they follow instructions in implementing the new curriculum (for example, see Chall, 1967). Failure to take this factor into account and attempt to control it is probably a major reason why most curriculum evaluation studies have produced negative results.

Even when studies have produced positive results favoring a new curriculum or method, they usually have not provided data that would allow us to draw inferences about effective teaching (exceptions will be noted in Chapter 4). The usual reasons are that such studies did not use the classroom as the unit of analysis (lumping together the results from different classrooms rather than looking at them separately), neglected to include both observation of classroom teaching and measurement of student learning, and/or failed to control for important variables such as student social class or class size.

The research on early elementary grade classrooms that were studied as part of the evaluation of Project Follow Through (Stallings, 1972) is one example. Project Follow Through is a federally funded experimental program which provides financial support so poor school districts can install special experimental curricula in the first three elementary grades. These same districts have Project Head Start classrooms for preschoolers and the idea is to "follow through" on the gains presumably produced by the Head Start programs. The Head Start children are moved into the specially enriched "follow through" classrooms rather than into traditional ones. Different Follow Through models involve various curricula and methods, and one aim of the evaluation project is to compare the differential effectiveness of these models. The research has comprised collecting demographic data on students and teachers, observing in the classrooms, and testing children.

Comparisons of different Follow Through models with one another have shown that teachers' methods differ according to which model they are using. Thus, the curriculum sponsors have been successful in training teachers to follow the specifications of their models. However, to date very little has been accomplished in the area of finding out which models are more successful than others or why.

Comparisons of Follow Through classrooms with non-Follow Through classrooms have produced impressive data suggesting that students in the former outperform control students taught with traditional curricula and methods. Such comparisons have shown, among other things, that children in Follow Through classrooms had a richer program because of the greater availability and variety of materials, that they more often worked independently even though more adults were available to them, that they received more attention from adults when basic skills were being taught (because more adults were available), that they had access to a greater percentage of teacher aides who actually functioned as teachers, that they were asked a greater percentage of thought-provoking questions by adults in the classroom, and that they were less often taught in large groups. Furthermore, when adults in the classroom frequently asked thought-provoking questions, the children tended to have higher achievement scores and better attitudes towards school and learning. Finally, when the children themselves were observed to ask more questions of the adults in the classroom, they tended to have higher achievement scores and better attitudes towards school and learning, as well as lower absence rates.

Taken together, these data seem to establish that the Follow Through program is more effective than traditional curricula and methods. However, we cannot be sure exactly what made the program a success—certainly many factors contributed to it. First, the extra money available to Follow Through classrooms enabled them to purchase more materials and hire extra adult help, particularly teacher aides. Also, the sponsors of the various Follow Through models usually provided workshops and other teacher training help in addition to teaching manuals and materials. These factors made it likely that a strong Hawthorne Effect was operating. (The Hawthorne Effect, so named after an assembly plant in Cicero, Illinois, where the effect was first observed and documented, refers to an enhancement of expectations and effort that usually occurs when people are aware that they are part of an experimental group receiving the benefit of some useful innovation.) In addition to the extra materials, teachers, and training, participants in Follow Through had the attention of education experts, the opportunity to be involved in a new and prestigious program, and other experiences likely to raise their expectations and motivation levels. Perhaps most important of all, the Follow Through classrooms had a much lower child-to-teacher ratio than the traditional comparison classrooms so the teachers could intensify and individualize their teaching.

Given all of the above, we cannot simply take the Follow Through evaluation data at face value and assume that the differential effects observed were due to the new curricula and better teaching behaviors. For example, the increased independent work by Follow Through children, and the greater frequency of adults asking thought-provoking questions may have resulted simply from these differences or from the supplementary training and educational materials. Stated another way, perhaps the comparison classrooms would have done just as well or better if they had been given an increased materials budget, access to training experiences, a reduced child-to-teacher ratio, and reasons for expecting better results than had been achieved in the past.

As noted above, most curriculum evaluation studies have tested the students before and after the course or the school year in order to assess gains and compare effects with control classrooms; but usually there is no actual classroom observation to see whether the program is being implemented according to instructions. Rather than use the individual classroom as the unit of analysis, investigators lumped together the data from many classes. In short, individual differences in teaching were not taken into account. The Follow Through evaluation project avoided both of these problems: the teachers were observed, and data were used to score the teachers on the degree to which they implemented the program. Preliminary data are sketchy, but they do suggest that teacher success as measured by student test data is partly determined by the degree to which the teacher implements the program according to the instructions of its designers.

An additional difficulty with curriculum evaluation studies lies with the control group. Experimental classes have typically been compared with groups receiving either no curriculum or some ill-defined "traditional" curriculum, rather than with one or more control groups that had a well-defined but *different* curriculum. Thus, even where positive results are observed, their meaning remains ambiguous. The experimental group might show better results than the control, but for what reason? Is their success due to the innovative aspects of the new curriculum, to special teacher training, to the quality of the teachers in the experimental classrooms, to Hawthorne Effect, to some combination of these, or to other variables? Without data on how each teacher actually instructs in every classroom, there is no way to know.

Also, if the individual teacher is not used as the unit of analysis, the degree to which each taught the curriculum as instructed is glossed over when group data are compared. Even where a significant group difference is observed, it is likely that some of the experimental teachers were more effective than others and that some of the control teachers were more effective than others. It is also likely that some of the control teachers did better than some of the experimental teachers. These important teacher differences typically have not been studied until very recently. Instead, whenever a significant group difference was observed, it was usually attributed to the new curriculum, when this was not necessarily the case. Experienced classroom researchers and observers have seen that teachers do not always teach an experimental curriculum precisely the way the designers want them to (Katz, 1972; Rosenshine, 1971). Often this is just a failure of communication: The curriculum designers don't provide sufficiently specific instructions. Consequently, the teachers have to improvise in some areas and usually do so in unique and individual ways.

A second and more fundamental reason for a difference between the intentions of the curriculum designers and what actually goes on in the classroom is active or passive resistance by the teachers. Most teachers have beliefs, based on previous teaching and classroom experience, about what is good and bad teaching. If the new curriculum violates one or more of these credos and if the curriculum designers fail to convince them that their belief is wrong or that they should at least suspend judgment and give the new idea an honest try, the teacher is very likely to ignore the intentions of the designers. Some teachers will deliberately change or omit unacceptable aspects; others will teach them but in a mechanical way that indicates lack of enthusiasm and negative expectations about student interest and learning probabilities.

The main point here is that *inferences about effective teaching can only be made when the individual teacher is monitored.* It is not enough to show that the children exposed to a new curriculum learn more than children in a control or traditional curriculum. Without observations of what goes on in the classrooms, we can only know that children are receiving the experimental curriculum as it is interpreted and implemented by the teachers, and this may or may not be what the designers had in mind. To judge the relative success of a new curriculum we would have to show that the experimental classes actually received it. Furthermore, to the extent that there may have been important variations in how the individual teachers implemented the new curriculum, such differences should show that the teachers who followed it most faithfully were the ones who obtained the best results. Such data would provide convincing evidence that student gains were actually due to the new curriculum rather than to some of the extraneous factors discussed above.

Teacher Training and Process Change Studies

Several teacher training traditions have stressed inculcation of certain "approved" behaviors, but typically they have failed to provide process-prcduct[1] data which show that these changes lead to improved student performance. The usual reason that such investigators have failed to check that changes in teaching process variables have led to changes in product variables (measures of student learning or improvement in student attitudes) is usually that the process behaviors taught by these teacher trainers are *assumed* to be effective, either on the basis of data or on sheer faith (Dunkin and Biddle, 1974).

Much of the impetus for this line of work has come from Ned Flanders and his associates, who have developed classroom observation scales and completed several studies of teaching methods. These provide evidence that indirect teaching (questioning and discussion versus lecturing and demonstration, frequent pupil-to-pupil interaction, frequent praise and infrequent criticism) is associated with improved student learning and/or better attitudes towards teachers and schools (Flanders, 1970). Although these data are certainly suggestive and worth following up, they are not in themselves convincing, for two major reasons.

First, "indirect teaching" is an umbrella term that includes a wide variety of separate and perhaps unrelated behaviors. Consequently, lumping "indirect teaching" instructors together on the basis of this umbrella measure is like combining apples with oranges. Second and more important, studies of the indirect teaching tradition usually have not taken into account SES (socioeconomic status) and other student differences which probably affect the success of indirect versus direct teaching methods. Consequently, there is reason to believe that indirect teaching may be as much an effect as a cause of student behavior. It is much easier to be "indirect" in a classroom full of bright, well-motivated students than it is in a classroom populated by disadvantaged students who find school difficult and are not particularly interested in its curriculum. In the latter type of classroom, teachers are virtually forced to be more direct. Furthermore, there are data to suggest that direct teaching is actually more effective than indirect teaching in this type of classroom (see Chapter 4).

In any case, many of the studies which *appear* to support indirect teaching over direct teaching can be interpreted more simply and perhaps more ap-

---

[1] *By process we mean how teachers and students behave in the class. By product we mean the attitudes, behavior, etc. that students learn over time, as a result of participating in the classroom process.*

propriately as showing only that teachers working with brighter and better motivated students will be more successful than teachers working with less bright and less well motivated students. Unless such student differences are controlled, these studies do *not* prove that teachers using indirect methods succeed better than teachers working with more direct methods. More recent studies (particularly those instigated by Flanders himself) have begun to introduce such controls; nevertheless, contemporary teacher-training textbooks frequently state that indirect teaching is more effective than direct, even though this is an inference not supported by the available data.

This problem is not confined to the proponents of indirect teaching; commitment to certain favorite teaching methods on the basis of faith rather than data is rather typical (Dunkin and Biddle, 1974). The work of Flanders and his associates is stressed here partly because other investigators assessing both experienced and student teachers on process variables and then training them to improve in areas of weakness have borrowed heavily from the Flanders tradition, usually taking it for granted that indirect teaching has been established as effective (to his credit, Flanders himself has not done this). The idea of assessing teachers on process behaviors and then training them in their individual areas of weakness is the basis underlying the concept of Competency Based Teacher Education (CBTE).

Although CBTE is widespread and takes many forms, most versions are derived from the microteaching methods developed at Stanford University (Bush and Allen, 1964; Allen and Fortune, 1966) or from the methodology of the mini-course, a specialized version of microteaching developed by Borg, Kelley, Langer, and Gall (1970). In microteaching, the student teacher receives instruction about how to perform a teaching behavior or a set of related teaching behaviors, and perhaps also sees it modeled in a live or video taped demonstration. He then tries to perform the behavior or set of behaviors himself in a short (usually five minutes) mini-lesson which he teaches to a small group (five or six) of his peers. Following this teaching, the peers provide feedback about his success in demonstrating the intended teaching behavior. Behaviors practiced during the mini-lessons usually are limited and specific (praising; asking high-level questions; summarizing before going on to a new point; etc.).

The mini-courses are specialized and commercialized refinements of the microteaching model, in which learners complete an individualized learning module including written materials and videotapes demonstrating the desirable teaching behavior. Then the learner attempts to implement the desirable behavior in a mini-lesson which is itself videotaped. The videotape is then played back so the teachers can observe themselves and get objective feedback about their performance. Both microteaching in general and the mini-courses in particular have three things in common: (1) the attempt to focus the learner's attention on a single teaching behavior or a set of closely related teaching behaviors; (2) the provision of opportunity to practice the relevant behaviors in mini-lessons conducted in an instructional context, but kept shorter and simpler than classroom lessons, and (3) the provision of objective feedback about the teacher's success in implementing the desired behavior.

It is assumed that behaviors learned in this way will be retained and generalized, so that they will be used in appropriate situations in the classroom. This assumption could be self-defeating, since it has led to an emphasis on the practice of isolated, discrete teaching behaviors under artificial conditions. In contrast, teachers working in the real world of the classroom must blend these behaviors into an integrated approach, "putting it all together" while dealing with the entire class.

It is also assumed, although sometimes not quite so explicitly, that the behaviors being taught are well established as aspects of effective teaching. This is clearly an assumption however, and not a fact. Sometimes it is demonstrably wrong. The most obvious examples occur in cases where different microteaching programs train teachers to do contradictory things in similar situations. For example, one program has teachers always repeat the student's answer (presumably to provide repetition and reinforcement), while another says that answers should never be repeated (lest the student learn to listen only to the teacher, and not to other students). Obviously, both assumptions cannot be right if one behavior is effective and the other is not. If the situation is more complex than this (for example, if one behavior is effective in some contexts and the other behavior is effective in other contexts), neither program is appropriate since neither takes contextual variables into account and both teach the behavior as something that should be done at *all* times.

Another problem with microteaching, especially when it involves videotape feedback and explicit evaluation, is that it can be threatening to the learner. Even where there is nothing to fear objectively, some learners become extremely anxious about microteaching and/or depressed if their performance does not meet with their expectancy (Fuller and Manning, 1973). As a result, some learners tend to stick with familiar and preferred teaching patterns during microteaching (Emmer, Good and Oakland, 1971), rather than take a chance on trying something new and unfamiliar. Special instructions and provision of emotional support may be needed to overcome this problem, especially with anxious learners.

In summary, the microteaching and mini-course programs and other CBTE efforts have shown that teacher process behaviors can be taught and have provided some evidence that these behaviors which are acquired in specialized learning situations generalize to teaching done in ordinary classrooms later. However, the behaviors themselves tend to be *assumed* rather than *known* to be effective. Thus, the CBTE effort is effective as a *technology* for training teachers, but its present usefulness for improving teaching effectiveness is dubious because of the lack of a data base to support the assumptions that a given set of teaching behaviors is in fact effective and worth teaching. In short, we know more about *how* to train teachers than about *what* to teach them.

Needed Research

By now it should be obvious that we need research both to measure teacher behavior and to link this behavior with measures of student outcome. So far, a remarkably small number of studies of this kind have been done (see Chapter 4), and these have had relatively little success, usually because they lacked one or more of the characteristics to be discussed below.

Following is a list of aspects of process-product teacher effectiveness research which seem to be needed if such research is to yield definitive information about effective teaching. There is no special theoretical orientation underlying the list, only a concern for making it possible to draw more definitive inferences about effective teaching. However, there are a few assumptions underlying the list which should be made explicit.

First, it is assumed that the relationships between teacher behavior and student outcomes are complex, and that the effectiveness of a given teacher behavior will sometimes depend on such student variables as age, sex, or personality traits. For example, certain teaching behavior might be helpful to younger students rather than older students, to girls rather than boys, or to anxious students rather than confident ones.

Second, it is assumed that effective teaching will vary according to the context or circumstances. For example, an effective method of introducing a topic does not help during review of the lesson, and vice versa. Thus, in sum, what works with one student or in a particular situation will not necessarily be effective with a second student or at another time.

Third, despite these complexities, we assume that lawful relationships can be discovered between how the teacher acts, and how the student reacts, although we also take for granted that most teaching behaviors will prove to be necessary but not sufficient as antecedents of student outcomes. That is, we believe that most student performance results from a combination of several different teaching behaviors being present at or above a minimally necessary degree, and that there are relatively few simple one-to-one relationships between teacher behaviors and student outcomes. One implication here is that a teacher who is above the necessary level on warmth, clarity, *and* managerial skills will be more successful than one who is extremely good in one or two of these areas but below the necessary level on the other one or two. With these assumptions in mind, we offer the following suggestions for improving research so that inferences about effective teaching can be drawn with greater validity and confidence.

Naturalistic Settings

Research on teaching should be conducted in the settings to which the investigator wishes to generalize his results. If first grade reading groups are of interest, the research should take place in the first grade classroom during reading lessons. This eliminates the problem of "generalizability" (or "external validity") that exists when findings coming from research carried out in laboratory settings are applied to the real world classroom. Microteaching and other CBTE activities are useful as teacher training devices, but they are inadvisable as research settings. They contrast in so many ways with naturalistic classrooms that their findings cannot be generalized confidently without first redoing the entire study in a naturalistic setting. Thus, researchers interested in the naturalistic setting in the first place should conduct their study in a real classroom. This may seem obvious, but a remarkable percentage of educational research projects have been carried on in laboratory settings, even though the explicit intention was to develop knowledge about effective teaching strategies for use in the classroom.

Include a Variety of Student Outcome Measures

Most studies completed to date have included only one or just a few closely related student outcome measures, usually measures of the variables most central to the interest of the investigator. This makes it impossible to know whether improvements on these points have been accomplished at the cost of deterioration of others (for example, are cognitive gains in learning achieved at the expense of a decline of good student attitudes towards the teacher and school?). Ideally, a battery of student measures should be administered both before and after the teacher behavior is studied. The battery should include both criterion-referenced tests of the student's knowledge, attitudes, and/or behaviors directly relevant to the experimenter's interest, as well as a broader range of tests of other variables which might conceivably be affected by the experiment. These would include both high level (abstract) and lower level (concrete) measures in the cognitive sphere, as well as one or more measures in the affective sphere. The affective measures might include, for example, measures of student self-concepts in general and self-concept of learning ability in particular, attitudes towards the teacher and school, and achievement motivation.

In studies where the teacher is trained to change behavior towards a single student or subgroup rather than towards the entire class, data should nevertheless be collected on the entire class. This will be necessary to check for either of two kinds of possible side effects of the experiment. The first is the possibility of "radiation effects," in which the teacher may begin to show the experimental behaviors towards certain other students in the room (perhaps even the entire class) in addition to the experimental student or group.

For example, a behavior modification experiment might be training the teacher to ignore misbehavior and praise and reward positive and desirable behavior in three students who are among the most disobedient and troublesome students in the room. If the training succeeds, however, the teacher may end up reducing attention to misbehavior and increasing rewards of desirable behavior in *all* students in the room, not just the three experimental students.

The opposite of a radiation effect occurs when the treatment produces compensatory or "boomerang" effects. Here, the gains enjoyed by the experimental students come at the expense of the rest of the class or of certain members of it. For example, if the teacher has been instructed to spend more time with the experimental students, this means that he will probably spend less time with the others. Or, to return to the behavior modification example, the teacher may succeed in reducing his attention to misbehavior and in increasing his reward of good behavior in the three experimental students, but at some cost to himself or to other students in the class. For example, he may become irritable because he finds it difficult to implement the treatment, so that he is resentful and punitive towards the rest of the class, even though he is more rewarding towards the three experimental students. Or, even if he does not change his behavior towards the rest of the class, they may become jealous and angry because the teacher is treating the three experimental students differently in a way that they perceive is unjustified favoritism. In general, then, research in the classroom needs to adopt an ecological standpoint, with *any* event that might be affected by the treatment being monitored, not just those events directly related to the treatment.

Include Both High and Low Inference Measures of Teaching Behavior

Classroom observation systems and other methods of measuring teaching behavior are frequently classified as either "high inference" or "low inference." Despite the common use of these two terms, these represent two ends of the same continuum; there is no clear-cut line between high inference methods and low inference methods. It is a matter of degree.

In general, however, high inference measures are rating scales that characterize the teacher as high or low on some variable. Or they can be ranking scales in which the rater compares the abilities of two teachers or lists teachers in order from best to worst, either in general or on some more specific criterion (such as warmth). High inference measures are so called because they involve a high degree of deduction on the part of the rater, who must take into account everything that he has observed about the teachers involved and arrive at a judgment in some complex and idiosyncratic way. Because high inference methods allow so much room for judgment, they are often strongly affected by the biases of the rater, and are open to all the drawbacks of any subjective rating system as compared with more objective measurement.

In contrast to high inference measures which rely on complex subjective judgments, low inference measures, usually classroom observation schedules designed so that observers can code the frequency and/or type of teacher behavior within a narrowly defined range, require minimal subjective judgments or inferences on the part of the observer. The behaviors included on the measurement instrument are usually easy to observe and count reliably, often being brief segments of behavior that occur frequently during typical everyday classroom interaction (questions, correct answers, incorrect answers, hand raising, warnings and criticism about misbehavior, and so on). Because minimal judgment or inference is required of the observer, low inference measures are much less subject to observer bias and usually produce higher percentages of agreement across independent raters or observers.

Thus, low inference coding systems provide the most objective measurement of teacher behavior, but they tend to be most suited to measuring teacher behavior that occurs in short, concrete units. Consequently, reliance on low inference coding measurement alone often means that the measurement of a given study will be rather trivial and that many important teacher variables will not be measured at all. Rating scales or other high inference measures are needed to get at certain teacher attributes that cannot be validly measured by counting the frequency of discrete behaviors but must instead be measured by rating the teacher with a more general scale (i.e., variables such as warmth, enthusiasm, interest in the subject matter, organization, and orientation towards the students).

So far, these general teacher variables have defied successful measurement through low inference coding, but they can be quite reliably and apparently validly measured with high inference ratings. Yet, investigators should avoid reliance on high inference ratings alone because they are notoriously vulnerable to different types of rater bias. One is *halo* effect: If the rater generally likes or is impressed by the teacher he will probably rate the teacher favorably on virtually any scale in spite of whatever weaknesses the teacher may have; if he dislikes or is negatively impressed he is likely to rate the teacher unfavorably on virtually any scale, even though the teacher has certain strengths. A related source of rater bias is *logical error*: If the rater believes (correctly or not) that two attributes tend to be highly correlated or go together, he will tend to rate a teacher high on one of the variables if he has already rated the teacher high on the other (although this teacher may be an exception to the general rule and be high on one variable but low on the other). Another source of error in high inference ratings is straightforward bias on the part of the rater. Thus, suppose a group of teachers is being appraised by two raters, one of whom favors well organized lecturing and teacher-dominated instruction, in contrast to the other who favors avoidance of lecturing whenever possible and reliance on classroom discussion and discovery method. The two raters are going to show large disagreement in their measurement of teacher effectiveness because they are biased by conflicting opinions about "good teaching."

Because of the difficulty of rater bias, one of the thorny problems of teacher evaluation has been that ratings by principals or supervisors (which typically have been done with high inference instruments) have been notoriously contradictory (two raters don't agree with each other) and invalid (they don't correlate with more objective measures of teaching effectiveness). Thus, although high inference measurement appears to be necessary if certain important teacher variables are going to be measured at all, because of the problems of observer bias, investigators using high inference ratings should be sure that two or more individuals familiar with the teacher make independent ratings, so that reliability (agreement) data can be computed and ratings can be averaged to help minimize the bias.

When both high and low inference measures used in the same study address the same areas of teacher behavior, investigators can compare them to determine their probable validity. When the two sets of data complement each other and suggest the same general conclusions, it is likely that both sets are valid. However, where such internal validity checks show up contradictions, investigators should attempt to determine the reasons for them and to assess the relative validity of each data set.

This can be done in several ways when teachers are monitored to provide feedback. For example, if one supervisor rates the teacher as affectionate and student-oriented on a high inference form, but on a second occasion another superviser fails to find any evidence of such behavior or attitudes in low inference coding the supervisors could trade notes to see if any obvious contextual differences explain the contradictions. For example, the high inference ratings might have been made during a discussion class in an atmosphere of high interest and excitement. In contrast, the low inference codings made by the second supervisor might have been made when the teacher was introducing difficult and/or uninteresting material and (possibly for good reasons) spent most of his time giving lectures and demonstrations with little or no questioning or discussion. If this were the case, the low inference coding data would not be surprising. However, in order to give the teacher useful feedback on the variables of concern for students and general warmth, it would be advisable to make repeated observations using high inference ratings (especially by the supervisor whose low inference codings previously showed unfavorable results). This would enable the supervisors to get a better idea of the degree of warmth and concern shown by the teacher across a variety of contexts.

A different approach would be required in accountability evaluations or evaluations of curriculum or method. Here, where it is important to show that teachers are covering particular content and/or that they are teaching it in a particular way, data should be collected with observation instruments designed to obtain this information as specifically as possible. These should be low inference instruments, and any disagreements should be resolved by repeated observation and measurement. In this instance it would be important to have two or more supervisors/coders observe the teacher at the same time to discover whether any disagreements occurred. In this case, the teacher may have varied his method or the observers simply may not have been reliable in their coding. If investigation data taken at the same time by different coders show disagreement, the observers will need to discuss the coding and determine who is doing it incorrectly. Eventually they will be able to accumulate reliable and valid data on the teacher. In cases where the coders are using extremely objective, low inference methods to measure discrete teaching behaviors, different observers should reach extremely high levels of agreement, approaching 100 percent. Where this does not occur, disagreement cannot be resolved simply by averaging the codes; the observers must pursue the problem in order to identify the sources of their disagreement and to eliminate them so that everyone is using the measurement instrument reliably and validly.

Test Students Before and After Observation and Use Adjusted Rather Than Raw Gain Scores as the Criteria

Adjusted scores rather than raw scores should be used as the criteria for comparison in studies concerned with the degree of student learning gains and/or the amount and type of change in student attitudes. Simple gain scores[2] (post-score minus pre-score) should not be used because they can be influenced by many extraneous factors unrelated to teacher behavior or teacher effectiveness. For example, IQ or standardized achievement test scores almost always show greater gains in a given unit of time by students who started out *higher* than by students who started out lower at the beginning of the school year. This merely reflects the fact that brighter students will gain more in a given unit of time than duller students. Unless classes have been matched in the first place to eliminate student differences in certain areas, use of raw gain scores would unfairly penalize teachers who were working with primarily low achieving students and would unfairly inflate the scores of teachers who were working with primarily high achieving students.

These problems with raw gain scores or gain scores can be eliminated through repeated measures designs in which each student's prescore is used

[2] *A simple gain score represents the difference between a student's prescore (his raw or actual score at the beginning of the year) and his postscore (his score at the end of the year).*

as a covariable in computing his adjusted gain score (these adjusted scores are usually referred to as "residual gain scores"). These adjusted or residual gain scores are computed using standard statistical procedures which are well worth the time and effort involved because they enable the investigator to compare teachers directly. The statistical adjustment procedures have the effect of "holding constant" or eliminating the influence of differences in pre-scores, so that students and groups of students who differed in their pre-score level can be compared directly. Briefly, these statistical procedures accomplish this by converting the student's raw gain score into a score that represents the amount of change he showed divided by the amount of change that he was expected to show. For example, if students with pre-test scores of 50 averaged 75 on post-tests, their expected gain would be 25 points. Similarly, if students scoring 75 on the pre-test averaged 125 on the post-test, their expected gain would be 50 points. Using raw gain scores, a group averaging 75 on the pre-test would appear to have made twice as much gain in the course of the experiment as a group who averaged 50 on the pre-test. However, when adjusted or residual gain scores are used, the gains made by these two groups would be considered equal. That is, an average gain of 25 points in a group that averaged 50 on the pre-test would be considered equal to an average gain of 50 in a group that averaged 75 on the pre-test. Teachers of these two respective groups would be considered to have done an equally good job. If a teacher working with a group who averaged 50 on the pre-test succeeded in producing an average gain of 35 points in his class, he would be considered as having done better than a teacher who produced an average gain of 40 points in a class whose expected average gain was 50 points. On the other hand, a teacher working with low achievers who succeeded in producing an average gain of only 15 points when a gain of 25 points was expected would be considered less successful than a teacher who succeeded in producing an average gain of 60 points when a gain of 50 points was expected.

Without getting into statistical procedures involved, these examples illustrate how the use of adjusted or residual gain scores enables the investigator to compare teachers directly even if they are teaching students who are significantly different in ability (or whatever other relevant variables are measured on the pre-test) at the beginning of the experiment. Comparisons involving such scores are much more likely to reveal genuine differences among teachers, in contrast to comparisons of raw change scores which are likely to penalize certain teachers.

Match Classrooms

Even when adjusted or residual scores are used, investigators still are well advised to match classrooms on any relevant student variables, particularly on pre-scores on the criterion tests. Ideally, each teacher involved in the study should have approximately equal numbers of high versus low achieving students, boys versus girls, whites versus blacks, or any other student variables of interest. Also, teachers should each have approximately the same number of students in similar classrooms and have access to similar equipment. Many such differences can be taken into account through statistical procedures to adjust gain scores, but these statistical corrections are less desirable and reliable than matching teachers on the relevant variables in the first place.

There is evidence to indicate that even the use of adjusted or residual scores does not sufficiently take into account or correct for certain "class" or "cohort" variables which can affect a teacher's effectiveness from one year to the next (Brophy, 1973). In this study, the average scores for classes on a battery of standardized achievement tests showed clear year-to-year fluctuations. This was true even after statistical procedures which theoretically eliminate the effects of student differences by "holding them constant" were applied. Apparently, variables which are not reflected in individual student scores, such as year-to-year differences in class leadership or morale or in health and attendance, affect student learning gains. Obviously, such differences could exist between different classes in the same year, not just between one year and the next. Thus, matching classes on all relevant variables is the only way that an investigator can be really sure that his classes are truly comparable and that any differences in student outcome measures are logically attributable to differences in the teachers and not to some extraneous variable.

Analyze the Distribution of Gains

Virtually all investigators to date who have used student learning gains as a criterion of teacher effectiveness have used only the *mean* gain or mean residual gain, paying little or no attention to the *distribution* of individual gains across individual students. A question worth investigating is "Where does the teacher get his gains?" That is, does the mean residual gain for the class as a whole represent the gain for boys and for girls equally well, or does this teacher have greater success with boys than with girls or vice versa? Do teachers who produce similar gains on class means also produce similar gains among high versus low ability students, or is one teacher especially good with high ability students and the other with low ability students? Are some people better able to teach dependent and passive students while others work better with assertive and independent students? Such questions concerning the interaction between teacher effectiveness and individual student differences have barely begun to be investigated, but the few available data suggest that they are important and worthy of investigation in any process-product study. This assumes, of course, that the individual teacher (or classroom) will be used as the unit of analysis, as discussed below.

Use the Individual Teacher (or Class) as the Unit of Analysis

This matter has been discussed at length several times, but it is worth repeating here. Studies using groups of teachers rather than individuals as their unit of analysis tend to mask rather than reveal process-product relationships. Even where predicted group differences show up, it is important to look at the relationship between each individual teacher's behavior and his success in achieving gains in student outcome measures. Such analyses will yield a much greater volume of information, and usually much more important information, than a simple analysis of the hypothesized group difference.

Use a Large Sample of Teachers

This is necessary in part because the idea of using the teacher as the unit of analysis assumes that for statistical reasons the sample includes at least 30 or so teachers. At minimum, the sample should be large enough so that it can be cut in half to compare teachers high and low on some variable of interest (e.g., the type and difficulty level of questions they ask) to see if there is any relationship between that variable and teacher effectiveness. Frequently such "variables of interest" are not known ahead of time, but they become obvious in the course of the investigation. In other words, the investigator may discover that he should have controlled the teachers on one or more variables that appear to be significant in differentiating effective from ineffective teachers. This may come to light after the study has already begun and it is too late to institute such controls. It need not ruin the study if the teacher sample is large enough for the investigator to score the teachers on the variable of interest and thus take it into account in evaluating teacher effectiveness. However, where there have not been enough teachers included in the study, the existence of even one such variable can ruin an otherwise well designed study by making it impossible to do meaningful statistical analysis.

Use a Sample That Is Selected Rationally Rather than Randomly

Most process-product studies have used convenience samples (the teachers were available and willing to participate) or random selection. Neither selection method is as valuable for this kind of research as using a sample carefully chosen on the basis of its special appropriateness for the study. For example, in a naturalistic study which is intended to relate teacher behavior to student gains on outcome measures, a carefully selected sample composed of teachers who had shown consistency in the gains that they produced on student learning measures over a three- or four-year period would be preferable to a random sample of teachers. The former group would be composed of teachers who were experienced at their grade level and who probably had established a style or pattern of teaching that reasonably could be expected to continue with roughly the same relative success as in previous years. In contrast, a random sample of teachers would probably include a large number who were changing their teaching styles because they were new teachers, or new to the grade they were teaching, or were experiencing difficulty in adjusting to some problem. Also, a random sample would include a number of teachers who were highly inconsistent in their effects on students from one year to the next (for unknown reasons).

Thus, samples chosen on the basis of rational selection are much more likely to yield consistent and interpretable results. Such selection insures both consistency and variance in the sample. Consistency is insured by selecting teachers who have a "track record" of consistency on the variable of interest, so that their relative standing on this particular variable compared to other teachers is somewhat predictable rather than simply unknown. At the same time, sufficient variance can be introduced into the sample by selecting from among consistent teachers individuals or groups who differ from one another and represent a full range or at least different points on the range from high to low on the variable of interest. For example, consider a study of the relationship between authoritarian versus democratic leadership styles and student learning gains and attitudes towards school. Careful teacher selection can insure that teachers who consistently show these contrasting leadership styles are included in the study. In contrast, suppose the investigator were to take a random sample of teachers and simply split at the median on some measure of authoritarian versus democratic leadership styles. He might find that his data were artificial in that 90 percent of the teachers had democratic leadership styles, so that in effect he was comparing a group of extremely democratic teachers with a group of moderately democratic teachers and a few authoritarian teachers. This is quite different from comparing a group of democratic teachers with a group of authoritarian teachers.

Actually, in cases like these, it is ideal to include a third group who would be neither authoritarian or democratic but balanced in between the two extremes. This helps guard against nonlinear relationships that might be missed if only the two extreme groups of teachers were studied (Soar, 1972). The problem will be discussed in more detail in the following section. In any case, it is often assumed that a random sample of teachers is ideal for research purposes. This is often, but not always, true. Sometimes the best sample is one which is rationally selected according to where teachers stand on the variables of interest to the study.

Random selection of students is not always optimal either. Instead, students should be deliberately assigned to teachers in a way that would equalize the proportions of different kinds of students in different classrooms. This would provide greater insurance that study results would not be affected by contrasting student samples in different classrooms. In general, investigators should rely on random assignment only when they lack information that would allow them to select teachers or students on a more rational basis. Where such information is available, rational rather than random assignment may better produce the desired results.

It should be noted that there are also disadvantages to rational assignment. These might occur if the investigator wants to generalize his results to a population of teachers which is wider than that included in the sample. One important advantage of random assignment is that any results obtained can theoretically be generalized to the entire population of teachers, or at least to the subpopulation of teachers like those in the sample (elementary school teachers, science teachers, and so on). When a sample is chosen through rational rather than random selection, technically the results can be generalized only to a population of similar teachers (that is, teachers who are consistent in obtaining student learning gains as opposed to teachers who are not consistent). However, we believe that the advantages of using a rationally selected sample outweigh the restrictions on generalization of the results, because results from a rationally selected sample are more likely to be unambiguous. Also, the general thrust of research on teacher effects shows the need to subdivide both teachers and students into smaller, more clearly defined groups based on meaningful classifying categories, rather than continue to treat them as homogeneous. Thus, clear-cut data that apply only to certain teachers and students are preferable to data that apply in theory to all, but in practice do not have any application because they do not hang together.

In summary, the effect of rationally selecting teachers and/or students according to variables of interest is to insure that the investigator gets the sample he wants to study. A related effect is to increase variation on the variables of interest, either by insuring that the full range of scores is represented in the sample or by deliberately choosing groups that are high and low (or high, middle, and low) on these variables. Studies are likely to yield important and meaningful results to the extent that investigators insure that they have maximal variance on these variables, and the best way to do this is to select appropriate samples in the first place.

Analyze Data for Nonlinear as well as Linear Process-Product Relationships

Recent process-product research (see Chapter 4) has shown that many relationships between teaching process variables and student outcome variables are nonlinear. A *linear* relationship means that the process variable and the student outcome variable are simply and directly related. That is, the more that the teacher shows the process variable in the classroom, the more favorably the student outcome measure is affected. In contrast, *nonlinear* relationships are more complex. One kind of nonlinear relationship, shown graphically in Figure 3.1, is that in which increases in the teaching process variable lead to increases in the student outcome variable only up to a certain point but no further. In cases like this, increasing the teacher process variable is important if student outcome is to be maximized up to a certain point, but once this key point is reached, further increases in the teaching variable are unnecessary and do not affect student outcome. A second, and perhaps more typical and important, type of nonlinear relationship is shown graphically in Figure 3.2. This is the "inverted-U" or "crescent" relationship referred to above. In this kind of relationship, increases in the teaching process variable lead to increases in the student outcome variable up to a certain point, but beyond that point *decreases* take place. This type of relationship indicates that there is a certain *optimal level* of the particular teaching process variable in question, and that teachers who have either too much or too little of this behavior do not succeed as well as teachers who have just the right amount.

"Inverted-U" nonlinear relationships are examples of the assumption mentioned earlier that student outcome usually results from *a combination of teacher behaviors which must all be present at or above some minimal degree.* One example of the "inverted-U" relationship is the difficulty level of teacher questions. Measures of student success in answering teacher questions show "inverted-U" relationships to student learning (Brophy and Evertson, 1973b). That is, teachers whose questions are either too easy or too difficult are less successful than teachers who appropriately match their questions to the

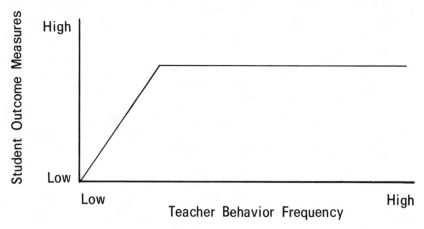

Figure 3.1   Illustration of a Positive Process-Product Relationship Which Is Linear but Levels off at Some Point

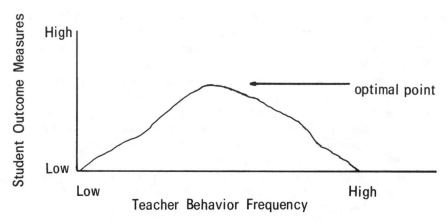

Figure 3.2 Illustration of an "Inverted-U" Curvilinear Process-Product Relationship

readiness levels of their students. Process-product relationships like this are easily interpreted and applicable to classroom teaching, but they will not be discovered unless investigators routinely search for nonlinear as well as linear relationships.

Failure to check for nonlinear relationships has been one reason why previous process-product research has failed to yield very impressive results. Where process-product relationships are nonlinear, simple linear measures such as correlations may not reach statistical significance, but a test for non-linear relationships might show a strong and clear-cut relationship. For example, in the extreme case where a perfect "inverted-U" relationship exists between the process variable and the product outcome measure, a simple correlation coefficient would be at or near zero. This is because the teachers scoring lowest on the process measure as well as those scoring highest would both have low scores on student outcome variables compared to teachers who scored medium high.

This example also illustrates why investigators using groups of teachers should always include a middle group as well as a low and high group on the teaching process variable. If only teachers low and high on the process variable are included, and if the process variable has an "inverted-U" curvilinear relationship with student outcome, the investigator will have selected an inappropriate sample by choosing only teachers high and low on the process variable. Of all the teachers that could have been included, these are the lowest teachers on the student outcome measure. Meanwhile, the teachers moderately high on the process variable, who are most successful in changing the students on this particular measure of student outcome, would have been excluded from the sample altogether (Soar, 1972).

Thus, the possibility of nonlinear relationships between process and product measures should be investigated routinely. Many such relationships have already been discovered and replicated, and many more will no doubt appear in the future as investigators begin to search for them more consistently.

Collect Enough Data To Insure Reliability and Validity

The quantity and quality of data on teaching behavior should be sufficient to insure reliability and validity. For example, little confidence can be placed in data which are based on only one or two visits to the classroom, because so many different situational and contextual factors can influence a teacher's behavior during a short segment of time. The only way to be sure that the process measures accurately reflect the teacher's general style, as well as the degree of variability in a teacher's behavior on a variable of interest, is to visit the classroom many times and in many different contexts (mornings and afternoons, different days of the week, during introductions to units and during completions of units, and so on). Often it will be necessary to subdivide the observations into smaller sets based on different contexts.

For example, in a series of studies on teacher expectations and attitudes conducted at the early elementary grades (Brophy and Good, 1974), it became obvious that teacher-student interaction during reading groups was different in many ways from interaction during whole-class discussions. Consequently, separate measures of the same kinds of behavior were developed and used in these two different contextual situations. This proved to be worth the trouble; although in many cases the process-product relationships were the same for measures taken in reading groups and in whole-class discussions, they were also different in many cases and these differences often were illuminating.

One way to solve the problem of reliability and validity of sampling, as well as to avoid situational and contextual differences which might affect observations, is to ask the teachers to teach standardized lessons. Each teacher can thus be observed teaching the same material in the same way and in roughly the same amount of time. This is often a good method, but it has certain assumptions that should be kept in mind. The method is a good one to the extent that: the standard lessons are identical for each teacher; they are equally relevant and appropriate for all students; the lessons are taught and observed under standardized conditions (time of day, day of week, time of year); and instructions about what and how to teach are sufficiently detailed and explicit so that all teachers will be working towards the same goals.

Gather Information about Teachers' Values, Goals, and Perceptions

This is another caution that should be taken to avoid putting one's self in the position of comparing apples with oranges. Teachers often are very different in their definitions of their teaching roles, their approaches to teaching, their goals for student outcomes, and other important variables of attitude and beliefs. In order to truly make sense out of data gathered from different classrooms, investigators should either find out this information by interviewing the teachers. Or they should attempt to insure that teachers have a common set of goals by requiring them to comply with a standardized set of instructions for teaching standardized lessons (although the latter method reduces variance that would show up in more natural situations). Even in the latter case, information about teachers' naturalistic inclinations is important, because data exists to show the teachers will be more likely to follow instructions that are compatible with their pre-existing values and goals than they would be to comply with instructions that conflict with these (Rubin, 1971).

Information about teacher values and goals should be looked at in connection with a description of their behavior in the classroom in order to make sense out of each data set. Often it happens that teachers appear to have contrasting values and goals (for example, one teacher may talk only about affective goals and the personalities and individual characteristics of his students, while another might concentrate on cognitive goals and the work habits and learning progress of his students), but they might turn out to be quite similar in their patterns of interaction with students. Conversely, teachers who espouse quite similar goals verbally may turn out to contrast sharply in their classroom behavior. However, usually there is a close correspondence between the teachers' stated goals and values and their classroom behavior. Thus, to the extent that values and goals differ, it is likely that classroom behavior will also differ. Where such differences are of interest to the investigation, they should be measured and taken into account in matching teachers, in the first place when assigning them to groups and in analyzing the data later. Where the differences in teacher values and attitudes are not of interest, they should be avoided whenever possible by rationally selecting teachers either to confine the sample to one or two types of teachers or to balance teacher types across each group (recognizing, of course, that the sample will be artificially homogeneous and that this must be kept in mind when discussing the results).

Data Should Be Based on Psychologically Meaningful Teaching Units

Many classroom observation systems have used time sampling, in which the observer watches for a fixed number of seconds and then codes his observations, then observes again, then codes again, and so on. However, simple time is not a very meaningful unit, since neither teachers nor students use it as a basis for carrying out their activities. Consequently, it is not surprising that research based on time sampling has generally proven unproductive.

More productive research has used sampling units of actual behavioral events occurring regularly in the classroom. For example, one common unit is "teacher asks question, student gives answer, teacher gives feedback." Another is "student comes to teacher for help with work, and teacher provides feedback." A third is "student acts out disruptively, teacher responds with some kind of disciplinary move, and student responds to teacher." These and other naturally occurring sequences are more psychologically meaningful to both students and teachers than a simple time unit, and they tend to yield the most meaningful process-product data.

Often it is important to keep track of the *sequence* in such a unit, noting in particular who started the sequence (the teacher or the student), and keeping track of the series of actions and reactions involved as it winds through to conclusion. Different classrooms can be compared conveniently when such psychologically meaningful units are used, because variables can be expressed as percentages based upon the total number of units observed.

For example, one classroom might have 200 instances of teacher disciplinary moves in response to student misbehavior, while another classroom might have only 50. However, by using variables such as "percentage of time that the teacher criticizes a student for misbehaving" (as opposed to merely warning him or ignoring him) or "percentage of times that the misbehavior appears to be directly caused by the teacher," meaningful comparisons of two classrooms can be made, even though one had four times as many instances of misbehavior as the other.

One probably important reason for the slow accumulation of useful process-product data in classroom research has been the slow progress in identifying such psychologically meaningful units. It appears that investigators often are using measurements at either too molecular or too molar a level (the units used are either too small or too large to be very meaningful), and consequently are unaware of many important relationships because the appropriate unit of measurement required to illuminate them has not yet been discovered. There is still much to be gained by simply observing in classrooms and developing taxonomies of teaching behaviors which might be useful for later investigations. Much progress has been made in this area in recent years, but it is likely that most such work remains to be done. The kinds of units used in conceptualizing and measuring the teaching process or teacher–student interactions still are fairly primitive.

For example, most studies of lesson presentation techniques have used the entire lesson as their unit. This seems inappropriate on intuitive grounds. At the very least, we should be differentiating between the introductory aspects of the lesson when the teacher is trying to get student attention and present the material, practice periods in which the teacher is asking questions or making response demands in order to get answers or responses from the students and provide them with feedback, and teacher review or summary at the end of the lesson. If the lesson is followed up by some kind of seatwork, this should be a fourth part of the lesson analysis (type of follow-up, clarity and thoroughness in giving instructions, and so on). Study of teacher behavior during lessons would probably yield much better results if it was recorded separately during these separate segments rather than being lumped together as is typically the case at present.

Another example is the long-standing lecture versus discussion controversy. Many studies have been done in this area, but they have yielded almost totally contradictory results (despite suggestions to the contrary by certain writers who firmly believe that discussion is almost always good and lecture is almost always bad). The reason for the conflicting results is most probably that the data have been collected at too molar a level, with teacher lecture versus discussion per time unit being the measure used. Again, by using such molar measures, we are comparing apples with oranges. We fail to take into account important situational differences that would affect the appropriateness of the method. In particular, it seems that lecturing should be especially appropriate and likely during introductions to units when teachers are giving new information, and discussion should be apropos during later parts of a lesson when students are expected to use the information given earlier, draw conclusions, and discuss it. If investigators measured amounts of lecture versus discussion separately according to these different situational contexts (and especially if they took into account the teachers' stated goals in carrying out the unit), it is more likely that they would gather more orderly and interpretable results.

A related point is that the selection of variables to be studied and the design of measurement instruments to be used should be related to a model or theory of teaching that ties together the different variables and facilitates interpretation of the data. Many process-product studies completed so far have involved variables selected without any apparent rationale, so that the findings are often puzzling and difficult to interpret even when they appear to be clear and replicated. Or, the hypotheses in one study might flow from a fairly clear-cut theory, but the measurement methods used may bear no observable relationship to the theory itself. Often one gets the impression that a particular measurement method was used simply because it was available, not because it was especially approriate for the study in question. Thus, in addition to stressing that measurement should be conducted with the appropriate instrument scaled to psychologically meaningful units, we would add that the variables selected for study and the measurement methods used to study them should stem from a concise model of teaching, and thus should be logically related to one another. Often this will mean that the investigator must create his own observation or data collection system tailored specifically to his needs, because the existing systems are inappropriate. Where this is the case, it should be done. The alternative, using already available but inappropriate instruments, usually produces only ambiguous or meaningless data.

Summary

Studies intended to evaluate the effectiveness of new curricula or to assess the impact of interventions involving changing teacher behavior were reviewed. Although these lines of research have produced a variety of interesting data and some promising leads about effective teaching, most of them have involved weak research designs that do not allow us to draw clear inferences about effective teaching from their data. The more frequent weaknesses were reviewed, and suggestions were made for improvements that might lead to more clear-cut results. These suggestions concern such matters as the variables and settings selected for research; the instruments used to measure the variables; the need to control extraneous teacher and student differences and contextual factors that might bias the findings; the need to use the individual class, or in some cases, the individual student as the unit of analysis; the need to check for nonlinear as well as linear relationships; the need to collect a quantity and variety of data large enough to allow for clear interpretation; and the need to switch from random samples of teachers to the use of rationally selected samples based on their particular appropriateness for the study in question. The net result of these suggestions would be to insure that the investigator has enough of the right kinds of teachers in his sample, so the teachers will show enough difference on the variables of interest to allow meaningful analyses. In addition, he requires enough information on teacher, student, and contextual variables to be sure that the findings are really due to the process variables he is studying and not to some extraneous variables. Finally, it was stressed that investigators should seek to identify psychologically meaningful and appropriate units for conceptualizing and measuring teaching. Non-meaningful units such as time, or inappropriate measurement devices should not be employed simply because they are available. Studies which incorporated these suggestions would go a long way towards producing more meaningful and interpretable process-product data than most of the studies done to date. However, some useful and interpretable studies have already been completed, and these will be reviewed in the following chapter.

Chapter 4 Teachers Can Make a Difference

As noted in Chapter 2, certain educational studies go against common sense experience and expectations by suggesting that teachers, curricula, and schools do not make a measurable impact on students. However, we have pointed out that these studies have serious design and methodological deficiencies that make it difficult to draw any confident conclusions from them. None of them even approaches the criteria for a good process-product study described in the previous chapter. Thus, these data are not definitive. On the other hand, they should not be dismissed lightly or thoughtlessly.

These data merit serious consideration not only because they are disturbing but because of the great amount of publicity and acceptance they have received. Also, in addition to acceptance and publicity, the large studies by Coleman, *et al.* (1966) and by Jencks, *et al.* (1972) have received support from other sources. First, as noted in the previous chapter, most process-product studies of teacher behavior have failed to identify specific behaviors that consistently affect student learning in predictable ways.

Second, the evaluation data from compensatory education programs, especially from Project Head Start, have been overwhelmingly negative. Comparisons of children in these compensatory programs with control children who were not in such programs usually failed to show any significant advantage to the children in the special program. Furthermore, even when significant differences favoring the children in the compensatory program were found, they usually disappeared within a year or so after the children left the special program. Such data led Arthur Jensen (1969) to proclaim that compensatory early education had failed.

Third, most comparisons of two or more curricula have revealed no differences. Students taught with a new and supposedly improved curriculum usually failed to show any measurable advantage over students taught with a traditional curriculum. Such data lead to the suggestion that different curricula and/or methods do not make a significant difference in student learning.

A fourth source of disturbing data has been generated by a series of studies completed by Popham (1971). These studies seem to show that even teacher training and the presumed expertise that it produces in teachers does not make a measurable difference in student learning. In a series of related studies, Popham compared learning by students taught by experienced, certified teachers with the learning of students taught by individuals whose work involved application of the skills being taught but who had not ever had teacher training or experience. For example, a course in auto mechanics would be taught by a group of teachers certified to teach the subject, and a comparison group would be taught by auto mechanics who were experienced in applying the concepts involved in auto repair but who had had no teacher training or experience. In various experiments like these comparing certified teachers with nonteachers experienced in the field, Popham regularly found no differences in student learning.

The implications of these studies are even more extreme than those previously reviewed which suggest that certified teachers are not significantly different from one another. These studies suggest that certified teachers have no more impact on students than practitioners who have knowledge of the field but no special expertise in teaching. In fact, Popham's studies raised the fundamental question of whether or not teachers have any special expertise at all! One could conclude from them that teachers learn nothing in the process of becoming certified that untrained practitioners do not already know intuitively (or, at least, that they do not learn anything that makes a difference with regard to student learning).

Popham himself has sharpened these disturbing conclusions by drawing comparisons with other professions, noting that teachers presumably have some professional expertise that sets them off from individuals with no specialized professional training. He points out that if a professional really has specialized expertise, an untrained nonprofessional should not be able to step in and do the professional's job competently. He notes, for example, that the average person would be unable to perform a medical or dental operation, or to draw up a contract, conduct a trial defense, or perform some other specialized aspect of the lawyer's role. Yet, it appears that untrained nonteachers can teach just as effectively as certified and experienced teachers!

Popham's results have been replicated by Moody and Bausell (1971, 1973), who also found that teacher training and experience was unrelated to the amount that students learn. These studies involved an improved research design that avoided the confounding of teacher training and teacher experience which had been present in Popham's research, but the same results were obtained. Dembo and Jennings (1973) also found no differences between experienced teachers and inexperienced teacher interns in ability to produce student achievement gains in mini-lessons, in the quality of their teaching as measured by observational coding, or in their ability to solve simulated classroom incidents. However, differences favoring the experienced teachers were found in a measure of attitudes towards education.

Although such data are disturbing, the methods used in these studies hold up to question their generalizability to naturalistic classrooms. Glass (1974) has criticized the methods used by Popham and his associates on several grounds. In particular, he objects to the use of a standardized test as the measure of teacher success, favoring instead observations and ratings of teacher behavior and student evaluation of teachers. Glass rejects the idea that a standardized test is more valid than these alternative methods, particularly the brief tests used by Popham which measured only a narrow range of teaching goals. The brevity and narrowness of these tests causes them to be unreliable and therefore inappropriate as measures of teacher effectiveness.

Glass goes on to suggest that the methodology used by Popham and his associates tends to "stack the cards" against demonstrating any differences between teacher groups. First, given the brevity and unreliability of the tests and the fact that the tests were not related to teacher goals, there is serious question as to whether the tests were measuring what the teachers were teaching. Second, although both teachers and practitioners were teaching in their general area of expertise, the experiments involved the use of materials unfamiliar to both, so that the experienced teachers had no special advantage owing to their familiarity with and expertise in using particular curriculum materials. Also, the experiment required the teachers to work with learners whom they did not know. Therefore they could not gear their lessons to the individual characteristics and learning styles of the students as they would have done in their own classrooms. In short, Glass argues that the experiments were designed so that teachers could not put into practice the special expertise that they presumably have.

The criticisms of Glass apply in particular to the results of Popham and of Moody and Bausell. They are less applicable to the study of Dembo and Jennings, because this study used observation of teaching behavior and a test of teacher ability to generate solutions to simulated classroom problems. Nevertheless, the observational data revealed no differences favoring the experienced teachers. Even this study, however, is open to the more general criticism that it did not allow the teachers to call upon the specialized expertise that they use in naturalistic situations.

For example, teacher skills such as lesson and unit planning, diagnostic reteaching, managing classes of thirty or more students, and individualizing instruction to each of these students were not involved in any of these studies, including the one by Dembo and Jennings. Yet, it is precisely these kinds of abilities which probably would be most obvious in comparisons of trained and untrained teachers in more naturalistic settings. Thus, all of the studies reviewed above raise important questions worth pursuing, but their results should not be accepted naively or generalized simplistically. In particular, these studies do *not* establish that experienced teachers have failed to acquire any special skills that are not possessed by untrained individuals. It is likely that comparison experiments in more naturalistic settings and over long time periods would reveal consistent and important differences between experienced teachers and untrained novices.

The Importance of Positive Findings

Other data suggesting that teachers, curricula, and/or schools do not make an important difference in student outcomes could be discussed, but these would not resolve the issues that they raise. The problem is that a negative hypothesis, such as the hypothesis that something makes no difference, cannot be proved scientifically. No matter how often negative findings are replicated, they are never proven in the sense that they can be taken as established facts, because there is always the possibility that positive findings may turn up.

Questions concerning effects on students must be resolved by analyzing the positive findings which have been reported. If it can be shown that such findings are suspect due to faulty experimental designs or other reasons, we can at least say that the proposition that teachers, curricula, and/or schools make a difference "remains unproven." On the other hand, if some of the positive findings stand as scientifically acceptable, and especially if they are validated by different investigators using different methods and populations, such data *can* establish cause–effect relationships even though negative findings may be more frequent.

It is possible, of course, that a small percentage of positive findings might be obtained by chance alone, but there are ways to check out this possibility. One way is to carefully investigate the specifics of a particular study in order to make sure that the research was properly carried out and that the findings are clear and consistent. Another and more important way is to survey these positive findings to see whether or not some of them replicate consistently. Findings that consistently replicate, especially if produced by different investigators working with different populations, are very unlikely to be due to chance. A third way, which is most convincing of all if done properly, is to move from correlational designs[1] to experimental designs, systematically varying the teaching behavior of interest to see if it has the expected effects upon students. When a study has been well designed to control for extraneous influences that might affect the results, confirmation of the expected relationship between teacher behavior and student outcome in such experimental studies constitutes strong evidence that the teacher behavior in question does in fact influence student outcomes. Most existing data relating teacher behavior to student outcomes are correlational rather than experimental because of the relatively primitive state of development of research in this area. However, improved research designs have begun to yield consistent correlations between teacher behavior and student outcome (to be discussed below), so that it is likely that experiments yielding consistent positive findings will appear with increasing frequency in the near future.

Research Relating Teacher Behavior to Student Outcomes

Although most process-product research has produced ambiguous or negative results, some variables have been correlated consistently with gains in student achievement and/or attitudes. Usually these teaching behaviors do not correlate very strongly with student outcome measures, but the fact that they usually correlate strongly enough to reach statistical significance in different studies conducted in various settings by separate investigators suggests that they are in fact related to student outcomes. This conclusion is further supported by the fact that most studies have failed to control for context differences, and we now know that most teaching behavior is optimal for certain contexts but irrelevant or even inappropriate for others. Thus, although the strength of the relationships revealed in these studies is not impressive, the consistency of findings across different studies by different investigators is.

Rosenshine and Furst (1973) reviewed most of these studies and concluded that students learned best when the following teaching characteristics were present: clarity; variability in teaching methods, curricula, and/or

[1] *In correlation research we can only say that variables co-occur. For example, by observing in a classroom we may see that students are more attentive when the teacher moves around the room during recitation period. However, before we could say that teacher mobility caused greater attentiveness, we would have to* manipulate *teacher mobility (ask teachers to move every minute, some not at all, etc.) and see directly the effects of teacher movement patterns on student attention. Without manipulating variables, we can only say that two variables share some association but not that one causes the other. (It is possible that teachers walk around the room when they see students becoming more attentive.) Correlational designs do not involve the manipulation of variables whereas experimental designs do.*

media; enthusiasm; task-oriented and/or businesslike behavior; indirectness (questioning rather than lecturing, frequent use of praise and frequent pupil-to-pupil interaction); student opportunity to learn the material; teacher use of structuring comments; and multiple levels of questions or cognitive discourse (as opposed to heavy concentration at one level of discourse). Also, teacher criticism consistently has an adverse effect on student learning.

Other variables that appeared to be effective in single studies but which require substantiation include: teacher redirection of student comments for reaction from other students; teacher expectations for achievement (the extent to which the teacher requires 100 percent correct responses from *all* students); thoroughness in teaching (the extent to which the teacher corrects errors by repeating the entire task and testing the student to make sure he knows the answers); and the extent to which the teacher follows the specified lesson formats.

Most of these relationships come from correlational rather than experimental studies, so that it is premature and incorrect to claim that the teacher behaviors *caused* the student learning gain. However, the consistency of these correlational data strongly suggest that the process-product associations are real, and that well designed experimental studies involving these teacher behaviors are likely to yield positive results.

In addition to the support they receive from research, these variables (in this case, effective teaching behaviors) have face validity. That is, they hang together well and fit well with theoretical and common sense expectations. The variables all seem to be compatible with one another and are likely to be intercorrrelated. In short, they suggest that a teacher who is determined to teach the content that he is supposed to teach, who is well prepared and organized in his instructional behavior, who is enthusiastic and skilled in motivating students, and who encourages the students to become involved in an active way in the learning process is more likely to be successful than a teacher who lacks one or more of these characteristics.

Another major review of process-product studies has been conducted by Dunkin and Biddle (1974). This review included not only studies linking teacher behavior to student learning gains, but also studies linking teacher behavior to affective variables such as student attitudes towards themselves as learners, towards teacher or school, and the like. In general, Dunkin and Biddle reached conclusions about process-product relationships similar to those reached by Rosenshine and Furst, although they caution that few of these correlational relationships have been borne out by experimental studies and that some have been negated by the few experimental studies which do exist. They also criticize many of the correlational studies for such defects as failure to take into account differences in students (SES, IQ, etc.), failure to include control or comparison groups, and failure to investigate possible nonlinear relationships between teacher behavior and student outcome.

Also, where Rosenshine and Furst chose to focus on the commonalities across studies, Dunkin and Biddle stressed the ambiguities and contradictions, seeking to find explanations that might resolve or explain them. However, despite their more critical approach, the latter authors still acknowledged that most, if not all, of the variables listed by Rosenshine and Furst appeared to be related to student outcome. They also noted some additional variables that appeared to be related to student learning and/or student attitudes. Most of these are in the area of classroom management, especially the kinds of teacher behavior stressed by Kounin (1970).

Kounin's research, since replicated by Brophy and Evertson (1974a, b, c), suggested that the teachers who are most successful in managing their classrooms are: more alert in monitoring the classrooms and remaining aware of what is going on at all times ("withitness"); able to sustain one activity while doing something else at the same time ("overlappingness"); able to maintain continuity without unnecessary interruptions or confusion ("smoothness"); able to sustain proper lesson pacing and maintain group momentum (avoiding overdwelling on minor points or wasting time dealing with individuals rather than groups, and so on); able to keep the group alert by creating suspense before asking questions, by asking questions frequently, or by presenting novel or interesting material regularly; successful in holding their students accountable for attention and learning (attending carefully to verbal responses and checking work carefully to let the students know that their performance will be monitored); attempting to generate enthusiasm directly and often; and providing variety in work assignments and general classroom activity.

In short, Kounin's findings indicate that the secret to successful classroom management is keeping students actively engaged in productive activities, avoiding periods of inactivity or confusion that lead to restlessness and misbehavior. The most successful classroom managers (the teachers who least often had to deal with disruption and other undesirable classroom behavior) were successful because they planned their instruction and organized their classrooms so that the students were continually engaged in productive activities, thus preventing problems from getting started in the first place. For the most part, they were not notably more successful than other teachers in dealing with problems once they had gotten started (Kounin, 1970). Brophy and Evertson (1974a, b, and c) replicated these findings and extended them by showing that such teachers also tended to produce greater learning gains in their students on standardized achievement tests.

Like the variables discussed previously, these classroom management variables are supported by classroom research and by their own internal consistency. Thus, they appear likely to be confirmed as causally important in future experimental research.

Several other promising variables were also identified by Dunkin and Biddle. One, related to teacher expectations, is the nature of the *steering group* in the classroom. Steering groups (Lundgren, 1972) are groups of students that the teacher uses as "benchmarks" for pitching their levels of instruction and for deciding when material has been learned and it is time to move on to something new. In general, the higher the ability and achievement level of the steering group in a classroom, the higher the learning shown by the class as a whole. Teachers who aim higher generally produce better results.

Group size also proved to be important, despite the typical finding that class size is not. Regardless of class size, teachers who worked with smaller groups tended to get better results than teachers who spent most or all of their time working with the class as a whole. In short, a high quality lesson with a small group of students appears more worthwhile than lower quality but longer lessons conducted with the entire class.

In general, the reviews by Rosenshine and Furst (1973) and by Dunkin and Biddle (1974) have identified a number of teaching behaviors which consistently correlate with student learning gains and/or positive student attitudes. Although most of the data remain correlational at this stage, the literature concerning correlates of student outcome measures provides one set of evidence that teachers do in fact "make a difference."

Preschool Studies

Jensen (1969) proclaimed that compensatory preschool intervention had failed. Using a box score approach, we would have to agree with him. However, as noted previously, such negative statements cannot be settled with a box score. Instead, they must be assessed by carefully examining the positive evidence. Most of this can be found in two recent reviews (Beller, 1973; Gordon and Jester, 1973) which reveal that most early education programs have failed to produce meaningful and sustained gains in student IQ's or school achievement test scores. However, the reviews also name several studies which have produced impressive results showing statistically and practically significant gains maintained over a long time period in certain well designed and implemented preschool programs.

Early evaluations of Project Head Start usually showed no advantage to the Head Start children. Furthermore, even where positive findings were obtained, the advantage to the Head Start children typically disappeared a few months after the end of the program. That is, where Head Start children were significantly above control children on measures of IQ or achievement at the end of the program, follow-up measures taken later usually showed that this advantage had disappeared and that the control groups had caught up to the Head Start groups. Such findings indicating a dissipation of the effects of experimental intervention are typical in preschool evaluation studies.

Early education enthusiasts reacted to such findings with concern and consternation at the time, because they had hoped that Project Head Start and other experimental preschools for the disadvantaged would make a strong impact on IQ tests and standardized achievement tests. In retrospect, we can see now that these were pie-in-the-sky hopes, rather than realistic expectations. Project Head Start affected the children only a few hours each day and for only a relatively short period of their lives, and thus, at best it could have a minor impact on their general development in comparison to the combined effects of the rest of the children's environment. Also, the vast majority of Head Start classrooms had little or no planned teaching and a relatively poor child-to-teacher ratio, so that they provided little more than custodial care rather than a true educational experience. In addition, most early Head Start programs had little or no meaningful parent involvement, so that this valuable resource was untapped. Given all of this, it is hardly surprising that such programs had only slight impact on the children.

However, better designed and implemented programs do have worthwhile and sustained effects upon young children. Several studies (summarized in Bissel, 1971, and in Stallings, 1972) show that a planned curriculum tends to structure teacher behavior. Teachers implementing an experimental model tend to teach according to the methods prescribed by the model. Also, such studies show that children enrolled in experimental programs benefit from them significantly more than children in traditional programs. Although there is no clear-cut evidence suggesting that any one program is superior to all the others, existing data do indicate that certain features of experimental programs are consistently associated with success when they are compared with programs that do not achieve such success.

Long-term studies by Klaus and Gray (1970), Karnes (1969), Weikart (1971) and others have shown that children in well designed and implemented preschool programs can achieve significant gains in IQ and/or achievement test scores compared to children not enrolled in preschools or attending preschools without an educational focus, and that these gains are sustained over a number of years. The more successful programs tend to have in common: a low child-to-teacher ratio; a parent involvement program that strongly stresses the development of close relationships with the parents; the provision of opportunities for parents to have input in the program and to participate in it; and the presence of a planned and structured curriculum with preselected objectives and concise lesson plans. These factors appear to be the most crucial in determining the degree of success a preschool program achieves. For more detailed discussion of this point and for suggestions about teaching preschool children effectively, see Brophy, Good, and Nedler (1975).

Parent involvement appears to be important for two reasons: first, directly, parents help and support the program both in school and at home with educational activities planned for them to use with their children; second, indirectly, parental expectations, attitudes, and school–home relationships are improved. A planned curriculum with preselected objectives seems to be important because programs lacking this feature tend to be traditional middle-class oriented nursery schools which provide disadvantaged children with experiences that they usually get at home anyway (warmth from adults and opportunities for social interaction with peers), while failing to provide them with the intellectual stimulation that is usually characteristic of advantaged homes to a far greater degree than of disadvantaged homes (Hess, 1970).

The *specifics* of the planned curriculum which is used appear to be less important than the *presence* of such a curriculum, although Karnes (1969) has provided data suggesting that programs featuring stress on verbal modeling and instruction are more successful than Montessori programs (which stress nonverbal modeling and discovery learning) with disadvantaged children. These findings fit common-sense expectations, in that disadvantaged parents usually provide a lower quantity and quality of verbal modeling and instruction to their young children than more advantaged parents, whereas they apparently provide at least as much opportunity for observation of adult behavior and for manipulation of objects. The findings concerning child-to-teacher ratio also make common sense: Even the most talented teacher cannot accomplish much if he must work with 30 to 40 children.

So far, preschool studies have failed to produce evidence that certain kinds of teachers or teaching behaviors are superior to other kinds, but this is mostly because research done at this level has concentrated on curriculum evaluation. It is likely that studies that concentrate on teachers and their behavior will identify types of teachers and teaching behavior that are especially successful with young children, but such research has not been done to date (Gordon and Jester, 1973).

Many studies conducted in laboratory situations as well as in naturalistic classroom settings have demonstrated the effectiveness of *behavior modification* principles for improving the classroom behavior of students and, in some cases, student achievement. Klaus and Gray (1968) and Bereiter and Engle-mann (1966) have employed behavior modification principles heavily and apparently successfully. This was also true of the Durham Education Improvement Program (Spaulding, 1968). In addition to providing evidence for the general effectiveness of behavior modification procedures, Spaulding's study showed that supportive, approving, and receptive teacher behavior functioned as rewards for the children; aversive or dominative teacher behavior had a generally punishing effect on the children; and limiting and goal setting teacher behavior which tended to clarify, regularize, organize, or otherwise structure the environment tended to have positive effects on the children. Each of these three types of general teacher behavior was significantly related to both pupil performance and reported self-concept.

Studies of behavior modification or other methodological variables might produce more impressive results if teacher implementation data were regularly collected. Such studies share the same problem noted previously in curriculum evaluation studies: There is no guarantee the teachers will use the desired method simply because they are asked or instructed to do so. For example, Rowe (1972) experienced great difficulty in trying to train teachers to execute the apparently simple behavior of pausing at least three seconds to wait for a student to answer a question, and behavior modifiers frequently report that teachers have difficulty learning seemingly simple techniques (praise desirable behavior, ignore undesirable behavior, and so on). Thus, investigators interested in assessing the effectiveness of a given teaching method should monitor the teachers in the study, since some experimental teachers will not use the method despite instructions and some teachers in the control group will use the method naturalistically. Clear and interpretable findings will be difficult to achieve unless such problems are overcome through better research designs.

Elementary School Studies

In this and the following sections of the chapter we will review some specific studies that illustrate or elaborate upon the conclusions drawn in the two general reviews by Rosenshine and Furst (1973) and by Dunkin and Biddle (1974). First, several studies have shown that attendance at elementary school makes a difference and/or that some elementary schools are more successful than others.

At the most fundamental level, several studies have compared children who have gone to school with children who have not, or who have left school early. These studies all show that school has considerable impact, not only in infusing knowledge but in developing children's cognitive abilities and problem-solving skills.

One such study was conducted in Prince Edward County, Virginia. This county closed its public schools from 1959 to 1964 rather than comply with a court order to integrate them, so that some children in the county did not go to school during this period. Comparisons of children who stayed in the county but did not go to school with peers who went to private schools in the county or who left the county to attend school elsewhere showed that the children who did not attend school failed to progress and in many cases seriously regressed in their intellectual abilities (Green, et al., 1966).

A second study yielding similar results was conducted by Schmidt (1966). This research was done in a South African community where education is not compulsory. Children who started school early and stayed in school longer were compared with children who began later or did not stay in school very long. Among other things, his comparisons revealed a strong relationship between years of schooling and intelligence test scores, even with age held constant and SES controlled statistically.

A third study of this type conducted by Vernon (1969) involved children in Nigeria and Senegal, South Africa and canal boat children and gypsy children in Britain. In each sample, comparisons of elementary school age children not attending school with age mates who were in school revealed that the children attending school not only knew more on tests of school-related learning but scored higher on intelligence tests also. Finally, Walberg (1974) notes that children in school tend to maintain or gain in measured IQ, while school dropouts tend to lose IQ points, at least for the first few years after they drop out.

All of these studies no doubt involved a certain amount of selection bias, because even where SES was controlled it is likely that the children who attended school came from families who placed a greater value on education than the children who did not. Thus, the differences seen in these studies reflect not only the effect of school but probably also differences in family values. Nevertheless, these and similar data leave little doubt that schooling has important effects upon cognitive development. Children with more schooling not only learn more facts; they develop their thinking and problem-solving abilities more fully.

The previous studies all compared children attending school with children who had not gone to school or who had had minimal schooling, and all favored the children with more schooling. In addition to these studies showing absolute effects of schooling versus no schooling, data are beginning to appear showing that some schools are more effective than others. An especially interesting study in this tradition was reported by Brookover, Gigliotti, Henderson, and Schneider (1973). In contrast to the approaches taken in the studies reviewed and criticized in Chapter 2, these investigators took into account the SES and racial composition of school populations by matching schools within categories before making comparisons. As noted previously, this is preferable to attempting to control these factors statistically. Based on demographic data and standardized achievement test scores attained by fourth graders, elementary schools were assigned to categories based on SES and racial composition of the school populations and on whether the school was urban or rural. Then, the investigators identified pairs of schools within each category that were similar on every variable measured except student achievement. Thus, they identified pairs of schools virtually identical in SES and racial composition and in being either urban or rural, but contrasting in the levels of student achievement that their students attained on standardized achievement tests. These data demonstrate that schools can differ significantly from one another even when student populations are carefully matched.

After identifying pairs of contrasting schools, the investigators asked the students, teachers, and principals of 24 schools to fill out questionnaires. The responses were then analyzed and related to measures of school success in producing student learning. These results showed that the most important single negative factor was the students' *sense of futility*. Students in the schools that had the worst records showed the strongest sense of futility. These students were cynical and apathetic, feeling that very little of value went on in their schools and that they had little or nothing to say about it. Other important differences between successful and unsuccessful schools included teacher perceptions of future evaluations and expectations of the students (a measure of the general level of teacher expectations) and teachers' reported willingness to push students to achieve. In short, when teachers believed that the students could learn and worked hard to see that they did, the students learned; when teachers did not think the students could learn and did not work very hard to see that they did, the students did not learn much.

These data are consistent with those from many studies (reviewed in Brophy and Good, 1974) which show a relation between teacher expectations and student achievement. Whether the unit of analysis is the individual teacher or the entire school, teacher expectations and student learning tend to go together.

Although teacher expectations are to some degree unique to the individual teacher, several studies indicate that the curriculum materials provided to teachers tend to set the pace for the class by fixing the expectations of both teachers and students concerning what is appropriate for the students to learn. This was shown very clearly in a cross-cultural study conducted by Pidgeon (1970) which compared elementary school students in England and in California. Pidgeon found that British students of similar age and intelligence to students in California had learned much more mathematics, as evidenced by their much higher scores on identical tests. However, an additional analysis comparing the percentage of students in each group who passed each specific item showed no difference between groups on items which had been taught in *both* school systems. The advantage to the British students was due solely to the fact that they had been taught more during the year than the students in California. Apparently expectations for mathematical learning in this grade were higher for the British schools (appropriately so, judging from the test scores), so that British children learned more than the American children even there was no difference in student ability.

Related data were reported by Chang and Raths (1971). In this study, the achievement scores of fourth and fifth graders from seven low-SES and seven middle-SES urban schools were analyzed. As expected, the middle-SES students scored higher than the lower-SES students. However, analysis of the items revealed that the SES difference was due to a set of items that the middle-SES children passed and the lower-SES children failed. To find out why, Chang and Raths questioned the teachers involved to find out how much emphasis they placed on teaching the particular skills involved in each item. These interview data showed that the middle-SES schools placed emphasis on all of the items, while the lower-SES schools emphasized on only some of them. The items taught in the lower-SES schools were the ones on which the lower-SES students did reasonably well when they took the test. Thus, again, the biggest reason for the difference in scores between the two sets of students was the degree to which the material was taught (although in this case there was also a difference in student ability levels).

Similar findings resulted from a review of 32 studies of innovative curricula, covering elementary school through college (Walker and Schaffarzick, 1974). Almost all of these comparisons favored the innovative curricula over the traditional curricula, at least if the test data were taken at face value. However, the authors inspected the tests used in each of the studies and assessed whether the test tended to favor the innovative curricula by emphasizing items taught in it, to favor the traditional curricula by emphasizing items taught in it, or to favor neither. When this information about the nature of the tests used was included in a reanalysis of the data, the findings were clear: innovative curricula looked good when the criterion test favored the innovative curricula, and traditional curricula looked good when the criterion test favored the traditional curricula. In short, the students had learned what they were taught.

The preceding studies indicate that much of what students learn is a function of teacher and student expectations, and that these are determined in large part by the curriculum used. Thus, the quantity and quality of student learning is partly determined by what school officials or other decision makers decide is relevant and appropriate. Within limits, at least, students will learn what they are taught.

Differences in Teaching Methods

Some teaching methods are more effective than others, even when the curriculum is identical. Many of these method differences have already been discussed in connection with the reviews by Rosenshine and Furst (1973) and by Dunkin and Biddle (1974). However, there are a few additional ones that are worth mentioning.

One important matter relevant to early elementary school instruction is the controversy over the importance of phonics and word attack skills versus sight reading and the whole-word approach in teaching initial reading. Chall (1967) reignited this old controversy in her book *Learning to Read: The Great Debate*. She reviewed many studies which had been completed before that time and concluded that a strong phonics or word attack component should be included in teaching beginning reading. Unfortunately, some schools overreacted to this and went to an approach that overstressed phonics, far beyond what Chall suggested. Nevertheless, her conclusion that initial reading programs which included a strong phonics element would be more successful than initial reading programs restricted to the sight reading or whole-word approach was strongly supported by the studies she reviewed, and it has received further support since (Della-Piana and Endo, 1973; Hoover, Politzer, and Brown, 1973; Nelson, 1973).

Studies agree in finding that children who learn initial reading with a method that includes a strong phonics component tend to acquire better word attack skills and generally better reading skills, other things being equal. This qualification is important, however. As Chall (1967) pointed out in her initial review, the teacher is at least as important as the curriculum and teaching guide in determining student learning, because some teachers use the curriculum as it was intended to be used (with or without specific instruction), while others do not (sometimes despite instruction).

Once again, we see that simple purchase of an innovative curriculum will not insure its effectiveness; teachers must be motivated to desire to teach the new curriculum properly and be trained to do so.

This is one reason why some of the more recently developed learning systems devised by educational development laboratories and research and development centers funded by the federal government have achieved success when earlier innovations did not. These nonprofit institutions usually have more time and funds to devote to careful development and testing of new curricula and methods, and they typically include good staff development and training materials with the teaching materials. These intitutions also tend to research and evaluate their products before attempting to disseminate them widely, making sure that the learning package involved not only has a clear rationale behind it but also is appropriate for use in typical classrooms. These improvements make it likely that the products being developed by these institutions will produce genuine educational improvements rather than passing fads. Such careful development of new educational materials, coupled with improvements in research on teaching methods, have already begun to pay off in educational improvements and are likely to continue to do so in the future.

Another promising method that is receiving increasing attention lately is *tutoring*. Although tutoring by classmates is sometimes attempted, the more common and successful methods involve the use of adult volunteers or older students to tutor young students. For example, Keele (1973) used tutoring in a remedial reading program for nonreaders. Twenty-eight children tutored by Mexican-American paraprofessionals who had been trained in a tutoring method were compared with twenty children taught in the school's traditional remedial reading program. Even though the tutors were paraprofessionals with minimal training, the tutored children outperformed the children in the traditional group on all five tests, significantly so on four. Apparently these results were due to the tutoring method, independent of the ethnicity of the tutors (Mexican-American paraprofessionals were also used as teachers in the traditional remedial reading program).

Such studies show the power of tutoring as a teaching method and illustrate that nonprofessionals using prepared materials and given sufficient training can tutor successfully, sometimes even accomplishing more in less time than certified teachers are able to accomplish in typical classroom settings when they are trying to work with the whole class or with a group. Studies involving the use of fifth or sixth grade children to tutor younger children have usually produced equally impressive results, often showing that the school work and general school attitudes of the tutors improves at least as much as those of the children whom they tutored (Good and Brophy, 1973).

Thus, tutoring is one teaching method that has proven valuable as an adjunct to ordinary teaching practices. Another is computer assisted instruction (CAI). For example, Fletcher and Atkinson (1972) studied reading achievement in 22 pairs of first grade boys and 22 pairs of first grade girls who had been matched on readiness test scores. All of the children received first grade reading instruction as part of their ordinary school experience, but one child in each pair also had eight to ten minutes of CAI per day during the second half of the school year. Reading achievement tests given at the end of the year showed that the children in the CAI program outperformed their matched controls, and that these improvements were general and not limited to the phonics-oriented goals stressed in the CAI program. Sex comparisons showed that boys benefited more than girls. Thus, this study further illustrates the importance of word attack skills in teaching initial reading, and it also suggests that CAI is a useful teaching adjunct, especially for boys. A number of studies have suggested that CAI and other special teaching innovations that involve gadgets in addition to more traditional teaching methods are especially effective with boys (Brophy and Good, 1974).

Another promising innovation is Individually Prescribed Instruction (IPI), although the program is still new and the available data tend to be sketchy. A study by Rookey (1973) is perhaps typical. Rookey compared student learning in eight IPI schools and eight control schools. A total of 150 IPI teachers and 145 control teachers in grades three through six were included, along with their students and most of the students' parents. Teacher interviews showed few group differences, but the differences that did show up favored the IPI schools. The IPI teachers were more positive in describing their pupils as independent and self-directed, and more positive in seeing teacher aides as more productive, necessary, active, valuable, and desirable. Parent interview data showed large differences favoring the IPI schools, with parents of IPI pupils reporting them to better motivated, more self-directed, and more independent. Since both the teachers and the parents were aware that an experimental innovation was involved, these self-report data may be affected somewhat by the "Hawthorne Effect." Nevertheless, all of the significant differences in this research favored the IPI schools.

Sears, *et al.* (1972) are conducting a five-year study designed to discover what classroom teacher behavior will improve achievement, self-concept, and internal locus of control (the sense of power over and responsibility for one's own successes and failures) in low-SES children. Following the first year of the study, data were available on six first grade classrooms in a low income school district. They showed that:

1. Achievement was greater when teachers directed attention more often to individual children than when they spent more time with groups or with the class as a whole;
2. Achievement was greater when these private interactions were related to the students' work rather than to their behavior, and when the teachers gave the children their undivided attention;
3. Achievement was greater when teachers spent a greater proportion of their time giving individuals information publicly (thus, even in discussions, reading groups, and other public situations, interactions with individual students were especially important);
4. In contrast, achievement was reduced when teachers frequently initiated interactions with the entire class in order to provide information about subject matter.

Summarizing, the authors note that the more successful teachers did more tutorial teaching. They spoke to the class as a whole in order to provide structure and give general directions, but most of their actual instruction was given in small groups or to individuals. These data reinforce several previously reported findings, especially the importance of individualized attention to children and of stressing academic work in private interactions with children rather than nonacademic content.

Recent studies are also providing increasing support for applied behavior modification, particularly contingency contracting (Homme, 1970). Contingency contracting means "contracting" with students to do a certain amount of work or to accomplish a certain set of goals in exchange for a specified reward. When used most successfully, contingency contracting programs individualize the "contract" so that each student is given an assignment which is appropriately time-consuming and at the level of difficulty that matches the individual's rate of progress and the time available to complete the assignment. Ideally, the content of the assignment is also matched to the individual's interests (for example, if the assignment involves writing a composition, the students can be allowed to select a topic or range of topics of interest to them).

Although there is no necessary logical connection, contingency contracting methods are usually used in combination with behavior modification methods (rewarding desirable behavior and ignoring, as much as possible, undesirable behavior). Thus, students who work hard and carefully enough to complete their contracts successfully are rewarded (usually by allowing them to choose from a variety of rewards referred to as a "reinforcement menu"), while children who fail to fulfill their contracts go unrewarded (they are not punished in any direct way, but they are deprived of the rewards they could have enjoyed if they had fulfilled their contract). Contingency contracting and behavior modification methods have been developed mostly by psychologists and educators interested in applying the work of B. F. Skinner (motivating through reinforcement) to practical classroom problems. Many writers have objected to this approach on philosophical grounds, arguing that students should not be rewarded for what they should be doing anyway, that the approach is too manipulative, that it tends to degrade the student, and/or that the heavy dependence upon extrinsic rewards will erode intrinsic motivation so that students will lose interest in doing things or learning things for their own sake. These objections seem to have face validity, and there are laboratory data to back up the assertion that rewarding people for doing things that they would have to do anyway may erode intrinsic motivation and make the people unwilling to work unless rewarded (Deci, 1972). However, a number of counter arguments and a much longer and more impressive list of laboratory studies exists to back up the contingency contracting/behavior modification approach.

Until recently, the argument was largely academic, because behavior modification and contingency contracting were used mostly in laboratory experiments or in classroom studies involving only one or two students. Most observers, including many proponents of these methods, dismissed them as impractical for use with entire classrooms by individual teachers. However, recent data suggest that the methods might be more feasible for use in everyday classrooms than was previously suspected.

Thompson, et al. (1974) taught elementary teachers to use contingency management principles as their basic approach to classroom management in dealing with their entire class. Most teachers implemented the principles successfully, and 12 of the 14 classes showed higher task involvement and fewer disruptions. Rollins, et al. (1974) studied the effects of a contingency management program on 16 elementary teachers and their students compared with matched control classes. Data on the teachers showed that they successfully learned to use the techniques and enjoyed using them, and data on the students revealed less disruption, more task engagement, and gains in IQ and school achievement. A third study (Brophy, Colosimo, and Carter, 1974) was conducted in an elementary school which had been run along traditional lines previously. All teachers, not just volunteers, were *required* to shift to the new system after four days of training, and then were monitored to see how well they implemented it and what effects it had on the students. The findings were mixed but mostly positive. Teacher attitudes were generally favorable, and observation data showed that they implemented the procedures as instructed. Student achievement measures showed mostly gains over expectations based on previous years, and school attendance improved significantly. There were no effects on tardiness rates, teacher ratings of students' behavior, or student self-concept.

These studies reveal that contingency management and behavior modification principles can and do work in real world classrooms, including situations in which teachers are using them with the class as a whole and even where the sample is not restricted to willing volunteers. Longer term studies are needed to insure that the gains from these procedures hold up over time and that the procedures do not involve undesirable side effects, but the presently available data are certainly encouraging as far as they go. Contingency management and behavior modification techniques appear to be effective for both student achievement and student affective development.

Affective Variables

So far we have concentrated mostly on various methods of instruction and their relative effectiveness. However, several studies have indicated the importance of certain aspects of teacher personality, especially the affective or emotional aspects of teaching. For example, St. John (1971) studied 36 white urban sixth grade teachers whose classrooms contained both black and white students. She found that the warmer, more student-oriented teachers were more successful with black children. Black children showed the greatest growth in reading when their teachers were rated highly on traits such as kindliness, adaptability, and optimism, and when the teachers did *not* consider tests scores to be a good indication of student ability. Such teachers not only obtained better reading gains from the black children, but also obtained better conduct and attendance as well as a greater belief in the importance of teacher approval.

In contrast with the findings for black students, white students showed the greatest reading gains under teachers characterized as task oriented (fluent, confident, stimulating). These teachers were more concerned with putting across subject matter than they were with their relationship with students. Although they produced greater reading gains, their students did not think that teacher approval was very important. In general the findings were much more striking for black students than for white students, perhaps because all the teachers were white. Along with the data of Kleinfeld (1972) and others, this study suggests that teacher warmth and student orientation are especially important to minority group students who are (or feel that they are) disliked or discriminated against by teachers and students who belong to the majority group (Brophy and Good, 1974).

Several studies by Aspy (1973) also illustrate the importance of teacher affective variables. These studies all involved what Aspy calls "interchangeable responses," a concept adapted from Carl Rogers' writings about effective psychotherapist behavior. "Interchangeable responses" are teacher summations of student statements which are interchangeable with what the student has actually said (in other words, teacher responses which show that the teacher has heard and understood the student completely and accurately).

Aspy's studies involved coding teacher statements as to whether or not they were "interchangeable" and then computing the percentage of such interchangeable statements for each teacher. In one study, the standardized reading achievement scores of 120 third graders were positively related to the scores on teachers' interchangeable responses: Students of teachers high in interchangeable responses scored better than students of teachers low in interchangeable responses. A follow-up study showed that reading teachers who had been given specific training in making interchangeable responses were twice as successful in increasing student reading achievement during a summer session than were untrained teachers. A third study revealed that when elementary school teachers increased their frequencies of interchangeable responses, student absences significantly decreased, reaching their lowest levels in the school's 45-year history. Similar findings were reported in two other studies. Research on student teachers also yielded favorable results when those who had been trained to make interchangeable responses were compared with those who had not.

These studies provide impressive evidence of the importance of teachers' showing empathy for children by being able to make interchangeable responses. Their ability to do so shows that they are paying careful attention to the students and are interested in what the students have to say. Teachers listen carefully to get the full nuances and emphasis of the students' statements, and their behavior suggests that they think that what the students have to say is important and worth listening to.

Teachers' ability to make interchangeable responses probably is one central aspect of the *quality* of teacher–student relationships, and this in turn is probably one reason for the impressive correlations that this variable shows with student outcome measures. Also, note that studies involving this variable have been experimental as well as correlational, so that, taken together, the data seem to demonstrate that the improved student gains are a direct result of interchangeable responses by the teachers, rather than a result of some extraneous variable. This line of research is particularly interesting and important, partly because it is programmatic (the studies build on one another in order to answer a variety of related questions) and partly because it represents an improvement in identifying the crucial aspects of the affective side of teaching which previous investigators have studied under overly broad terms such as "warmth," "acceptance," "praise," "student orientation," and the like. The ability to give interchangeable responses is more narrow and operationally defined than these broader concepts, and thus it is both easier to study in the classroom and easier to explain to teachers.

Large Scale Studies

Recently, several large scale process-product studies have been initiated in an attempt to identify teacher behavior that correlates with student learning gains. Although similar in general concept and intent to previous process-product studies, these more recent ones differ in that they involve larger numbers of classrooms, larger numbers and kinds of teacher behaviors, the use of improved and/or more appropriate classroom observation techniques, and other improvements which make them more likely to succeed in finding systematic relationships. Many of these efforts are so new that data are not available yet, but data from two studies are available and will be discussed.

The first is the work of Robert Soar and his colleagues at the University of Florida who have been studying teachers in Project Follow Through classrooms. These are first, second, and third grade classrooms located in schools that have Project Head Start programs. They attempt to adapt the traditional early elementary programs to take into account the benefits gained in the Head Start program. The schools involved are populated substantially or totally by students from low income families. Soar and his colleagues have done several studies to date, each producing some confirmation of earlier results and also some findings which surprised both the investigators themselves and the research community at large, at least at the time.

A study by Ragosta, Soar, Soar, and Stebbins (1971) is typical. Data were collected in 70 Follow Through classrooms by making twelve 5-minute observations on a single day in each classroom. The observational data then were correlated with several measures of student learning. Unsurprisingly, it was found that teacher emphasis on simple and highly focused learning tasks was positively related to student learning on tests of simple, concrete skills. However, the same teacher behavior was also *positively* related to learning gains on more abstract and complex tests. In other words, both kinds of gains were associated with the same kinds of teacher behavior: giving and receiving information (in other words, teacher structured lecturing vs. pupil-centered learning experiences); simple as opposed to complex questions; low frequencies of evaluation questions and other difficult questions; high frequencies of narrow answers as opposed to broad answers; moderately focused (as opposed to child-centered and child-directed) learning tasks; and general frequency of information giving and receiving by the teachers (as opposed to high levels of pupil-to-pupil interaction and a generally indirect teaching style).

Thus, this study revealed that the more heavily structured, teacher-dominated, and slower paced classrooms were more successful in producing student learning on both low level and high level tasks than were the more indirect and pupil-centered classrooms. These data are not anomolous, because they have been supported and expanded by data from the project by Brophy and Evertson to be described below.

Another important set of findings from this research is that many teacher behavior variables relate to student learning curvilinearly rather than linearly. In particular, many teaching behaviors show an "inverted-U" relationship to student learning, indicating that the ideal teacher behavior is somewhere in between the low and high extremes, and that teachers who are moderate on the variable tend to be more successful than teachers who are either low or high. This makes intuitive sense for many teaching variables, and it indicates the need for regularly checking for such curvilinear relationships in any process-product study, although this has not been done until recently (Soar, 1972). Research by Soar and his colleagues is continuing (Soar and Soar, 1973), and it should continue to make significant methodological and substantive contributions to the search for teacher behavior that optimizes student learning.

A second large scale study is being carried out by Brophy and Evertson and their colleagues at the University of Texas (Brophy, 1973, 1974; Brophy and Evertson, 1973a, 1973b, 1974a, 1974b, 1974c; Evertson and Brophy, 1973, 1974; Peck and Veldman, 1973; Veldman and Brophy, 1974). This series of studies is the largest investigation of its kind today, involving several methodological and design innovations which should help it succeed in identifying process-product relationships more consistently than most previous studies have. One important feature was the selection of teachers included in the sample. This research was a two-year replicated study, involving 31 second and third grade urban school teachers in the first year and 28 in the second year. These teachers were drawn from a larger sample of 165 because they were the most consistent in their relative success in producing student learning gains on the standardized achievement tests.

The sample selection process itself provided evidence that teachers differ significantly from one another in the amount of learning their students accomplish. About half of the teachers showed consistent patterns from one year to the next, and among these, some teachers were consistently quite successful in producing student learning gains while other teachers were consistently unsuccessful. The other half of the teachers were inconsistent, producing high gains one year and low gains the next, or vice versa. In any case, the data clearly showed that teachers have differential effects on student learning which are both statistically and practically significant (Brophy, 1973; Veldman and Brophy, 1974). Acland (1974), studying the stability of teacher effectiveness in a sample of 89 fifth grade teachers, produced similar results. These data revealed that teacher effects are much stronger than was previously suspected. They do not show up, however, unless the appropriate controls and statistical procedures are used to insure that teacher differences are not masked by student differences.

Although the studies by Brophy, Evertson and their colleagues are still in progress, many interesting results have already appeared. First, there were striking differences between the kinds of teaching behavior that appeared to work best in high-SES schools in contrast to the kinds most effective in low-SES schools. Textbooks usually discuss teaching behavior as being *generally* either good or bad, thus failing to take into account important contextual differences such as student ability levels, student ages, subject matter, types of lessons and activities, and so on. The data from this study suggest that high-SES students do in fact learn more when taught with methods stressed in most textbooks (indirect teaching, use of student ideas, frequent pupil-to-pupil interaction). However, students in low-SES schools tend to learn more when taught in a different way that might be characterized as "overteaching." This includes: going through the material at a slower pace; using smaller steps and including more repetition and redundancy; more teacher direction and more teacher implemented activities; fewer student-initiated activities; more teacher lecture and demonstration and less student talk; and more tightly teacher-organized classrooms.

In general, the data strongly support Soar's findings from the Follow Through classrooms, since they indicate that similar kinds of teaching behavior appear to be optimal for low-SES students in the early primary grades. The data do not necessarily invalidate or even conflict with the claims that indirect teaching is more effective than direct teaching, since most data supporting this proposition come from studies conducted at higher grade levels. Low-SES students in the early elementary grades have not yet mastered the fundamental tool skills of reading, writing, and arithmetic and the work habits involved in independent completion of assignments and independent learning generally, so that they are still relying heavily upon the teacher for instruction. In contrast, by second and third grade, high-SES students usually have mastered these skills for the most part and thus are more capable of benefitting from independent learning efforts. So in general, it appears that indirect teaching is probably effective, but only after students have mastered the fundamental tool skills and work habits required to assume responsibility for initiating and maintaining their own learning efforts.

The Brophy and Evertson study also bears out Soar's contention that many process-product relationships are curvilinear, although many of the nonlinear relationships they report are not of the "inverted-U" type that Soar postulated as typical. Some are rising or dropping curves which tail off at a certain point, suggesting that certain teacher behaviors are either good or bad only up to a point, beyond which further increases in the teacher behavior will make little difference in student achievement. Other teaching variables do show the "inverted-U" relationship to student learning, suggesting an optimal level of teacher behavior on this variable and indicating that teachers moderate on the variable will produce greater learning than teachers with either lower or higher scores.

One especially interesting curvilinear relationship has been discovered linking the percentage of teacher questions which are answered correctly to student learning gains. Contrary to the assumptions and expectations of errorless learning advocates who would suggest a direct relationship between this variable and student learning gains (assuming that learning gains will be greatest when errors are reduced to near-zero), the Brophy and Evertson research has shown that student success in answering teacher questions is curvilinearly related to learning gains, and also that the optimal rate appears to differ by SES. Low-SES students appear to make their greatest gains when they answer about 80 percent of their teacher's questions correctly, while high-SES students appear to make the greatest gains when they answer about 70 percent of the questions correctly.

These data suggest that optimal teacher behavior requires adjusting question difficulty level to the present knowledge and ability levels of the students, making the questions easy enough so that the students can understand and respond, but difficult enough to provide some challenge. If the success rate goes too high, approaching 100 percent, learning is reduced, apparently because the teacher is unnecessarily rehashing material that the students have already overlearned. In contrast, if the success rate falls much below 70 percent, the questions may be too hard for the students to fully comprehend and to benefit from; so that the teacher is generally "over their heads." The SES difference in optimal success rates is another example of the general difference mentioned earlier: Lower-SES students need the material presented in smaller steps and with greater repetition than higher-SES students, who appear to be able to proceed through a given amount of material more quickly.

The Brophy and Evertson study has also provided considerable support for the findings of Kounin (1970) concerning classroom management skills. Classroom observation variables based upon Kounin's descriptions of "withitness," "overlapping," "smoothness," and "momentum" produced some of the strongest and most consistent correlations with student learning gains among the several hundred variables included in the study. Thus, teachers who employ the techniques stressed by Kounin not only are better classroom managers in the sense that their students spend more time actively engaged in productive work and less time engaged in disruptive behavior; these teachers also achieve better results in producing student learning gains. This is probably related to what Rosenshine and Furst (1973) have called "student opportunity to learn." Put simply, students have more time and opportunity to learn in classrooms that are run smoothly with minimal disruption than they do in classrooms in which the teacher is often diverted by misbehavior or disruption.

Taken together, the findings suggest that lower-SES students with minimal skills will progress most rapidly in the early grades in a carefully planned and teacher structured learning environment. The teacher needs to give special attention to classroom management and to present material in small steps that the students can master to the point of overlearning before going on to higher levels. It should be noted, however, that although this appears to be the best *initial* strategy for teaching such students, the strategy becomes less effective to the extent that it succeeds! That is, to the extent that teachers are able to maximize the learning progress of such students, the students' need for teacher dominated and structured learning experiences will gradually decrease. As they learn fundamental tool skills, become more accustomed to school routines and more interested in school activities, and especially as they become more capable of independent and self-directed learning efforts, they will reach a point where they will learn more and better when taught with indirect methods. Thus, teaching is a matter of optimizing by matching curriculum and methods to the present needs of the students, and not just a matter of teaching one type of student one way and another type of student differently.

Another basic finding of this study is that *teacher behavior involved in maximizing student learning is not always the same kind of teacher behavior involved in maximizing student attitudes* (Brophy and Evertson, 1974c; Peck and Veldman, 1973). Student learning gains appear to be most closely related to how the teacher manages the classroom and organizes the curriculum, while student attitudes appear to be most strongly related to affective teacher variables such as warmth and student orientation. These are compatible for the most part, although the data suggest that extreme emphasis on one set of goals would probably interfere with progress towards the other type of goal. Thus, the most generally successful teachers are probably those who are equally concered with both student learning and personal development. Overconcern with either of these areas will probably mean that any extra progress attained in the area of emphasis will come at the expense of the area that is de-emphasized.

Summary

Although a variety of elementary school research has been reviewed in this section, the review has been illustrative rather than exhaustive. For more detailed reviews, see Dunkin and Biddle (1974) and Travers (1973), especially the chapter by Rosenshine and Furst (1973). The examples included in the present chapter were selected to illustrate two main points: (1) teachers differ significantly from one another, both statistically and practically, in their relative impact on student learning and student affective variables such as self-concept and attitudes towards learning and school; (2) much is already known, and more is being discovered every day, about what kinds of teacher behavior are appropriate or inappropriate for particular kinds of students in particular situations.

Although a teacher is partially an artist with a unique individual approach, teaching is (or should be) only partially an art. As knowledge about effective teaching accumulates, teaching should increasingly become an applied science, much like medicine, dentistry, or agriculture. The skilled teacher will be an individual who has mastered a large body of principles and skills, and who is capable of diagnosing a situation correctly and deciding which of the many options available to him are appropriate to the situation. In this sense, the teacher will be acting systematically and functioning as an applied scientist. However, once he has made his diagnosis and decided what to do, he will proceed in his own unique way, drawing on his unique experiences, talents, and interests.

Secondary Level Studies

Relatively few studies relating teacher variables to student learning gains have been done in secondary field settings, but the few which do exist have produced interesting data. Goodman (1959), in a study involving 70,000 seventh through eleventh grade students in New York State, found four significant predictors of adjusted student learning scores. These were: per pupil expenditures; number of teaching staff per thousand students; teacher experience; and classroom atmosphere. Classroom atmosphere was measured through observer ratings of the classrooms, mostly ratings of teacher attempts to relate subject matter to the interests and ability levels of the students. Thus, this study had only one measure of teaching process among those which predicted student learning gain, and it was a high inference measure of questionable meaning. Nevertheless, it illustrates that the observers were picking up something about teaching behavior that was significantly related to student learning.

A similar study conducted by McDill, Meyers, and Rigsby (1967) investigated sociocultural climate variables as they related to math achievement in high school. Even though many other investigators have attributed math achievement solely or primarily to student population characteristics, these investigators found that *climate variables* accounted for most of the variance in math achievement scores. School academic norms and related variables seemed to be especially important, again stressing the crucial role that expectations play in determining how much students learn.

Flanders (1970), reviewing a large number of studies done with variations of his classroom observation system, discussed several at the secondary level. These consistently showed positive and significant (but low) correlations between teacher indirectness and student learning. They also consistently showed negative correlations between teacher criticism and student learning, and these correlations were usually stronger than the positive ones for indirectness. Flanders also noted that the strength of relationships is related to student age and grade level, with stronger relationships at secondary than at elementary levels and at late elementary than at early elementary levels. These conclusions fit in with the data from the studies by Soar and his colleagues and by Brophy and Evertson and their colleagues discussed earlier, that is, in general, indirect teaching is increasingly appropriate and successful to the extent that students have mastered fundamental tool skills and are capable of assuming responsibility for their own learning.

Flanders also reported five experimental studies of teacher indirectness in addition to a large number of correlational studies. These experiments confirm the importance of teacher indirectness as teacher behavior that facilitates student learning although their findings are generally weaker than those suggested by the correlational studies. Flanders himself suggests, as noted above, that teacher indirectness might be less relevant or useful for teaching basic tool skills than for teaching the kinds of things stressed at the higher grade levels. Also, Soar's (1972) point should be kept in mind: perhaps the true relationships here are curvilinear (inverted-U) rather than linearly positive. That is, perhaps teacher indirectness is good up to a point, but that too much of it is not as good as just the right amount.

Taken together, the data from the secondary level suggest that student learning gains are most closely related to the general climate of learning that exists in the school, and that this in turn is linked to such variables as teacher expectations and teacher relationships with students. Affective teacher variables such as gaining student respect and forming good relationships with students appear to be particularly important.

Higher Education

Studies relating teacher behavior to student learning at the college level are also sparse, and those that do exist have produced similar findings to those done at the secondary level. A few representative examples will be discussed. Alexander, Elsom, Means, and Means (1971) studied the effects of teacher-initiated personal interactions on student achievement. Students in an undergraduate education course were rank-ordered according to grade-point average, and matched groups were then assigned to one of two treatments. The first treatment group received minimal attention from the instructor. Their classroom questions were answered politely but briefly and without personal involvement, and the instructor tried to avoid contacts with them other than those required by their own questions. In contrast, the instructor went out of his way to learn the names of the students in the second group, to initiate conversations with them in the hallways before and after class, and in general to form a personalized relationship with them that went beyond the minimal necessities involved in teaching. Test scores revealed that the students who got the personalized treatment achieved significantly better than those who did not, even though there was no difference in aptitude. In addition to this performance difference, observations of the students revealed that the students who had the personalized treatment increasingly initiated contacts with the instructor as the semester progressed, while the students who received impersonal teaching did not. This study again underscores the importance of affective teacher variables for student learning at the higher levels.

Welch and Walberg (1972) completed a similar experiment conducted as part of Project Physics. In this study, instructors who chose to use the Project Physics method were compared with those who did not. The Project Physics curriculum involved a humanistic approach to teaching physics, stressing among other things the place of physics in the history of ideas and its relationship to technology and social development. Thus, there was a greater attempt to make physics more relevant and personal to the students. Student feedback at the end of the courses showed that students in the Project Physics section saw their courses as more diverse and egalitarian than the control students. Compared with the others, the experimental students also found textbooks more enjoyable, the historical approach more interesting, and the subject itself as less difficult. However, they did not learn any more physics content as revealed by test scores than control students did. Thus, the effect of the Project Physics method was to improve student attitudes; it neither improved nor reduced learning.

Most of the research data on teacher behavior in higher education has been reviewed by Trent and Cohen (1973). They noted that only about 20 of over a thousand studies of "teacher effectiveness" used student learning as the criterion. Also, the sparse data that do exist suggest that teacher influence on student learning at this level is more specific than general. Teacher behavior that maximizes learning often is unrelated to student affect or even negatively related to it, and vice versa. Similarly, a given teacher or method often has a positive effect on one type of student but no effect or a negative effect on a different type of student.

Trent and Cohen call for more use of student learning gain as a criterion (as opposed to student evaluations of the teacher), noting that, among other things, students tend to favor younger teachers over older ones, higher level course teachers over lower level course teachers, and to prefer other attributes that seem unrelated to teaching skill. In general, student evaluations at the college level appear to take into account teaching skill, rapport with students, and classroom organization and management as three separate factors; in addition, students vary in how they weigh these factors.

A study by Turner and Thompson (1974) illustrates the evaluation problem that this poses and the need for taking into account student learning, as Trent and Cohen suggest. This study, replicated across two years, investigated the relationship between measured learning gains and student evaluation ratings as indices of how effectively graduate student teaching assistants taught introductory level courses to undergraduates. Both years of study produced similar results (the study was replicated because the investigators were amazed at the results obtained the first year!). First, the student ratings of teacher characteristics showed very strong evidence of halo effect, with students tending to see the teachers as either "all good" or "all bad." Second, and perhaps more surprisingly, the student ratings of the teachers showed clear-cut and consistently *negative* correlations with student learning gain. That is, the teachers rated most favorably by the students were the ones whose students performed most poorly on the tests, and vice versa. This was true even though the student ratings included such items as "explained clearly and his explanations were to the point," "seemed concerned that students learned," "provided appropriate corrections and guidance in spoken work," "gave vague explantions," "was well prepared for each day," and "showed concern for students as persons." In short, the questionnaire included all three of the general aspects of teaching mentioned by Trent and Cohen, but items related to all three factors correlated *negatively* with measured student learning.

In general, it appears that teacher behavior which facilitates student learning and that which optimizes student attitudes largely overlap at the preschool and early elementary school levels. However, as students get older and become more unique and differentiated in their personalities, interests, and learning styles, affective teacher variables assume increasingly greater importance in determing teacher effects on students, and the kind of teaching behavior that maximizes student *learning* shows less overlap (and often direct contradiction) with teacher behavior that promotes positive student *attitudes*. The data leave little doubt that teachers at the college level differ significantly from one another in their relative effectiveness, but drawing implications for teaching at this level is more difficult because of the complexities just mentioned.

In part, this is because the definition of effective teaching increasingly involves value judgments at higher levels of education. Although virtually everyone agrees that affective variables and aspects of personal development are important at any age, there is more agreement on the importance of student learning gains as the major criterion of teacher effectivenesss at the early grade levels than at higher grade levels. That is, most observers agree that teaching the fundamentals of reading, writing, and arithmetic is a major if not *the* major task of early elementary school teachers, but there is much less agreement on goals and priorities for teaching at higher levels. This question will be taken up at greater length in the following chapter.

Other Criteria

So far we have restricted discussion to relationships between teaching variables and student learning gains or student affective variables such as attitudes toward self, teacher, or school. A few studies have used different criteria, particularly creativity. For example, Harris (1973) found that students taught by a teacher who modeled flexible, divergent, or creative behavior increased their own creative behavior more than students in a control group with teachers who did not provide such modeling. Also, the modeling effect was more potent than simple instruction urging the students to be creative. That is, students explicitly asked to give creative responses in their assignments were less successful than students who had an opportunity to observe the instructor do so himself in the process of teaching them. This study demonstrates the potency of modeling as a teaching device. For more detailed commentary on modeling in teaching, see Good and Brophy (1973).

Anderson (1959) reviewed a large number of studies comparing authoritarian and democratic leadership styles. The studies agree in showing that student morale is higher in classes taught with democratic leadership styles, but the data for authoritarian leadership styles are less clear. These appear to be most effective when the tasks involved are simple and concrete, because students perform most efficiently when told exactly what to do and how to do it. However, the contrasting hypothesis that complex tasks would be best approached with a democratic leadership style has not produced clear-cut results. Most studies found no difference, and when differences were discovered they usually favored the authoritarian style on productivity measures and the democratic style on morale measures. Thus, democratic leadership and a learner-centered orientation appeared to foster student morale, while tight organization and authoritarian leadership appears to foster productivity.

Both of these variables are probably overgeneralized, however, and both are probably inappropriate when carried to the extremes. Other data suggest that a combination of teacher warmth, concern about students, and general learner-centeredness in attitudes is important, but at the same time so are a certain degree of teacher domination and structuring of classroom events. This finding is made further complex by the problem that *the optimal style for a given student will vary according to the subject matter, the age and ability of the student, and probably several student and teacher personality variables.* In any case, the frequently made generalization that democratic leadership styles are good and authoritarian leadership styles are bad is an overgeneralization not supported by the data. In fact, statements that particular teaching behaviors are *always* good or bad, regardless of context, are almost always overgeneralizations.

Summary

Data were presented in this chapter to show that some teachers consistently outperform others in affecting student learning or attitudes. It was noted that most data suggesting that teachers do *not* differ significantly from one another in their effects upon students come from studies with faulty conceptualization or design, and that studies with improved designs along the lines outlined in Chapter 3 indicate that teachers have effects which are both statistically and practically significant. Further, recent studies of teaching have begun to yield consistent information about relationships between teacher behavior and student outcomes, so that teaching should increasingly become an applied science involving systematic application of data-based principles.

However, the kinds of studies that are capable of yielding such principles are just beginning to be done in large numbers. Only a few studies completed to date have taken a broadband data collection approach, and only a handful have checked for nonlinear process-product relationships. Also, very few have taken into account context differences, and none have taken into account all or even most of the relevant context differences that probably affect process-product relationships. Thus, the data available at present are sketchy and probably overgeneralized, but even so they clearly establish that teachers can and do make a difference when they behave systematically and when the experimental or evaluational design of a study is appropriate for revealing such differences.

This is not to deny the primary importance of student ability and the general characteristics of the student population in a school in determining the performance levels of schools or of a particular teacher's classroom. *De facto* segregation along social class and racial/ethnic lines causes most schools, at least in cities, to be fairly homogeneous in their SES and racial/ethnic populations. Failure to take this into account has caused many previous investigators to jump to the false conclusions that *only* student characteristics make a difference and that teachers do not. While it is quite clear that student characteristics do make a difference and that they will serve as enabling or limiting factors affecting the amount that a given teacher can accomplish in a given year, it is also quite clear that teachers do make a difference.

Just as data suggesting that teachers do not make a difference frequently have been overgeneralized and accepted uncritically, there is a danger that these same mistakes can be made with the kinds of data cited in this chapter. While these data do establish that certain teachers consistently outperform others and that particular kinds of teaching behavior are always or almost always preferable to contrasting kinds, the present state of research in the area does not allow for the use of process-product findings for accountability purposes. Ultimately, findings of this type might be usable for making decisions about teacher tenure or pay raises, but at present they are too sparse and unsophisticated to be used for such purposes legitimately. We believe that officials charged with making accountability decisions must base them on reasonable and appropriate criteria. In our belief, such criteria do not exist at this time. Thus, before prematurely committing time and money to an imperfect and unjust accountability system, time and money should be allotted to the basic research needed to identify appropriate and inappropriate teacher behavior clearly and unambiguously.

Although the data reviewed in the chapter revealed much orderly and systematic information about relationships between behavior and student outcomes, it was noted that in order to measure teacher effectiveness you first have to define the term, and that such a task involves value judgments. There would be no problem if research indicated that the same teacher behavior fostered all desirable goals, but this is not the case. Many studies indicate that teacher behavior fostering growth in one area is unrelated to growth in another area or even inhibits growth in that area, especially at higher age levels. Thus, teacher behavior which leads to accomplishment of one set of goals may impede the attainment of others.

This raises the problem of ordering priorities among the possible goals that a teacher can or should set. As noted in the chapter, there is considerable disagreement among educational and psychological writers concerning appropriate and inappropriate teaching goals and the relative value of each. The problem of ordering goals and the value judgments associated with this process will be discussed at length in the following chapter.

Chapter 5 Goals for Education

In the previous four chapters it has been argued that experiments to find "desirable" teaching behaviors historically have suffered from a number of design flaws. But it has been pointed out that recent improvements in teacher effectiveness studies have paid off in the form of new insights about the conditions under which certain behaviors are likely to facilitate student learning. Similarly, research on teacher effectiveness has suffered from lack of a conceptual definition of what teachers are to accomplish in the classroom. Not only have researchers been handicapped by lack of goal statements (what should a second grade teacher of middle class students accomplish in a given year?) but so have teachers, superintendents, and test developers.

Most research studies concerned with the effectiveness of teachers and schools have produced information only about the effects of instruction on student learning. But surely teachers and schools exist for more than helping students to master subject material. However, little information has been collected to describe the influence of schools in noncognitive areas. The purpose of this chapter is to describe a variety of roles that schools and teachers are asked to play, to explain how lack of goal agreement inhibits instructional effectiveness, and to argue that, if research on teaching (or teaching *per se*) is to be improved, steps must be taken to clarify the goals of schooling.

In summary then, this chapter concerns itself with the problems involved in discriminating, setting, and meeting the diverse goals that can be set for education. The first section describes some common goals set for schools today and discusses a few of their implications. The second discusses mechanisms for debating and setting goals, and takes up the dilemmas faced by the teacher when, as is so often the case in America, no definite goals exist. The third discusses what can be done by educators to meet the goals of education once these have been clearly set and stresses the role of research in this enterprise.

Complex Demands

More than once in previous chapters we have noted that Americans are not always certain about what they want to accomplish in their schools. Part of the difficulty faced by teachers may be attributed to this fact. If teachers are told to do several different things, if those things are difficult to do, and if doing one or more of them well precludes doing the others well, it will not be easy to be successful as a teacher.

Once we had little difficulty stating the goals of education. The frontier community featured a simple, one-room school manned by a single teacher. That teacher's task was to train pupils in the time-honored Three R's, and teachers who failed in this mission—no matter how devout, humorous, or inspiring they might otherwise be—were deemed by their constituents as failures.

Today, the problem is no longer as simple. For one thing, success in the modern world requires more than simple literacy. For another, the school has grown in size and complexity, and it is tied to other schools as part of a complex system of education. As a result, today we demand that the school accomplish a broader range of more difficult tasks. This would be challenge enough, but we are also less certain about what tasks should be assigned to the school. Society is ethnically diverse and rapidly changing, so that we cannot be sure that the attitudes and skills we demand of pupils today will serve them twenty years from now. Moreover, we are assailed by prophets who advocate a staggering range of new tasks for our schools. Thus, not only is the catalogue of goals for the school broader and more complex, there is less consensus concerning these goals within society.

Nor does the problem stop with the fact that we hold confusing goals for our schools. Worse yet is the fact that we have few clear mechanisms for resolving conflicts among goals, and often we lack sufficient empirical information to know what to do even if we could all agree on established goals. Most other Western societies have well-established mechanisms to debate and make decisions about educational goals. Unfortunately, our mechanisms for this purpose are weak. Moreover, as education becomes more complex, as our goals for it become more ambitious, educators and other citizens become more confused about how to accomplish these goals. Questions of this sort require research, and too often the needed research is not available.

A Plethora of Goals

An enormous range of tasks has been advocated for American education during the twentieth century, encompassing teacher roles, classroom states, curricula, educational media, pupil achievements, and ultimate goals for the educational system. Rather than attempt to list them all, we will discuss a few of the more common goals manifested in the activities of the typical school system in America today. In short, our review will be restricted to the goals for which schools appear to strive in their current efforts (see Biddle, 1970), excluding those for which they *might* strive if they heeded the advocacy of ideologies (however, see Eisner and Vallance, 1974).

Pupil Socialization

One primary task of the schools is the socialization of pupils. The school's responsibility for socializing children is second only to the family's. Indeed, this task is so central to education that it is often used by anthropoligists as the defining criterion for recognizing the appearance of education as an institution in a primitive society. Wherever schools are found, at least some of their activities center upon the task of teaching to pupils those things that are valued by adults in the society. Thus, "education transmits a common cultural fund to the next generation and in the process helps to bring hordes of young barbarians to adult ways that are continuous with the past" (Clark, 1962).

The task of socialization is not the sole province of the school, of course. Socialization also takes place in the family, the church, the adolescent peer culture, and as a result of exposure to television and other information sources. However, schools exist "for the purpose" of socializing the young. Thus, for them the task of socialization is primary; it is only secondary in the church or the adolescent gang.

The socialization task is basically a conservative one. The school acts to preserve and transmit the traditions of the society, to constrain the pace of social change, and to produce a new generation who have learned to value the traditions of the past. The fact that socialization is basically a conservative business is occasionally forgotten by some educational philosophers or advocates who argue that the teacher's task is to induce "creativity" in pupils or to "loosen the shackles of the past." Indeed, so confused have some educators become that they are willing to tolerate indefinite delays in pupil acquisition of skills which are broadly agreed upon as needed for satisfactory adult behavior. One can find in some "progressive schools," for example, fifth graders who have not yet learned to read, or adolescents whose language and demeanor would be more suitable to the army barracks than the business office. Such events are atypical; most schools pay considerable heed to the goal of social-ization. By the same token, this conservative task sometimes conflicts with others we shall review below.

Pupil socialization is viewed in many ways among contemporary American educators, and conflict erupts from time to time concerning these different views and how the teacher should go about accommodating them. A sub-stantial, though possibly now declining, group of educators have always thought of pupil socialization in terms of specific content or skills to be learned. For this group, the task of socialization is to insure that pupils speak or spell appropriately, can handle science or higher mathematics, or know the history of their country in some detail. Another group conceives the educated pupil to be one whose cognitive processes are sufficiently developed so that he can cope with the rigors of higher education or adult life. For them, pupils are socialized if they can handle complex thinking tasks, regard-less of whether or not they know the details of a particular subject. Yet an-other group conceives education in terms of response acquisition and the task of the socializing teacher as providing appropriate schedules of rein-forcement. Still others speak of pupil self-actualization, or of teaching pupils to recognize and accomplish their own goals, and so on.

These and other curricular orientations will be familiar to many readers. We will not attempt to sort among them here. What should be recognized, however, is that each relates to the goal of pupil socialization. Each provides a recipe for *what* we should be trying to build in pupils, often adding stipu-lations about *how* we should go about the task. Each is conservative in that the teacher's task is conceived to be one of molding pupils to the standards of an adult society.

Pupil Allocation

"Every society must make some provision for deciding which of its mem-bers shall occupy the various positions in the society and perform the roles necessary for its continuation and development" (Goslin, 1965). As a rule, the task of pupil allocation is assigned to schools in contemporary Western societies. Other institutions, such as testing agencies and counselors, may help but the primary task of separating groups of pupils by ability or interest falls to the schools.

In older, more traditional societies, allocation is more likely to take place according to inherited or ascribed characteristics. Family background or title, race, religion, caste, ethnicity, birth order, and sex all have been used to determine occupation or access to desired experiences, including higher education. These criteria are arbitrary, however, and are not well suited for selecting persons who have the greatest aptitude and interest for jobs.

As a result, these criteria have either been abandoned altogether or are under attack in Western societies—witness attacks upon racial segregation and sexism in America.

One partially inherited characteristic still is used for pupil allocation in some Western countries, however, as we know from Chapter 2. This characteristic is intelligence, and some, perhaps most, countries use an early measurement of intelligence or achievement as a means (either formally or informally) for allocating pupils to differential education experiences. The theory behind this action concerns the need to provide appropriate education for those with high and low native ability, but in practice such measurements reflect social background as well as native ability. For this reason, allocation of pupils by intelligence is also being attacked in America.

But if allocation is not performed by examination, how is it to be done? Clearly, it is both uneconomic and unfair to pupils to assign them to educational experiences for which they are not fit. Some pupils should be encouraged to enter professional careers, some should become auto mechanics or secretaries; schools assume the primary task of making this allocation. In American schools this presumably is done gradually. Over time, it is assumed, the teachers and counselors develop "a feeling" for the interests and aptitudes of the pupil, and thereafter are able to provide him guidance for his future education and occupation.

Unfortunately, there are several difficulties with this sanguine description. For one, primary teachers sometimes form rather rigid opinions about the abilities of their pupils, opinions that thereafter serve to control their treatments of pupils in a prejudicial manner (see Rist, 1970). As a result, from their earliest school days pupils are probably sorted into groups of "sheep" and "goats" on an informal basis, and thereafter are treated in ways likely to encourage these descriptions. Also, pupils often are not known to counselors in larger schools, so that decisions concerning their futures may be made by quite arbitrary means (such as grades and test scores) despite the intention of the school to do otherwise.

However it is handled, the task of pupil allocation is always to some extent antithetical to that of socialization. The latter implies *motivation* and *encouragement* of the best pupils; the former implies *judgment* and *sanctions*. Many a teacher has complained that he would far prefer to teach and inspire pupils—and leave the testing to someone else. Alas, there usually is no one else.

The Control of Knowledge

Given the transcendant task of socialization, it is not surprising that schools have also been called on to conserve and develop knowledge for its own sake. This tendency appears more strongly within the university, but larger secondary schools also exhibit substantial investments in libraries and research laboratories.

But libraries and laboratories represent quite different functions associated with knowledge. Libraries conserve and preserve knowledge; laboratories discover and innovate. The first function fits well within the general task of pupil socialization, and only rarely is the maintenance of a library seen as controversial. The second function, research, is a radical task that may interfere with pupil socialization or cause the school to be challenged by its constituents. For these reasons, research is often seen to be antithetical to teaching. Teachers may resent the intrusion of researchers in their classrooms, parents may not understand the purposes of an experimental curriculum, and so forth.

Not all research takes place within schools and colleges, of course. Today, a good deal of it is conducted in industry or in independent research centers. But research *does* appear in schools, particularly research associated with curriculum or with the growth and development of children. When it does appear, it tends to complicate the lives of teachers and others who are involved in it. However, we shall argue in this book that such "complication" is the only way to provide dependable and usable knowledge that can be used to improve instructional programs.

Baby Sitting

Once upon a time parents were reluctant to send their children to school. Children were a source of labor. Boys and girls in farm families were needed to help bring in the crops and maintain the home. Children of urban families often worked as many hours as their parents, to supplement the family budget.

Contemporary conditions reverse this pressure. Parents are anxious to send their children to school. Not only does the school provide avenues to adult life, it also takes children off the hands of busy parents. Children are no longer allowed to work; nor are they needed on the farm. If they are not in school, they are likely to be found in gangs or engaged in deviant behavior. More and more mothers have acquired professional education or have entered the work force for reasons of self-actualization, boredom, or income. As a result, modern schools are sometimes viewed quite frankly as baby-sitting services, and parents often resent disruptions in the school year or seek to extend the hours their children spend in school.

One effect of this pressure has been to reduce the age at which pupils are allowed to enter school. Once upon a time, schools began at grade 1. Later, the kindergarten became nearly universal. Now, lower-class children are being given an even earlier school year in Head Start programs, and middle class mothers desire to have such programs added to their schools, too.

Time-Occupancy

A related task, time-occupancy, concerns the tendency of schools to retain pupils within their walls for longer and longer periods of time. Prior to World War II, it was common for sizable numbers of both boys and girls to drop out of school at the legal age for leaving. Today, completion of senior high school is much more common, and pupils are encouraged to stay in education for one or more years of college if possible. This not only helps pupils to "get ahead" in life, but also keeps thousands of potentially employable young men and women out of the job market, thus keeping down unemployment.

Time-occupancy has a number of effects on schools and society. For one, schools seeking to keep pupils of lesser ability within their walls must plan curricula for them. As a result, high schools have developed curricula concerned with subjects such as homemaking and auto mechanics, and even universities have begun to water down their academic standards or to offer more "relevant" subjects. This, in turn, produces conflicts between teachers who seek to protect academic standards and the traditional or scholarly endeavors of the school and those who are convinced of the need for the new curricula.

For another, the school is now viewed as a major avenue through which young men and women achieve adulthood. Formerly, the young man who had little interest in school could drop out and find gainful employment or seek an apprenticeship that would provide entrance into industry or a respected trade. Today, industries are looking for the young man or woman with college training, and a high school diploma is often requisite for employment as mechanic, clerk, beautician, or secretary. All of this makes the task of pupil allocation more important, for pupils who are misjudged by their schools may thereafter be forced to live with fewer alternatives for life adjustment open to them. It also places additional pressure on teachers to make schools pleasant and challenging places since pupils are to spend up to one-fifth of their lives there.

Finally, time-occupancy also produces an age-segregated society. In the past, adolescents were granted adult status as soon as they could do a day's work and hold their liquor. Today, the adolescent is sequestered in schools for longer and longer periods of time, during which he is interacting solely with peers and adult teachers. Adolescents are not welcome, or are prohibited by custom or law, from participating in adult work or recreational settings. No wonder the peer culture looms high among forces affecting adolescent socialization! Teenagers have their own styles of clothing, manners, music, and stimulants, but this is hardly surprising given the fact that we segregate them from adult society for so long. If Coleman (1961) and

Gordon (1957) are correct, the peer culture in the typical high school also operates to modify, to interpret, and often to vitiate the task of socialization. Clearly, high school teachers must be prepared to "take on" the peer culture. As an example, many urban high schools today provide drug and pregnancy counseling services.

Public Entertainment and Community Identification

Quite a different task is often taken on by large high schools, particularly those in small communities, when they provide plays, basketball games, and auditoria for community meetings. Such services provide entertainment for citizens of the community, along with a focus for identification and community pride. Citizens often are asked to contribute time or money to help these "auxiliary" school functions by providing funds for band costumes, helping to lead youth activities within the school, and so on.

This task should not be minimized when we consider the impact of the school on its supporting community. Frequently, the school is the *only* institution that brings together the majority of community members in a common cause. Its impact may be judged by studying what happens to communities when small schools are consolidated to make larger schools. The community losing a school may wither; the one gaining the consolidated school often grows.

Nevertheless, efforts devoted to entertainment or community identification are likely to interfere with other goals assumed by the school. Minimally, funds spent for entertainment are not available for instruction, but the problem does not stop with funding. Some teachers, particularly coaches or sponsors of debating teams or school plays, are likely to focus more on the excellence of the performance than on providing pupils with "worthwhile educational experiences." Parents and alumni also may confuse winning with participation and may seek to influence school policy to that end.

Courtship

Yet another task concerns courtship. Schools are now counted upon to provide a setting in which boys and girls can interact informally, under supervision. In this they are gradually taking over functions that formerly were performed by churches and families. Numerous social events are now programmed in the typical high school, ranging from various types of clubs to dances and parties. These appear to have little relevance for the traditional tasks of instruction. Indeed, like baby sitting and public entertainment, they often are attacked by traditional teachers as being "frills." Nevertheless, most parents prefer to have pupils involved in such activities in the schools than have them courting in unsupervised conditions.

Maintenance of Subgroup Traditions

Two additional tasks are sometimes taken on by schools, although neither is ever seen as a "frill." The first of these is the maintenance of subgroup traditions, which is seen most clearly in parochial schools or in urban schools that serve an ethnically homogeneous clientele. Thus, one is likely to find moral philosophy taught in Catholic schools, African history in schools serving black populations, or courses in Armenian, Hebrew, or Portuguese in schools serving students from these ethnic groups.

Such curricula pose a dilemma for American education—how much curricular homogeneity will we enforce on American schools, and how much will we encourage ethnic diversity and the maintenance of subgroup traditions? There is no simple answer to this question, for an answer presupposes agreement about whether America should become ethnically homogeneous or pluralistic. Many forces are driving us in the direction of ethnic homogeneity, particularly television and other forms of mass communication. Minimal common curricula for public schools have always been argued as a means for socializing pupils to the point that they can live fruitful lives in a common society. And yet, respect for ethnic diversity is widely argued today, and schools are also viewed as a means by which ethnic traditions can be maintained.

Social Reform

Finally, schools are also viewed as a means for the accomplishment of social reforms. As we saw in Chapter 2, schools are assumed to be means for the equalization of opportunity and income, and as instruments for the alleviation of racial and ethnic prejudices. Whether or not schools *can* accomplish these reforms is moot. The fact is that parents (and educators) expect they can, and educational policies are planned with such expectations in mind. Thus, schools are asked to accept pupils that are bused in from another district; pressures are placed on schools to institute curricula, testing programs, or streaming procedures; citizens are to participate in various school activities —all in the name of equal opportunities or racial integration of schools. Once again, these activities may (to the traditionalist) appear to interfere with time-honored tasks of pupil socialization or allocation.

Confused Mechanisms for Decision

Nine goals for education have now been suggested, and this list is far from exhaustive. Yet, to have schools accommodate even this partial list would seem a superhuman task. How can the school possibly provide for pupil socialization and allocation and at the same time accommodate needs for public entertainment and courtship, let alone maintain subgroup traditions and provide for social reform? How does the school determine which of these goals to emphasize and which to let slide? How does it determine where funds shall be invested or how it might accomplish the tasks of allocation, instruction, or racial integration?

Most Western countries have well-established means by which such decisions are made. In other countries, the management of education is largely a state function, although some countries feature a combination of state and religious control over schools. Much of the day-by-day decision-making concerning schools is done by bureaucrats hired to manage the school system. These men (and most of them *are* men) are usually trained educators who have been in the system a long time. Since they are older, their decisions concerning education tend to be fairly conservative, which fits in well with the traditional task of pupil socialization. Major decisions, however, usually are made by educational commissions called together periodically to debate the goals and means of education, although implementation of their recommendations is a matter for the state legislature.

These procedures have a number of shortcomings, of which three are particularly worthy of comment. First, such systems often constitute bureaucracies whose activities are organized from the top downwards and are not subject to much input from teachers or principals. Like all bureaucracies, large school systems are capable of generating vast collections of rules and policies which may or may not apply to the individual school, and rare is the teacher in such a system who has not longed for greater autonomy or flexibility. Second, such systems often are somewhat less than responsive to the needs of a particular region or ethnic constituency. It is possible to decentralize decision-making in even the largest bureaucracy, of course, but bureaucrats often do not know how to do so or dislike doing so because it involves giving up some of their power. This problem is particularly knotty when constituents are physically distant from administrators who are responsible for making decisions concerning their schools, or where administrators represent one social or ethnic group and constituents another. Third, the typical state system does not involve parents in the management of schools. Parents are brought to the school only occasionally, and then only to be told of the status of their children's progress and what they might do to encourage same. Parents typically have little to say about what goes on in their school, nor are they encouraged to think that they might have such a voice. It is possible to build a role for parents into the state system (this seems to be provided by local school councils in New Zealand, for example), but most state systems don't bother.

On the other hand, such procedures also have advantages. Clearly, they facilitate the distribution of funds to provide equal opportunity for education for pupils in rich and poor districts. They also provide clear avenues whereby decisions can be made about the goals of education. A clear forum exists wherein the advantages and disadvantages of a new curriculum or development in educational media can be debated and a firm decision about whether or not it will be adopted can be made. Moreover, the citizen, be he an educator or "merely" a parent, has a clear map to show him how he may seek to change the system. For openers, he has the option of appealing to the principal of his school for a change in policy, then up the ladder of responsibility to the director or his assistants. If this does not work, he may try appealing to his local legislator. If this, too, is fruitless, he can provide testimony at the next educational commission or can work for the election of a new government. The point is that in such a system educational policies are articulated, goals are set, and efforts are set up to accomplish those goals within the system.

All of this sounds strange, if not exotic, within the American setting. As many readers know, American schools are fractionated into more than 20,000 local school districts across the country. Each of these districts has its own school board and administrative staff. Little state control is exercised over decisions by such boards, and remarkably little federal supervision. The result is a remarkable pluralism of effort. Some schools in this country still use McGuffey's Readers (really!); some have earthen floors; some have desks that are bolted to the floor; some have a flexible curriculum or a "school without walls"; some have no books at all, others a massive library; and some have their own radio stations, television facilities, or a modern digital computer. In part, this pluralism is a good thing, since school boards usually are responsive to their local communities. In addition, pluralistic standards allow schools to try out any number of innovations to see whether or not they will work. On the other hand, pluralism also implies gross inequality in expenditures for the education of pupils from rich and poor districts, and disagreement about what schools are supposed to be doing abounds.

Given that we have no state or national means for debating educational policy, how *do* we arrive at decisions concerning our schools? How is it, for example, that we have settled on a national system that allows pupils to enter at a given age and progress through grades K through 12 before they enter college? How are educational media innovated? Why have we adopted a standardized code of football rules for the country as a whole?

Such questions are sufficiently complex to have generated research on the processes of decision-making in American schools (Miles, 1964). Several means for making decisions can be discriminated. For one, some innovations (such as new media and textbooks) are "sold" to schoolmen at conventions, in the same way as dental chairs are sold to dentists or coffins to undertakers. Other innovations come about through the appearance of a controversial book or a new curriculum that is being pushed by a foundation. Still others are promoted by special interest groups, such as school architects. Still others (few, too few) result from the publication of research. However, each of these innovations must be decided upon by the local school board or superintendent, and decisions made in one corner of the country may not match those made elsewhere. Rarely is there a statewide or national decision concerning educational policy. Instead, decision-making involves 20,000 local decisions by school boards, schoolmen, and in some cases by teachers themselves. How does common practice coalesce from this clumsy chaos? This tends to happen either through the pragmatic discovery by schoolmen and women everywhere that a given innovation works or does not, or through the activities of regional or national associations that set and enforce standards for schools in different communities.

Such a system is not only chaotic; it is also fiscally irresponsible. Untold millions of dollars have been invested by American educators in innovations that don't work particularly well, such as language laboratories. Curricular innovations by the dozens have been sold to schools without benefit of supportive research. Literally hundreds of new school buildings designed with "open-plan" architecture are under construction, even though we have little information about the effects of such structures on teacher or pupil behavior or on the achievement or attitudes of pupils (see Chapter 8 for a review of this research). Until recently, most Americans have not been concerned with "waste," either in their homes or in their schools. Today, however, Americans are becoming conscious of the limited state of our resources. Perhaps the time will come when citizens will insist on public debate (and evidence) concerning the means and ends to be adopted by their schools. Surely we need *some* sort of mechanism for rationalizing and evaluating our educational decisions. But the call here is not for "standardization" of the curriculum but rather for periodic review, discussion and goal clarification.

To say this does not mean that *all* or even most decisions concerning educational policy should be made "on high." Even if it were possible to debate and decide upon national goals for education, there still would be room for considerable variation in the means by which these goals were accomplished in local school districts. Moreover, national goals concerning school policy would cover but a fraction of the issues with which a local or regional school system might concern itself. Thus, there should always be room for local autonomy and variation in large areas of the curriculum. But we need a public mechanism for debating and deciding *some* aspects of school policy.

Coordination of resources is perhaps more essential for clarifying possible and reasonable goals and devising educational procedures for reaching and measuring goals than in establishing goals *per se*. The funds for developing research priorities, instruments, and conducting effective school-related research is more than many local school districts can afford. Some of this coordination has already begun to occur (see the discussion of National Assessment in Chapter 6), and in time shared resources (information about present progress on educational goals, ways to measure progress, and so on) may help schools to plan more meaningful ways to mobilize resources for accomplishing their desired goals.

Thus, we suggest that national efforts to clarify educational goals and to provide information about how such goals can be realized would be a considerable improvement over the way in which educational decisions are presently made (curriculum testimony without data, and so on). However, independent of national, state, or district efforts in goal setting, we feel that *schools and individual teachers need to clarify their own goals* if their own resources are to be used effectively (more on this in Chapter 10).

Also, national leadership is needed to insure that equal opportunities are provided for access to public education to all Americans, be they from the South or the North, be they from poor urban ghettoes or rich suburbs, and be they black, white, or green. Moreover, we need a sharply expanded national effort to provide educators with the empirical information they need to make rational decisions in matters of educational policy. These needs are appropriate to plan for and fund within our federal educational budget. To fail to solve them at this level is fiscally irresponsible and contrary to the interests of American pupils.

Research and Goal Accomplishment

It seems truistic to say so, but the more complex the goals taken on by the school, the more we need the help of researchers if we are to accomplish those goals. Let us assume for the purposes of argument that we could all agree on the goals of education. Let us assume that we had had a national debate concerning educational goals, and that we had arrived at a list of priorities for our schools. How would we tell whether or not we were achieving those goals, and what methods worked best?

Back when our goals were simpler and education was under the control of the isolated classroom teacher, questions such as these did not arise. Where the goal is simple literacy, teachers find it easy to judge whether or not one of their pupils has learned to read yet. Moreover, many strategies for developing pupil literacy are open to the teacher, and if one does not work with a given pupil, another is likely to succeed. As long as goals are set at such a low level, then, evidence about goals and the means for their accomplishment are under the direct control of the teacher. To the extent that "research" appears in the classroom, it is an intrinsic part of the teaching process. Little need is felt either by educators or by ordinary citizens for more formal information concerning goal accomplishment. Teaching is not viewed in problematic terms, and there is little demand for formal research in education.

All of this changes when we set more complex and sophisticated goals for education. Let us assume that one of our goals is that pupils will attain a high standard of accomplishment in terms of a specific content or skill to be learned. First of all, how are we to tell whether that standard has been reached? To do this, we must institute and validate some sort of an instrument, an achievement test that will tell us the degree to which the standard has been reached by the pupil. This requires research. In addition, how can we best encourage pupils of various dispositions to attain the standard? Is our best strategy to lecture to pupils *en masse*, to lead them in drill, to provide individual instruction and encouragement? What of reinforcement? Will different textbooks or curricular packages work equally in encouraging a high standard in pupils, or is one clearly better than the others? Such questions require additional research.

In short, the more complex our goals, the more we need the help of researchers to accomplish them and the more we need to build research into our educational institutions on a regular, ongoing basis. All of this seems fairly obvious—except that it doesn't occur in our schools. Numerous critics have noted the fact that of all the vast sums that are spent on education annually in America, only a pittance is set aside for research (and how sharply this contrasts with other fields, such as the drug or automotive industries, where research commands a much larger portion of revenues). Other critics have commented on the poor, starved quality of much of the published research in education today. Still others (for example, Chall, 1967) have noted how rarely evidence from education research is used for making decisions concerning educational policy. Though the need is there, we have yet to include research among the customs and practices of our system of education.

Let us examine some of the many things that are presently missing in education which research might provide us. Perhaps most surprising is the fact that few "polished" instruments are available for educators to use in detecting whether they are accomplishing the stated goals of education. There are numerous instruments available for measuring noncognitive student growth, but few that have been widely used for sufficient time to build normative data that can be used to tell "what a score means." For example, there are countless measures that purport to measure a student's self concept but the following are unknown: whether teachers can influence student scores on such instruments; how these scores change as a function of school size and student age; or the relation between a student's reported self concept and his classroom behavior. For convenience, let us focus on only the goal of pupil socialization. As we know, some educators conceive this goal in terms of content or skill acquisition. Others view it in terms of cognitive development, response acquisition, pupil self-actualization or creativity, goal recognition, the ability to perform adult roles or be good citizens, even simple pupil happiness. So much for what we might be attempting to induce in pupils. But how are we to tell whether pupils have attained these states? The sad fact is that today we use instruments only for measuring pupil content, or skill acquisition, and general attitudes that students have toward teachers and schools. Educators interested in the many other things pupils might learn in schools are unlikely to find instruments that will tell them how well they are doing. Needed are specific instruments designed to measure noncognitive school goals directly.

The fact that we use instruments only for measuring pupil content and skill acquisition has some interesting ramifications. For one, educators and researchers alike tend to reify data from such instruments and, in effect, to claim that they measure the "success" of educational efforts. Evidence from such instruments forms the major data base for such studies as the Coleman Report, the Jencks study of inequality, and the IEA studies of achievement. Interpreters of these studies have concluded that our educational system was "succeeding" or "failing" to the extent that high levels of achievement were reported for a given population of schools or pupils. Similar thinking has also appeared recently among commentators who have decried the fact that our national averages on Scholastic Aptitude Test scores have been declining for the past decade. To conclude that our educational system is "succeeding" or "failing" in terms of a single standardized test of achievement seems silly, and yet when educators are offered no other criteria of success, who can blame them for clutching at this one straw? Surely if we are to conceive education to have many goals, it is time that we developed more sophisticated means for establishing whether or not some of these other goals were reached.

As we shall see in Chapter 9, work in the past few years has provided some promising instruments that could be used by schools or teachers to assess their effects on students. However, if generalizable information is to be produced it will be necessary to develop such instruments further and to incorporate them in comprehensive studies that relate scores on noncognitive measures to classroom behavior.

Another surprising lack that might be remedied by research is the paucity of evidence concerning the effects of classroom practices on goal accomplishment. Let us assume, for the purposes of argument, that adequate instruments were available for assessing the subject-matter achievement of pupils. What, then, are the effects on pupil achievement of lecturing versus discussion or self-directed pupil exploration? Which induces more achievement, standard instructional methods or Montessori methods? Do new curricula actually induce changes in classroom procedures, and how are these related to achievement? How do teachers and pupils respond to open-plan school buildings, and how are these responses related to achievement? All these are questions which could be answered through research. Yet, even today few comprehensive studies have been attempted.

What does the educator do to solve problems in education, given the lack of effective research information on which to base his decisions? How can teachers, principals, superintendents, or school board members make up their minds whether to adopt a given classroom strategy, curriculum, building plan, or educational innovation? Today, most of these decisions are made on the basis of plausible argument and the enthusiasm of proponents. Enthusiasm is not a bad thing to find in education. The principal or teacher who is convinced that a new curriculum will be a radical improvement over the dull practices of the past may induce all sorts of positive effects in pupils with his enthusiasm alone. But enthusiasm alone is not enough to fuel the educational engine; we also need hard facts concerning the relationships between the activities of teaching and the accomplishment of goals. Until these facts are provided, along with explanatory theories to lace them together, much of our educational practice will be based on fads, biases, or other nonobjective rationales.

The more complex and sophisticated our goals for education, then, the more we need research evidence to help us accomplish those ends. Teachers make a difference, but we won't know much about the nature of that difference until we subject the activities of teaching to serious scrutiny and learn a great deal more about the effects of those activities on our goals for education than we know now. And until such research evidence is available, many of our most important decisions concerning education must be made in the dark.

Despite the confusion over the goals for American education, the paucity of developed instruments for measuring noncognitive objectives, and the lack of definitive information about how to accomplish any educational goal, there are some who would hold educators accountable for their effects on students. We suspect that accountability prior to agreement about the importance of various educational goals is premature and hence self-defeating. Others would argue that accountability will force goal clarification and is both possible and desirable. In the following chapter we will discuss the origin, the methods, and the possible effects of accountability.

Chapter 6 Accountability

Educational accountability has been defined in a variety of ways and various procedures have been suggested for achieving accountability. In general, present-day usage of the term accountability includes: (1) the statement of student outcome goals, evaluating whether these goals have been achieved and at what cost, and (2) acceptance of responsibilities for inadequacies (Mehrens and Lehmann, 1973). Emphasis in accountability arguments is on the need for schools to be responsible for results. Accountability pressures have become more intense in the last five years. For example, Elam (1970) notes that in the first year of performance contracting (1969) only $25,000 was spent on the project; however, he estimated between $100 and $150 million would be spent in 1971. The purpose of this chapter is to review the source of accountability pressures and to discuss various methods of accountability (performance contracts, voucher plans, national assessment, teacher assessment) and to discuss the general effect that accountability may exert on schooling in America.

Source of Accountability Pressures

Popular cries for accountability resulted from a series of pressures rather than a single specific source. The chief cause, however, was the dramatic failure of education to offset the consequences of poverty. In the 60s, massive amounts of money were spent on educational projects that were designed to aid the disadvantaged. Much of this money was not spent on improving the quality of existing schools, but instead to mount new efforts in preschool education.

Despite the fact that virtually no money had been invested in preschool research (to determine the learning conditions necessary for improving the educational skills of disadvantaged youth such that their success in subsequent schooling would improve), vast amounts of monies were awarded to mount early intervention effects. Educators were not hesitant to accept the money, but in general preschool educators were more likely to escalate public expectations than to attempt to develop more realistic and appropriate public expectations.

No doubt part of the problem was that, without a research base, it was impossible for educators to predict the difficulty of the task that they were implicitly accepting: Namely, to reduce drastically the effects of poverty on school performance. Educators joined with popular writers in saluting the avalanche of federal support and many made wild, sweeping claims (for example, "Children's IQ's will be raised 30 points in a year").

Politicians, too, were quick to support such claims with even more congressional support. This support, however, was based only on *claims* and *promises*. Seldom did the public or Congress demand to see proof that a program had (or was likely to have) desirable effects on learners *before* funding it. These were exciting times. Education was receiving the support and recognition that had never been accorded it previously. Confidence abounded that the lives of significant numbers of Americans would be improved.

Eventually, though, research data began to surface suggesting that certain types of programs were more beneficial than others, and that only under certain conditions were preschool gains likely to be sustained. However, deep public disappointment was registered before these results could be widely replicated and built into explicitly research-based curricula. Similar problems and failures were noted with other poverty problems, and the political support for these programs also began to dissipate.

Disappointment in large measure registered because IQ's were not radically increased. That more children were able to achieve *up to potential* was not noticed, because the public was "cued" to inappropriate expectations (IQ gains) rather than more realistic indices (reading, developing skills, and so on). Fragmentary good news was lost in the disappointing flood of data suggesting that preschool *per se* was ineffective. The fact that some *were* working was unobserved.

Parallel with its displeasure with early education programs, the public was expressing disillusionment toward education in general. The civil rights movement of the 60s targeted the school as society's agent for correcting injustices *now*. Schools were exposed to scrutiny as never before in American education. People wanted to know about schools. Increased funding and exaggerated expectations (flamed in part by educators) were peaking just when results from preschool studies began to pile up, and the Coleman study published its disappointing results (that money was not necessarily related to educational progress in a simple, causal way). Thus, the general public's curiosity about schools was not met with satisfying information. Futhermore, countless critics began to publish popular books about schools, and their descriptions systematically painted schools as unresponsive and inadequate (see Chapter 2).

Needless to say, the general public was disappointed in the performance of their schools and became suspicious about the efficacy of spending more and more money on education with little observable return. Given such views, it became politically advisable (if not mandatory) to cut back on educational funds and/or to place strong demands on schools to demonstrate effectiveness. For example, President Nixon's education message of March 8, 1970, emphasized that teachers and administrators should be held accountable for their performance.

There were other reasons for accountability cries—the depressed economy, youth demanding relevant experiences, and so on. But we feel that the basic cause was the series of events that created unrealistically high public expectations impossible for schools to meet. We stress the failure to develop *realistic* expectations, both because we think it is fundamental and because we suspect that schools that *mindlessly* heed accountability suggestions may touch off yet a new cycle of frustrations and disappointments (and eventually smaller budgets!). The only legitimate way to respond to accountability demands is to conduct extensive research *prior* to program implementation.

Teacher Education Programs

Accountability notions are not exclusively directed at elementary and secondary schools. Apparently, dissasisfaction with teachers has led some critics to focus their attention at the source of the Nile: teacher education programs. Lucas (1972) lucidly summarizes the criticisms that have been directed at teacher education programs and notes the increasing pressure to wrestle the licensing of teachers away from colleges and to place it in the hands of lay boards. No doubt much of the pressure stems from the inability of teacher education programs to provide evidence that their graduates can behave differently or exert more positive effects on student learning than other adults who have not been exposed to teacher training (see Chapter 4).

Such pressure has not been without its effects. For example, Wilson and Curtis (1973) report that eleven states have mandated performance-based teacher education. Also, much pressure is being exerted by ACCTE and other accreditation groups to "guarantee" that even more states will move in this direction. (Many university programs, to prevent action from the state legislature, will become more performance oriented.) The interesting factor, of course, is that no research base exists to provide direction for the selection of competencies that are to be mastered in teacher education programs. Research at present cannot tell us what teacher behaviors are unambiguously linked with student affective or cognitive progress. The obvious danger here is that money and talent which could be directed at finding such relationships may be *squandered* in setting up *competency programs*. In this case, agreed-upon competencies that become the Zeitgeist at teacher preparation programs are reified and begin to be respected as if they were legitimate goals in and of themselves. For example, the skills taught at a teacher training institution may be seized upon by local school officials, who will implement accountability legislation by rating teachers on these same measures.

What Is Accountability?

A universally accepted definition of accountability does not exist. Although a general meaning was given at the start of the chapter, the term's real definition has meaning only when expressed in the context of a particular application. The base question (and basic meaning) from a taxpayer's point of view is "What do I get for my money?" Disagreement arises because people vary widely in what they want to "get." Some are interested in teachers who behave in humane ways. Others are interested in student achievement. Still others simply want to know if schools use money wisely.

These examples implicitly illustrate why *accountability for products* (differences in students' achievement, and so on, associated with school attendance) cannot be meaningfully achieved. Let us make these two points explicit: (1) *Research does not* identify the mechanisms (teacher behavior, curriculum materials, homework, and so on) associated with student growth, and (2) There is no clear agreement on appropriate *product* goals. Few school districts have systematically identified possible school *products* and assigned priorities to the accomplishment of various goals (see Chapter 5).

However, before summarizing *possible* long range benefits and disadvantages of accountability, it will be useful to review a few of the plans that have been advocated for achieving accountability. We do this to illustrate that existing plans are quite varied and that the definition of accountability varies from plan to plan.

Voucher Plans

The notion of voucher accountability is seemingly quite simple. Parents are given their child's share of the public school budget and are free to cash it in at whatever school they care to select. Voucher plans in the form of the GI Bill have been in existence since World War II. Veterans who enroll in tertiary education or other approved training programs are given a stipend. However, they may use the stipend at whatever school *meets their needs.*

Advocates of the voucher plan argue that such a direct form of accountability would free parents from the monopolistic school market (that is, students attend the neighborhood school) and would let them buy their education at any school within the city in which they reside. Untested assumptions upon which the idea rests include:

1. Parents can pick rationally;
2. The choices are real (do disadvantaged parents have the time or money to take their children across town?);
3. Attractive alternatives will emerge as a result of the competition;
4. Safeguards can be built in to avoid segregation of certain students into certain schools.

None of these assumptions has been proved or disproved by empirical data. For example, concerning the first two points, Thomas K. Glennan, Jr., former Director of the National Institute of Education, has warned that the system may not help the most disadvantaged students because their parents are least likely to "hustle" them to other schools (Janssen, 1970). However, Christopher Jencks, an active supporter of the voucher concept, has claimed that if we entertain respect for the middle class parents' ability to discriminate among schools we should at least acknowledge the poor parents' potential capacity for doing so (if they had appropriate information, and so on) (Janssen, 1970). However, one wonders what criteria Jencks or anyone could provide to low or high income parents for distinguishing between two inner city schools utilizing traditional curriculums? What is good information? How can one pick the better school? Given the information that is likely to exist, it is probably an impossible task and will remain so unless appropriate data *are* collected.

The third assumption, that attractive alternatives will emerge, is a very interesting one. At first glance, it sounds plausible (and may well be), but in some ways it also has the gratuitous ring of Henry Ford's warm offer . . . you may have any color Ford as long as it's black!

If parents can choose among only very similar models, then the value of the choice is dubious. Similarly, if competition rules the market place and open, individualized programs begin to attract students, what would prevent *all* traditional schools from shifting to the new make? To survive, schools would have to adopt and adapt rapidly. But what, then are the alternatives for parents who want more structure (less religious material, socialization, or whatever)? The answer is obvious. Unless special arrangements are undertaken to assure that minority views are represented with a school model (within limits, although this raises yet another problem), parents of tomorrow's children will have to do just what parents of today's children do when no viable model exists: Compromise their goals.

Questions about the fourth point, the avoidance of segregation, appear to be tied to the creation of an Education Voucher Agency that would control the assignment of students locally. A chief responsibility of the agency would be populating schools that were undersubscribed. Rather than filling such schools on "tainted" criteria (aptitude, race, sex) enrollment presumably would be determined by lottery. Still, the functioning of such boards and the level of ethical standards the *average* board would achieve remains an open empirical question.

Comments here are not meant to suggest that voucher plans do not merit consideration. Indeed, from our point of view, they are an interesting educational idea and merit careful research. Perhaps the most attractive quality of voucher plans is that they could allow parents to select the skill/affective balance most advantageous to them. However, it would seem that careful debate and discussion of educational goals (and the identification of parents who prefer different goals, and so on) could profitably *precede* voucher money/experiments, since few communities are likely to answer directly such questions as, "Should our schools be responsible mainly for intellectual development? What percent of time and school budget should be spent in developing moral behavior, physical development, social growth, vocational awareness, and other goals?" Since such questions haven't been discussed, schools within a district probably offer but little choice. Allowing parents to "vote" for a preferred emphasis as represented by the schools they select (again, assuming that there is variance among schools) is one way to achieve value clarification. However, our interest in research does not mean support for implementing such plans widely; it means careful study of a few plans. Voucher plans are being implemented in some locations now, but it is premature to assess their general efficacy.[1]

Performance Contracting

Performance contracting is simply the award of a contract to an agent willing to guarantee results (typically a business firm). Cash is paid for

---

[1] *However, a newsnote in the December 1973 issue of the* Phi Delta Kappan *suggested that Thomas K. Glennan, former Director of the National Institute of Education felt that the voucher plan has been successful because it has proven to be politically viable and because interest (momentum) in the concept is growing. We would be much more interested in knowing how educational programs had been affected or the precise influence on teachers, students, and parents . . . before calling it a success.*

results. Essentially, such contracts mean that if students do not reach specified levels of achievement, the school district will *not* pay the firm or will pay the firm only a percent of the cost.

However, the obligations of "schooling" business firms may transcend the immediate contract. For example, at present the San Francisco School District is being sued for a million dollars by the parents of a high school graduate who cannot read. If the courts favorably react to this claim, business firms may be held responsible to parents and children for results as well as for fulfilling their contracts with schools. Such an occurrence might well dampen the interest of such firms in obtaining school contracts. Stucker and Hall (1971) have documented the fact that performance contracts (at least the early ones) are usually written in reading and mathematics. Thus, some emphasis exists for writing contracts in very specific terms and, of course, the only instruments that exist for measuring skills are standardized tests. Thus, the availability of instruments as well as the nature of "contracting" would seem to guarantee that most performance contracting will center on achievement in basic subject areas. We suspect that it will be some time before firms are willing to contract for alleviating drug abuse and other such problems.

Clearly, performance contracting is a direct form of accountability. Students' performance is the basis for results: no achievement, no money. However, contracts could be written to guarantee *teaching performance* just as easily. For example, "Ira's Inservice Insurance, Inc." might contract with a school to guarantee that after six weeks teachers could (and/or would) be able to ask questions from every cognitive level, maintain eye contact with all students, and demonstrate other skills. But most firms have contracted for student results, in part, no doubt, because of public interest in *student performance* and because of the difficulty in measuring the naturalistic classroom behavior of teachers. (However, as we shall see, ways have been devised to measure teacher behavior through the development of standardized teaching tests.) A variety of performance accountability studies have been initiated, but these results are not especially encouraging. Results of a six million dollar study conducted by the Office of Economic Opportunity in eighteen different school districts produced no support for performance contracting. An examination of the data in Table 6.1 shows no reason for optimism. Nonetheless, such data have not dampened the spirits of some enthusiasts. Mehrens and Lehmann (1973), for example, note that a Michigan Superintendent still allocated a half-million dollars for PC with private corporations. No doubt officials there felt the performance contract was still a viable concept worthy of continued investigation.

Carpenter and Hall (1971), in the course of reviewing several selected projects for a RAND report, note that performance contracts tend to focus upon a narrow range of objectives, that they are administratively complex

TABLE 6.1

Mean Gains in Grade Equivalent Scores in Performance
Contracting (PC) and Traditional (T) Programs[1]

	Reading		Math	
Grade	PC	T	PC	T
2	.4	.5	.5	.5
3	.3	.2	.4	.4
7	.4	.3	.6	.6
8	.9	1.0	.8	1.0
9	.8	.8	.8	.8

[1] *Drawn from W. Mehrens and I. Lehmann,* Measurement and Evaluation in Education and Psychology, *New York, Holt, Rinehart and Winston, Inc., 1973.*

and pose a variety of problems, and that they demand much time in selecting and administering tests. For example, the administrator who wants to be *responsible* (that is, *accountable*) to the public will have to spend a great deal of time in insuring that the gains can be attributed to the contractor, that the tests are related to important school goals, that the school could not achieve them more cheaply elsewhere. Thus to a heavy schedule of responsibilities administrators must add new (and complex) duties.

Although many would argue that the goals of performance contracting do not have to be narrow, limited subject matter-type goals (such as recall), the general structural characteristics of the situation work against any other type of focus, at least in the forseeable future. For example, school officials want to know the ability of a firm to produce results before signing a long-term contract (generally funding laws in most school districts prevent multi-year contracts). To demonstrate their efficiency, firms would be likely to argue for achievement gain in skill areas as the criterion, unless schools insisted on other goals.

Contractors' interest in helping children to advance in basic skills stems from the fact that testing vagaries virtually assure a regression effect when skill tests are repeated. Regression effect is the tendency for extreme scorers (either high or low) to score somewhat closer to the middle or the mean on the second test than they did on the first. Assume that 26 students take a 100-item test and score as shown in the table below.

On a reliable test, students usually maintain their relative rank (position in the distribution of scores) on separate administrations. Reliability is simple consistency of measurement. Thus, for example, we would expect students who scored high on the first test to generally outperform students who were average or low on the first test if retested on the same instrument or if given

TABLE 6.2

Fictional Test Scores Illustrating Reliability and Regression
Effect Typically Seen When Reliable Tests Are Readministered

	Test 1	Test 2	Sign of difference between test scores
Students having high scores on Test 1			
Student A	100	95	—
B	99	94	—
C	99	97	—
D	98	100	+
E	98	89	—
F	97	93	—
G	96	85	—
Students having near-average scores on Test 1			
H	89	92	+
I	88	88	0
J	88	87	—
K	87	86	—
L	86	87	+
M	85	86	+
N	84	85	+
O	83	81	—
P	82	85	+
Q	81	89	+
R	80	65	—
S	79	79	0
T	75	78	+
Students having low scores on Test 1			
U	65	67	+
V	64	65	+
W	64	75	+
X	63	59	—
Y	62	70	+
Z	60	69	+

$\overline{X}_1 = 82.8$ (appears beside row N)

a parallel form of the original test. When we look at the column of results
under Test 2, we see that this generally is the case, but there are several
exceptions. For example, it can be seen that student H, an average scorer
on the first test, exceeds the performance of two students (E and G) on
the second test.

Thus, even on a test with good reliability, there will be shifting of students on the second administration (if the reliability is poor, there will be wild shifting). However, as can be seen in the table, student results are generally consistent over the two testing occasions. But note that on Test 1 the number of score points separating students who scored within high, average, or low levels is considerably less than the score points separating students *across areas*.

Thus, while it is a reasonable expectation that the difference between a score of 100 and one in the mid 80s may represent a *real difference* in subject matter mastery, it is not reasonable to infer that a score of 99 is inferior to a score of 100. If the difference between 100 and 99 does not represent a real difference, then we do *not* know if student A would outscore student B on a parallel test. However, we do suspect that both students A and B would outscore most of the H–Z students.

When scores are close together (as they typically are at at least one of the extreme ends of the distribution), then the correctness of two items or even one additional item may cause considerable shifting of ranks. The odds are that extreme scores have a great deal of error built into them. (Frank guessed at items 26 and 27 and got them right. Judy guessed at item 14 and missed it. Bill was tired and worked slower than normal and did not attempt the last five problems . . . normally he would have completed the test.) At the extreme end, then, scores measure student ability but also represent a heavy chance factor.

This is especially true on survey standardized achievement tests, where most items are written at an average level of difficulty (roughly 50 percent of students will get the answer and 50 percent will miss). For example, out of a 100-item test, 70 may be written for the average student, (bright students get most of these questions correct) leaving only 15 questions to distinguish the scores of top students and 15 to distinguish the scores of bottom students. Consequently, it is generally possible to distinguish high, middle, and low achievement student reliably and sometimes possible to distinguish more finely within the average category. However, on most standardized tests, it is very difficult to distinguish individual scorers within the ranks of relatively high scorers and relatively low scorers. Since their score differences are based upon responses to just a few questions, random errors (sitting next to a restless student, guesses, and others) will have wide effects. As a result, we can *expect* the "very" top scorers (in our example, say students A, B, and C, to be surpassed by other highs on the second test. Similarly, one would expect low students, say X, Y, and Z, to be replaced at the bottom for random reasons. Thus, even without instruction, one would expect the very lowest scorer to move up in rank on the next test, unless he had been *much* lower than the others on the first test.

With standardized achievement tests as the measure of students' achievement gains, it is expected that extreme scorers on the first test will move toward the mean on the next test. This fact was advantageous to contractors in the first set of performance contracting experiments, because most early contracts were written so that contractors were only responsible for the gains of *low* achievers, not high achievers or the total group. Hence, contractors benefited from regression toward the mean by low initial scorers, so that the "gains" by these students were inflated.

Another closely related "mechanical" problem is the general unreliability of gain scores. To control for the regression effects cited above, one can use pre-scores to adjust for post-instructional scores. However, the reliability of gain scores is considerably lower than the raw scores on which they are based. Stake (1971) has noted, for example, that the reliability coefficient of gain scores is only .16 on tests where the reliability coefficient of the pre- and post-parallel test forms is .84. Thus, it is extremely difficult to estimate the degree to which gains represent real subject matter mastery versus statistical artifacts.

To illustrate his point, Stake notes that on a widely used standardized test, the *average* standard deviation is 9.5 items and 2.7 years on grade level equivalents. The *average* student raw score error is 2.5 items and .72 grade equivalent scores. But the error associated with average gain score would be 1.01. To know that the measured gain score is correct within one year or so is not very reassuring news. Under such circumstances, it will be difficult for administrators to know if performance contractors have delivered or not. To illustrate the utter unreasonableness in using gain scores, Stake notes that if a group of students are accepted in a contract program and *given no instruction* (only periodic tests), as many as two-thirds of the students could be graduated at the end of four tests!

One way out of this statistical morass is to use criterion-referenced measures rather than norm-referenced standardized tests. Criterion-referenced measures will be discussed fully in the following chapter; however, for the present, criterion-referenced measures may be viewed as a direct measure of the skills that a student has mastered. Rather than being tested on standardized instruments, student gain is measured by a specially designed test that tells whether the student has mastered specific skills taught in the *local* program. But the problem, as Stake (1971) notes, is that typical criterion-referenced measures do a poor job of predicting subsequent student performance (for example, is the mastered skill retained?) or their predictive power is unknown. Again, we see the *need for basic research* that precedes program implementation (use of criterion-referenced measures). Criterion-referenced measures are an attractive idea (independent of their use for accountability purposes), but the necessary data-based information for using criterion-referenced testing in a responsible fashion is largely missing.

Numerous studies of performance contracting have been completed or are in progress. For instance Dembo and Wilson (1973) provide an interesting case study of performance contracting. They note that despite questionable evaluation procedures . . . it was another successful (lucrative) venture for the contractor. However, the designs of most of the early studies are such that it is impossible to tell whether or not performance contracting worked and/or under what circumstances (Miller, 1973). Interestingly, where contracts appear to have worked (ignoring possible regression effects, unreliable gain scores, teaching for the tests [*as some contractors have admitted*], and Hawthorne effects), there is no reason to suspect that ordinary teachers couldn't have achieved similar results. For example, the results may be attributable to extra practice that the children weren't getting previously because of inappropriate teacher expectations or the age-graded curriculum. Teachers given more freedom to experiment (see Chapter 8), specified training, or, as Green (1970), suggested resources (money to buy children glasses, etc.) may be able to out perform contractors. However, the advantage of the contractor may be the ability to "break set" and try new strategies. Even if teachers can do or be trained to do the same thing, it may take an outside force to initiate change. Only careful research will tell, and only if process records are kept will we be able to understand how contractors work their magic when they are successful.

National Assessment

As Mehrens (1970) notes, the National Assessment of Education Progress effort is the most extensive assessment project ever initiated in this country. *Knowledge, skills,* and *attitudes* are being assessed in ten subject matter areas (*art, career* and *occupational development, citizenship, literature, mathematics, music, reading, science, social studies,* and *writing*).

Four age groups are included in each assessment cycle (9, 13, 17 and young adults—26 through 35). Roughly 32,000 individuals are tested at the younger ages, and 20,000 young adults. Thus, each year over 100,000 individuals are being assessed in the program. However, not all subject areas will be tested each year. The present cycling plan is:

Cycle 1		Cycle 2	
1969–70	Citizenship, Science, Writing	1975–76	Literature, Reading
1970–71	Literature, Reading	1976–77	Music, Social Studies
1971–72	Music, Social Studies	1977–78	Math, Science
1972–73	Math, Science	1978–79	Writing, COD
1973–74	Writing, COD*	1979–80	Art, Citizenship
1974–75	Art, Citizenship		

* COD *stands for Career and Occupational Development.*

Interestingly, in the early 1960s educators expressed concern that the National Assessment Project would be used *inappropriately* to make comparisons between specific states, cities within states, or particular school districts. These concerns were expressed sufficiently such that the data are collected only within the following three criteria (1) geographical region, (2) size and type of community, and (3) socioeducational status. Such a plan mitigates against the use of these data to make comparisons between *teachers, states,* or *schools*. Given that virtually all states are setting up their own assessment programs, many accountability enthusiasts regret the original sampling decision. However, the program still has the potential for providing useful comparative data. Perhaps collecting data this way will provide even greater potential for their use in intelligent ways and will minimize mindless formula applications (seemingly straightforward but erroneous applications).

Data are reported in national percentages by separate or relatively small subsets of exercises measuring the same objective. Comparisons on such exercises will be available by age, sex, socioeducational status, race, type of community, and geographical region.

As Mehrens (1970) notes, the assessment package in the National Assessment Project differs in several substantial ways from the "package" provided by standardized test results.

1. To begin with, eleven lay panels meet to review the adequacy of the measurement goals. Thus, a sustained effort was made to involve the public in determining relevant goals.
2. The assessment program includes a variety of question formats to supplement the normal objective–multiple choice format popular in standardized tests. Open questions and even structured interviews are being utilized to obtain an in-depth view of the *skills, attitudes,* and *knowledge* that the sampled age groups have obtained within the specific subject areas. Thus, the National Assessment Project has not limited itself to only those objectives that can be machine scored.
3. Attitudes are being sampled. Clearly this is an area where standardized testing on a wide scale has never existed previously.
4. The National Assessment Project in time will yield a record of student achievement describing what concepts students have mastered. This is because a large number of both easy and difficult items are included in the assessment. In the normal standardized test (as we shall see in the following chapter), most of the items are written at an average difficulty level (roughly half get the item correct and half miss it), such that the test makes for maximum discrimination among average students but provides very little knowledge about what the most and least competent students can do.
5. The test exercises as well as the results are to be reported in the

National Assessment Project. Approximately 40 percent of the exercises in each area will be made public after the initial assessment, and hence cannot be reused (the remaining 60 percent of the items in an area can be repeated in the second assessment, allowing for change over time to be measured). Thus, interested teachers and schools will have the opportunity to see how students in general are performing in skill areas, and also will have a chance to see a large number of the test items that were utilized in the assessment.

Such information is useful for two reasons. (1) Classroom teachers often are not allowed to see standardized achievement tests (for fear they will teach for the tests) and hence, they have no idea if tests are measuring *their* classroom objectives. (2) If the tests seem useful to the teachers they can administer them to their students and compare the performance of their students with similar students in the National Assessment Project. At least the actual test results should provide a great deal of information to many teachers about how to assess student attitudes and should help them to learn format styles for measuring their own objectives.

In general the National Assessment Project is a very interesting program which will provide a great deal of information about the attitudes and skills that students at selected ages have mastered. Data about the appropriateness (in the eyes of teachers) of the measuring devices as well as the use to which such results are put are necessary research areas.

Data from the first wave of national assessment are now available, but again we wonder how many teachers are familiar with these results and what, if any, effect these results have had on instructional behavior. Selected examples from writing and music appear in Tables 6–3, 6–4, 6–5, and 6–6. Eventually the National Assessment Project will describe what Americans know and can do in the basic subject areas . . . and in several years (when the second wave of testing is completed) help to assess the amount of progress that has occurred over a period of several years.

System Approaches to Education

Program–Planning–Budgeting System (PPBS), Program Evaluation Review Technique (PERT), and similar systematic planning schemes are yet another way to achieve accountability. Such systems are complex, and it is difficult to describe them fully in a few words; thus, the interested reader may want to consult other sources.

In general, PPBS has great potential for involving broader segments of the community in making school decisions and for spotting relevant budget information. Indeed, the program will take the cobwebs out of the budget and illuminate the priorities (in terms of dollar support) that the system has been explicitly or implicitly following. The cash flow can be seen, and this may prove to be revealing (no money spent on girls' P.E.; $200,000 spent to measure cognitive gains and no money spent in measuring attitudes, and so on).

Although the system approach can identify a number of problems such as anomalies, it cannot provide the empirical base for *solving* such problems when that base does not exist. In the case of girls' P.E., the answer is obvious: More money needs to be allocated. However when discussion centers on the *source* of money (Raid the budget of the men's program? Ask the school board for new monies?) the appropriate response is more elusive. Questions about attitude measurement are a bit complex, and it is not difficult to raise questions that cannot be answered. (Even if we find appropriate measures for collecting data on attitudes that we feel are important, can we increase positive school attitudes in sixth grade students? If so, does school achievement also increase? Does petty thievery decrease?)

Kaufman (1972) has noted, that the "System" process has six major aspects:

1. Identify the problem (based upon *documented* needs);
2. Determine solution requirements and solution alternatives;
3. Select strategies and tools (from among the alternatives);
4. Implement strategies;
5. Determine performance effectiveness;
6. Revise as required.

The first step simply says, "What is our problem? Where are we and how does our position compare with where we want to be? What are we to be held accountable for?" Assuming that this step is achieved by a wide body of community representatives (see Chapter 5), we have no quarrel with such goal-setting activities. However, if the problem is defined by the state department of education and has no relevance to the needs of a particular school district, valuable school resources are being wasted.

The immediate payoff of the process approach begins to break down at step two. Step two is the statement of overall objectives in the form of specific, measurable performance and possible strategies (performance contracting, teacher incentives, required books, teacher behavior, and so on).

The bind begins here, because there is no empirical base for determining solution requirements. For example, we have seen that performance contracting may or may not work. Thus, how can a superintendent know if he is better off in spending extra money for a performance contract, teacher incentives, or new materials for an individualized program? He can not. Only if priorities are firmly established can he even make an intelligent guess. Similarly, assume we have the goal, "Children are to be minimally satisfied in school" (even if it lowers average grade level achievement in skill areas by

TABLE 6.3

Example of a National Assessment Test Item, Scoring Criteria, and Results

Improvising Melody (1H)

In Exercise 1H, individuals were asked to listen to the following phrase and then improvise a concluding phrase.

An acceptable phrase was one which complemented the first phrase and ended with a cadence. About half of the individuals from all four age groups attained acceptable scores. Percentages of good responses were lower, ranging from about 20% for 9-year-olds to about 40% for adults, but criteria for good responses were far more stringent.

Scoring Criteria for Exercise 1H, Improvising Melody

Good
Acceptable
Poor

Three basic criteria separated the acceptable responses from the poor responses. To be considered acceptable, a response must have begun within two measures of the end of the stimulus, must not have deviated in tempo by more than 10% and must not have contained more than two unidentifiable pitches (pitches a little sharp or flat were acceptable).

Three other criteria separate good responses from other acceptable responses:

A good response must have lasted at least two measures, while other acceptable responses could have been as short as one measure.

Good responses maintained the key, while other unacceptable responses could establish and retain a new tonal center in a closely related key (dominant, subdominant, relative minor or parallel minor). Temporary dominant modulation with return to the tonic was not considered to be a change of key.

A good response must have ended on the first, third or fifth degree of the tonic chord with a definite feeling of finish, while other acceptable responses could end on any note in the same key in a clear cadence or half-cadence.

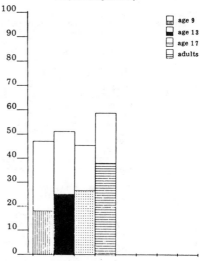

EXHIBIT 8
Percentages of Success for Exercise 1H,
Improvising Melody

age 9
age 13
age 17
adults

TABLE 6.4

Another Music Item from the National Assessment Project
with Scoring Criteria and Results

Improvising Harmony (1I)

In Exercise 1I, 13-year-olds, 17-year-olds and adults were asked to listen to the following line of music and then improvise a harmonic accompaniment to it.

Most individuals tried to improvise a harmonic accompaniment, but many did not: about 20% of the 13 and 17-year-olds and about 10% of the adults did not respond at all. Only 1 person in 10, at all age levels, attained an acceptable score.

<table>
<tr><td>

Scoring Criteria for Exercise 1I, Improvising Harmony

Good
Acceptable
Poor

An acceptable response must have met several requirements. It could not lose the tonality, and the cadence must have been in the key. At least 50% of the beats must have been harmonized with thirds or sixths (with the exception of pedal points using I or V^7) unless the response has the character of an independent melody, in which case only 25% of the beats need be harmonized with thirds or sixths. No more than 50% of the notes could have been in unison or at the octave, and no more than 33% could have been harmonized in seconds or sevenths.

The requirements for a good response were more stringent. At least 75% of the beats must have been harmonized in thirds or sixths (with the exception of pedal points using I or V^7), even if the response has the character of an independent melody. At least 50% of the notes should have been harmonized in thirds or sixths. The lines could not have included more than one measure of parallel fourths or fifths, and one of the two final notes must not have been in unison or at the octave.

</td><td>

EXHIBIT 9
Percentages of Success for Exercise 1I, Improvising Harmony

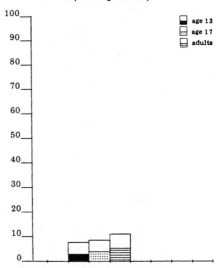

</td></tr>
</table>

It appears, then, that the generalizations developed in the last chapter are further verified by the results of the exercises in this chapter. Rhythm still seems to be the most comfortable element of music for most people; melody and harmony follow. Another generalization also seems apparent: that improvising is no more difficult than repeating an unfamiliar line. Even when individuals cannot remember the exact contour of a musical line, it may be that they often retain enough of the feel for that line to improvise upon it.

TABLE 6.5

Two Writing Examples of National Assessment Test Items,
Scoring Criteria, and Results

Exercise 103

(9:5-18) Similar to Exercise 203
and 301)

You are going to hear two people talking
on the telephone. One is a girl named
Mary Brown. The other is someone just
about your age. His name is Billy.
Pretend that YOU are Billy and LISTEN
CAREFULLY to what Mary asks Billy to
do. Children then listened to the conversation reproduced below. (It was not
printed in the children's booklet.)

BILLY: Hello.

MARY: Hello, who is this?

BILLY: This is Billy

MARY: Billy, this is Mary Brown. Is
your sister there?

BILLY: No, she's at the store.

MARY: Will you give her a message for
me?

BILLY: Sure, I guess so. What is it?

MARY: This is pretty important, Billy.
Can you get some pencil and paper
and write it down?

BILLY: O.K. Wait a minute. (pause)
I'm ready now. Go ahead.

MARY: Tell your sister that I'll
meet her at Jane's house at
6 o'clock tonight. Got it?

BILLY: No, don't go so fast. Say
it again.

MARY: Tell her to meet Mary Brown
at Jane's house at 6 o'clock
tonight. Got it now?

BILLY: I think so, let me see. Meet
Mary Brown at Jane's house at
6 o'clock tonight.

MARY: That's right, Billy. Don't
forget now. Goodbye.

Mary asked Billy to write a note,
didn't she? Now you will hear them
again. Pretend that you are Billy
again. Listen carefully, and this
time try to write the note that
Mary asks Billy to write.

(Approximately ½ page of lined
space was provided for the response.)

SCORING

Acceptable: The response must:

1) be a note that states:

a) meet Mary or Mary Brown
b) where: Jane's house
c) time: 6 o'clock
d) day: tonight

Not acceptable: Omission or
error in any of the above pieces
of information, or failure to
write a note. Copying the instructions or stating, for example, "Tell
your sister to meet Mary..." was
not in note form and therefore unacceptable.

RESULTS

Age 9
31%   Acceptable
66   Not acceptable
 3   No response
100%

Percentage including each piece 1
of information:

70%   meet Mary or Mary Brown
70   where: Jane's house
83   time: 6 o'clock
68   day: tonight

1   Includes responses judged acceptable and those judged not
acceptable.

EXERCISE 104

(9:2-21) (Overlaps Exercise 202)

Mary Smith lives at 100 Main Street in
Hopson, Ohio. The zip code for Hopson
is 45601. Mary's grandmother lives at
475 Cactus Lane in Sunshine, Arizona.
Her name is Mrs. Robert Smith, and her
zip code is 86001.

Pretend that Mary wants to send a letter to her grandmother. How should she
address the envelope? Fill out the
envelope below the way Mary should. Make
sure you write down everything that should
go on the envelope.

SCORING

Acceptable: All envelope parts had
to be written in the proper places. The
zip code was not required, but had to
be correct if written.

Not acceptable: Any errors or blank
spaces on the envelope.

RESULTS

Age 9
28%   Acceptable
69   Not acceptable
 3   No response
100%

Percentage placing each piece 1
of information correctly:

52%   Mary Smith
43   100 Main Street
37   Hopson, Ohio
51   Mrs. Robert Smith
42   475 Cactus Lane
39   Sunshine, Arizona

1   Includes responsed judged acceptable
and those judged not acceptable.

TABLE 6.6
Writing Sample from the National Assessment Test

Dear Pen Pal,

    We are preparing for our Thanksgiving holiday here in Memphis, Tennessee. We have bought a turkey and some stuffing. On Thanksgiving we will have turkey and dressing, cranberry sauce, corn, peas, beans, carrots, bread, milk, tea, and so many other dishes. That night we will have a hay ride. That is when we rent some horses and a wagon. We spread hay In it and an adult person will take us riding in woods. "Us" is all the children. I hope you are doing fine. Everyone is excited about Thanksgiving. Write me soon.

                    Your Pen Pal,
                    Pen Pal

                                          4141 Yutany Avenue
                                          Tokyo, Japan
                                          October 7, 1969

Dear Sir.

    We here in America will start to prepare for Thanksgiving soon. It is a day when all Americans give thanks to God for all the wonderful things he has given us. It is a day of jubilation. We eat turkey or something for dinner. Nice parades are shown on television and we watch them. In the afternoon we watch football games.

    It all began when the Pilgrims had a celebration with the Indians thanking God for their safe journey to America.

                                  yours truly,

Hi!

    How are you, fine I Hope. Well, another Holiday is coming Hope you are Having fun. I am celebrating christmas. WE Have a Big green pine tree for our CHRISTMAS TREE. We take paper and make ornaments and put lights on it. I will start buying presents for my family. I Hope to buy you something. We always wrap packages and put them UNDER OUR tree. THE Night BEFORE CHRISTMAS we all open one. OUR PARENTS buy us many things, But we are suppose to think Santa Claus BRings them. This is a tradition we have Santa is in almost all the stores. He is fat and dressed in Red, He Has WHiTE Rime all around his Suit. The Tradition has him living in the NORTH Pole with LITTLE Elves making toys. When CHRISTmas comes He gets in a sled and lets His Flying Rain deers pull him all over The WORLD giving gifts.

    PS. write Back soon.

                YOUR PEN PAl,

.2). We would *not* know precisely how to direct teachers to accomplish the goal. *The fear is that in the absence of program or substantive criteria, the only criteria that will be applied are cost-benefit or general efficiency measures.*

Few school systems in the country have the basic data they need to "plug" into a PPBS system for anything other than a rough financial audit (which may be valuable in and of itself, however). Basic program data are doubtlessly missing. For example, consider the following: What is each teacher's average residual gain score on a standardized achievement test administered to students in the district? What percent of the curriculum is mastered by students in the district? What are student attitudes toward school? Do black or low income pupils have attitudes similar to those of white or high income students? What is the morale of teachers in the district? Only when such questions are answered can a superintendent begin to plan a remedial program to help *students, teachers,* or *principals* as needed. Clearly, different teachers and schools would have individual patterns of strengths and weaknesses such that each would need a unique PPBS plan. However, a PPBS program applied indiscriminately to all school districts (and, in most cases, to all students in a district) would be self-defeating.

The chief danger in PPBS accountability approaches, as we see them, are summarized as follows:

1. They may be *applied inappropriately* as "formulas" to all school districts or schools within a system;
2. They may be used *prematurely* (arbitrarily agreeing upon certain solution strategies and then evaluating them *only* on cost effectiveness grounds).

Thus, economically "feasible" strategies become locked into standard operating practices, even though the strategies have not demonstrated that they help in reducing the original needs. (For example the "decision board," upon learning that no affective testing is done in the school district, might urge school officials to incorporate any affective measure the local school district finds useful. The testing proves to be relatively cheap and the procedure becomes standard, even though most teachers do not see their results until a year later and there is no attempt to see if teachers use the information (change behavior) and/or if student attitudes eventually improve in a particular room or in the school generally. Such superficial use of PPBS involves no actual solutions to anything.

However, it should be understood that very little research has been done on PPBS application in education, so that discussion here must necessarily be speculation. There are case studies praising the advantages of PPBS (see for example, Alioto and Jungherr, 1969). However, most of these reports have a Machiavellian ring to them (such as ways to get your budget passed), and as yet there are no substantive data to show that use of PPBS has substantially increased the *learning gains* of students when applied by any educational agency other than a professional research group or educational laboratory. PPBS systems may be effective, we feel, if they are used to collect a great deal of *decision making information* on schools (for perhaps as long as three to five years), and if such *program data* are then used to devise *program changes* whose efficiency is carefully measured in terms of progress in reaching *program goals*.

Teacher Evaluation: Teacher Incentives

Teachers have been found to be just as effective as performance contracting firms in several different experiments. Thus, at this point, if one wants to increase student performance in reading, the odds are just as good that a teacher could achieve these results as well as a performance contractor. Teachers also probably present fewer administrative problems. However, the same criticisms that were aimed at performance contracting could be leveled at teacher incentive plans as well (use of standardized achievement results, extra time, and so on) and one wonders if teachers will be willing to be "accountable" if present legal battles lead to the conclusion that it is possible to sue schools for their failure to produce student achievement gains.

Nonetheless, there are increasing pressures to hold the classroom teacher accountable. For example, Beller (1971) includes among the reasons for evaluating teachers these:

1. To see if educational objectives are being achieved;
2. To identify effective and ineffective teachers (for retention, pay increases, and so on);
3. To yield a basis for inservice and supervisory activity;
4. To provide a basis for self-improvement;
5. To provide evidence of the quality of services provided;
6. To determine to what extent education programs produce changes compatible with the goals of the culture.

Such goal statements are interesting, but generally unworkable. To begin with, in most school districts educational objectives, and the priorities within those objectives, have not been defined. Hence, goal one is impossible to achieve *until* these goals are established. Similarly, goal six is impossible to achieve in any school because universally accepted cultural goals have not been articulated. Goal two is an extraordinarily complex one to implement (we shall discuss one attempt below), and few *if any* districts have gathered the necessary variety of outcome measures to fairly evaluate teaching performance. Goals three, four, and five are possible, but we would suggest that such goals are more relevant for self-improvement activities or for gathering base line information about teaching that will lead to *eventual* remedial prescription and accountability, but not for *immediate* accountability. Even here data are only useful if they are collected in careful ways.

Despite the lack of a data base or a conceptual framework to guide evaluation activity, evaluating teachers remains a popular sport. Some of the more popular attempts to rate teachers' effectiveness include situational testing, student outcome scores on any measure (usually standardized tests), and naturalistic process measures of student and teacher behavior. Situational testing will be described in detail below. We feel that the use of student outcome measures and process measures of classroom behavior in tandem is a viable way to build up reliable data describing teacher progress and such process will be explained in Chapter 10; however, already the reader has been exposed to the necessary criteria that must be observed if viable data are to be collected (see Chapter 3).

Situational Testing

Another form of accountability is to test the teachers directly by observing their classroom behavior and by testing the "effects" of the teacher in special situations. Since we will discuss naturalistic observation in a subsequent chapter, our focus here will be on situational testing. Professor James Popham (1973) has described the situational test as a practical procedure consisting of 4 major steps to appraise teacher achievement in the classroom:

1. Teachers are given explicit instructional objectives, along with a few sample items of how students will be tested;
2. Teachers are given time to design a lesson;
3. Teachers instruct a group of pupils (ranging from six to the whole class) for a specified time period;
4. Pupil ability and achievement are measured.

Advantages to this system include *standardization* (same lesson, same test procedures, period of time controlled) and *randomization* (pupils are assigned to teachers such that sex, aptitude, race and other variables can be controlled) which makes it possible that differences in student achievement between teachers *can* be attributed to the teacher. However, the testing of teaching through such standardized procedures implicitly assumes that the essence of teaching is presenting information to a group of students (that is, teachers' skill in selecting appropriate objectives or ability to measure student gain is not being assessed).

The chief disadvantage to the use of situational tests as a measure of teaching effectiveness is (as the literature reviewed in Chapter 4 suggests) that many things other than instructional message variables (clarity, enthusiasm) are responsible for differential levels of teacher effectiveness. For example, other teaching skills include managerial skills; ability to break down the "class" and organize it so as to have time to spend with individual students in work-related interactions; ability to develop camaraderie; and ability to establish credibility with students. Such skills are unlikely to be exhibited in a relatively short time period when the teacher works with a strange group of pupils (who are tested only for knowledge). The real question is "What effect does a teacher have on students whom he sees daily?" Tentative data suggest that how a teacher responds before and after a teaching episode is as important as the teaching episode itself.

Popham (1973) has acknowledged the differences between teacher performance in situational testing and in the real classroom. However, rather than calling for empirical validity data, he chooses to dismiss the problem this way: "But is there any reason to believe that a teacher who has performed miserably on several short-term performance tests will suddenly blossom in a regular teaching situation? Hardly" (p. 27).

Even granting the assumption (that teachers who consistently do miserably on performance tests are relatively ineffective in the classroom), we are still left with a series of practical questions if situational tests are to be applied. For example, do top scorers deserve higher merit raises than middle scorers? It seems that no data are presently available to support the validity of situational performance tests. Needed are studies that depict the performance of teachers of known effectiveness on such situational tests. Do teachers who consistently outperform other teachers on important criteria (measured in real classrooms) score higher on situational tests than teachers of average effectiveness?

Granted, situational tests that correlated highly (or even moderately) with naturalistic teacher performance would be practical, useful tools for preservice and inservice programs, as well as for accountability purposes. However, at present no validity information exists. We again would argue that a *research base* should *precede* practical application, and that advocacy without data is a disservice to the improvement of teaching.

Reliability is also an issue. If teachers are high on one situational test, then low on a second test, which test is to be believed? Obviously, to clear up such discrepancies a third or a fourth situational test would be needed. But here the practicality of the situational test breaks down. Glass (1974) has shown that reliability is relatively low in situational tests. Studies of the reliability of top and low scorers are needed. Perhaps situational tests do a reasonable job of predicting performance (on other situational tests) for extreme performers. But if so, such data have not surfaced yet.

Lacking good reliability and validity data, it is impossible to argue for the use of situational tests in *applied* settings. However, experimental work on the reliability and validity of such tests is of value, and it may provide a strong tool that can be applied in the future for improving teaching efforts. However, we suspect that such research would be more fertile if conducted in concert with efforts to identify a pool of teachers of known effectiveness in order to test the validity of these tests directly.

A federal court recently ruled that a teacher could not be removed from her job on the basis of student achievement scores. However, in this case the U.S. District Court judge noted that "a teacher's professional competence cannot be determined solely on the basis of her students' achievement . . . especially where students maintain normal educational growth rates" (*Phi Delta Kappan*, News Note, 1973, 54, 580). Perhaps standardized test scores would hold up in court if the results from a class were clearly low and atypical. Only other court cases will answer this question. But given the low reliability of gain scores and other measurements, it is hard to visualize the use of student achievement scores as allowable evidence in competence cases. For similar reasons it appears that results from situational testing would be equally "unusable" given the present state of the art (with its low reliability and other factors) and the fact that performance is not measured in the classroom.

Mirror, Mirror on the Wall

We have talked about possible accountability plans and have seen that the possible ways of holding educators accountable are quite varied. In the tables which follow, the present accountability laws are shown in chart form. The data in Table 6–7 are summarized from the written descriptions of existing legislation in a document published by the Wisconsin Department of Public Instruction (Hawthorne, 1973).

The legislation is quite vague at present and hence difficult to describe (and, needless to say, in most states difficult to implement). Through August 1973, 27 states have enacted some form of accountability legislation. A state assessment program of student performance is mandatory in 15 states, and 13 have adopted a uniform accounting system (such as PPBS). Five states have been omitted from the chart because it was difficult to accurately summarize them in chart form. The laws of these five states (Alaska, Arkansas, Hawaii, Illinois, and Indiana) contain only *very general* mention of assessment; the laws usually apply to *all* state agencies and are primarily concerned with budget accounting.

Some points of general interest not included in the chart are the following:

1. California is the *only* state whose laws specify which tests are to be used (by name) in *some* of their testing programs.
2. *Remedial Programs:* Arizona, California (reading); Michigan, New York (urban aid).
3. *Use of Outside Experts for Planning and/or Evaluation:* Arizona, Ohio, and Nebraska specifically mentioned.

TABLE 6.7

State Assessment of Educational Programs[1]

State	Who Initiates	Kinds of Tests and/or Purposes	Results Go to . . .	Teacher Evaluation
Arizona	State Bd. of Ed., w/help of local districts	Pupil achvmt.; reading tests; performance objectives; *remedial* program	State supt., using experts, will assess reading program	No
California	St. Bd. of Ed. (assessment); Dept. of Ed., Legisl. and each school district (evaluation)	Achvmt., IQ, reading, physical fitness, aptitude tests; grades which are to be tested are listed; *remedial* program	St. Bd. of Ed., Legislature, St. Dept. Ed., funding priorities	Yes—Legislature/each school to adopt guidelines
Colorado	St. Bd. and an advisory committee also, *local acct. programs* estab. by Bd. Ed. of each district	Standardized tests, other means, evaluate performance objectives	St. Bd. of Ed. and *public*	No
Connecticut	St. Bd. of Ed., a legislative committee to oversee planning and evaluation in ed.	Evaluation and assessment procedure for vocational and occupational ed.; spec. ed.; federal programs; innovative programs; adult ed.; general ed.	General Assembly	Superintendent of each school district in charge of annual eval.; "minimum performance criteria" to be established by St. Bd. (presented to St. Ed. Comm.); additional local criteria

[1] *The authors gratefully acknowledge the assistance of Gail Hinkel in the preparation of this table.*

State				
Florida	Commissioner of Ed.	Student progress; criterion and norm-ref. tests; ed. objectives; comparison of school dists., *results by* grade and subject area for each district	St. Bd. of Ed. and *public*	Superintendent to estab. "procedure for assessing perf. of duties and responsibilities."
Kansas	Local school board (state will assist if requested)			A written policy of personnel evaluation procedure applicable to all employees; personal qualities and attributes to be considered are listed; administrative staff primarily resp. for making evaluation
Maryland	St. Bd. and St. Superintendent will assist local bd.	Dev. goals and objectives for subject areas; survey student achvmt. (each school)	Gov. and Gen. Assembly; St. Supt. of Schools	No
Massachusetts	Commissioner of Ed.	Assess "conditions and efficiency" of all schools = pupil achvmt. in terms of definable goals and objectives; *Independent Research Agency* created to study ed. systems and recommend policy		No

TABLE 6.7 (continued)

State Assessment of Educational Programs

State	Who Initiates	Kinds of Tests and/or Purposes	Results Go to . . .	Teacher Evaluation
Michigan	Dept. of Ed.	Statewide achvmt. testing —goals of achvmt. for elem. & sec. schools; *remedial* program; vocational assessment	Periodic Eval. reports of ed. progress of state	No
Nebraska	Commissioner of Ed. Dept. of Ed.; consult, experts and lay leaders	Statewide testing of achievement and accomplishment	Governor and local school district personnel, including public	
Nevada	Gov.-appt. committee which made $30,000 study of status of state's school system; comm. made 9 recommendations, 3 on accountability	(1) Identify & clarify ed. goals; (2) accountability implemented, wise use of ed. resources	Dept. of Ed. files report w/ Gov. and legislature	(3) Evaluation of teachers, supervisory staff, principals and superintendents.
New Jersey	Commissioner and St. Bd. of Ed.	Statewide test. program w/ emphasis on reading abilities done annually at appropriate grade levels		Voluntary coop. among Comm. and St. Bd.; univ., profess. organiz. and local schl. dists. will estab. criteria for *profes. teaching* competence based on a perf. eval. *prior* to issuance

				of initial teach. certif. minimum standards	Adequacy of staff preparation
New Mexico	Public schl. finance div. publish manual for uniform sys. of accounting and budgeting for all schools and school districts (doesn't specify who's responsible for testing)	Statewide testing program grades 1, 5, 8; criterion-ref. tests admin, to all high school seniors; ⅓ of public schools each yr. will be assessed and eval. "through visits by dept. personnel" for accreditation; will investigate pupil gain, activities, schl. dist. organiz.	Each dist. must report to St. Bd. effects of distribution formula and other financial arrang. on ed. program outcomes and student progress		
New York	Dept. of Ed.	Evaluation of and aid to urban schls.; dev. and implement comprehensive student eval. prog. for elem. and sec. schls.	Commissioner will report to legis. on how urban aid money spent		No
Ohio	St. Dept. of Ed. (use of experts)	Use *pilot schl. districts*; define ed. objectives; relate cost and efficiency to learning outcome; identify factors in teach.-learn. process which have greatest relevance to student performance	To develop "a uniform system" of reporting results to *all interested persons*		No

TABLE 6.7 (*continued*)

State Assessment of Educational Programs

State	Who Initiates	Kinds of Tests and/or Purposes	Results Go to . . .	Teacher Evaluation
Oklahoma	A state system of *local accountability* vs. a statewide assessment program; schl. dist. must initiate its own program to get state accreditation; local staff works under guidelines and direction of St. Dept. of Ed.—local patrons involved also	*Needs assessment* program in all grades; ed. goals and objec. to be dev.; *inservice training sessions* (regional) held by St. Ed. Department to effect changes in accreditation process		No
Pennsylvania	St. Bd. of Ed.	Achvmt., performance tests in all subjects, provide each schl. dist. w/relevant and comparative data	St. Bd. of Ed.—they will devise *performance standard* using results	No
Oregon	St. Bd. of Ed.; District Superintendents; more than 500 students	No assessment of ed. programs		St. Bd. will consider, in establishing professional requirements and experience (relating to *teacher tenure*), professional skills, educ., and experience *not* directly related to teaching

		exper. or training.; dist. superintendents still have an annual perf. eval. made for each teacher; a form to be prescribed by St. Bd. and completed by schl. dist. bd.; report goes in personnel file—bd. and teacher decide who has access
Rhode Island	Commissioner of Ed. (Appointed by Regents)	Uniform aptitude and IQ testing of all elem. and sec. pupils—to determine present and future needs of ed.
	State Bd. of Regents	Estab. master plan for *all* levels ed. (elem., sec., and *higher*); includes dev. goals and objectives and *continuous eval.*; "What men should know and be able to do!"
South Dakota	State professional *practices* Commission (7 people, 3 teach. rep. of St. Bd., etc.) w/help from atty. gen., St. Sup. and St. Bd. *when* requested	A resolution adopted to promote *total community* involvement to determine goals, philosophy, etc. of ed. by *local schl. dists.*	Estab. *Code of Ethics and Standards of Practice*; flexible ways to judge performance; (shall *not* estab. standards for minimum salaries, etc.); can reprimand

TABLE 6.7 (continued)

State Assessment of Educational Programs

State	Who Initiates	Kinds of Tests and/or Purposes	Results Go to . . .	Teacher Evaluation
	Local professional practices *committee*			or recommend disciplinary action; Adopt a policy stmt. on supervision and evaluation; prepare a feasibility study report for a merit and incentive pay system and submit to state commission
Texas	Legislature Budget Bd.	To have performance audits and evaluations of each state agency to review programs		Large 1971–72 study by Tex. ed. agency of competency / performance-based teacher ed.; as a result, St. Bd. of Ed. made major changes in teacher ed. and certification; all teacher ed. programs now c/p-based; under study now because of criticisms
Virginia	St. Bd. of Ed., subject to revision by assembly	St. and local schl. divisions try to achieve: *Standards of quality for schls.*		Yes, specific standards are set forth

132

		a. 8 planning and management standards b. 10 performance objectives c. School division objectives d. 8 indiv. schl. planning and management objectives e. Classroom planning and management—6 responsibilities of teacher	Establish "evaluative criteria and procedures" for all certified employees; annual eval.—every unsatisf. employee notified of his deficiencies w/ recommend. for improvement.; probationary period
Washington	(Local schl. bd.) Bd. of Directors		
Wisconsin	Bd. of Government Operations	Pupil achvmt. to be objectively meas. each year at several grade levels, on uniform, statewide basis	No

4. *Results to Public*: Colorado, Florida, Ohio, and Nebraska. However, confidentiality of results could change at any time. For example, Mehrens and Lehmann note that state assessment data collected with a confidential pledge in Michigan was publicly released after political pressure was applied.

5. *Local Accountability* (Education Assessment Programs which appear to be autonomous): Colorado and Oklahoma (to some degree).

6. *Florida specifies data analysis* by grade and subject area for each school district.

7. *Teacher Evaluation before Certification*: New Jersey and Texas.

8. *Pilot School Districts*—Ohio will use them to study accountability.

9. Oklahoma and South Dakota are the only states which allow the *public* to participate in assessment (not specific as to what way).

10. Virginia is the only state which goes into some detail on *standards of quality* which schools are to try to achieve, and the only state to mention specific factors relevant to teacher performance evaluation.

11. South Dakota is the only state which mentions a *merit* incentive pay system as a possible outcome of teacher evaluation; local committees instructed to prepare a feasibility study on this matter.

Thus, it is apparent in most states that accountability means very little at present, but has the potential for exerting far-reaching influences upon education in the future. Specificity is seldom provided in the laws, and local districts are often left to their own devices for achieving "accountability."

There can be no doubt that schools and teachers must be accountable to the society they serve. However, the research base for supporting specific accountability plans is meager. It would seem that the key to their eventual effects (good or bad) will depend upon how local school officials respond to the charges or pressures emanating from their legislatures or state departments of education.

The systematic pressure will be for quick and inoffensive formulas that are acceptable to all groups, perhaps also for minimal dialogue about the goals of education in local schools. Bowers (1971) notes that when accountability is applied in a community of diverse interest groups, the predictable outcome is a paralyzing politicization of the education process such that only safe, middle-of-the-road objectives are possible.

Virtually all advocates agree that the only way to make accountability responsive to the needs of children is to involve large numbers of people in the process of establishing priorities (see, for example, Marland, 1972). Similarly, many have predicted that accountability pressures will lead to national debates. For example, Sciara and Jantz (1972) suggest that questions such as the following will be debated: Shall cognitive goals such as literacy prevail over affective goals such as humanism?

However, as one looks at the accountability legislation that has been enacted to date, it is difficult to see much influence of "humanistic" values, and even little real interest in cognitive functioning. Legislation seems primarily concerned with the financial or mechanical use of achievement tests. Perhaps, though, such vague legislation will serve a catalytic function and urge interest groups to push for the specific recognition of needs they see as fundamentally important.

Again, however, if such debate does take place, the extent to which it is channeled into productive activity will be in the hands of local educators. If they hide behind accountability legislation as a way to prevent change ("We must have a consensus to change policy. We don't have money to evaluate attitudes because we have to test *every* grade level on standard achievement scores. We can't use criterion-referenced measures because they don't allow us to compare school districts.") much will be lost.

If, however, superintendents and school boards help their communities to become more responsive to the school, and the school to the community, progress may come about. One way in which local educational leaders can help is to provide the community with alternative goals and different school models that allow some degree of choice, so that local schools are held accountable for a core of overlapping goals but also for unique goals. Above all else, local educators can be responsive by insisting upon the collection of viable descriptive data (to tell themselves and the taxpayers what *effects* the schools are having), and to use accountability legislation as a vehicle for developing long-range, quality solutions to complex educational problems such that *responsible experimentation and documentation occurs*. What is *not* needed are untested solutions that are peddled as quick, overnight cures. We agree with Dyer (1970) that schools can be held accountable in the immediate sense only for (1) knowing as much as they can about the needs of students and their effects upon students and (2) using that information in the attempt to improve instruction.

Unfortunately, it is possible to free great expenditures of resources to develop PPBS approaches without the collection of such basic information! System proliferation and the drive for a unitary "order of sameness" has already been perceived by one educator; Gubser (1973), for example, has claimed that accountability has been used to justify budget cuts and as an excuse for cutting books from the approved state list because they did not exhibit the appropriate political philosophy. He also notes that the number of employees in the State Department of Education in his state has increased over 100 percent in the past three years. If accountability procedures are correlated with inappropriate standardization, hidden attacks on the curriculum, less responsiveness to public dialogue, unnecessary administrative growth, and less basic research on the teaching-learning process, then accountability will have been an excessive overreaction to education's inability to suddenly solve the inequities of decades.

Others too have voiced strong reaction against the dangers of accountability legislation. For example, The National Education Association (NEA) has suggested that passed and proposed accountability legislation is inoperative. Furthermore, the NEA has loudly argued that accountability laws are more likely to create a closed system of educational practice rather than to encourage educational renewal. Thus teachers as represented by a large and influential teachers' union have gone on record as saying that they strongly oppose accountability legislation. (See, for example, *Phi Delta Kappan, News Note*, 1973, *54*, 503.)

Proponents of accountability laws may interpret the teachers' stance as an attempt to avoid public scrutiny. However, we do not think this is necessarily so as there are some recent survey data to suggest that teachers favor the general idea of accountability (Good, Coop, Dembo, Denton, and Limbacher, 1974), and we suspect teachers' unwillingness to support accountability movements stems largely from their lack of faith in the validity of present modes of accountability.

State Assessment

Independent of a mandate for state assessment from the state legislature, most states have adopted some form of state assessment or plan to do so. Beers and Campbell (1973) recently divided the 30 operational programs into two groups: (1) data used by state personnel; (2) data used by teachers and local administrators. This division and the "who is the information for" effects can be seen in Table 6.8.

Although not mandated by legislative action, it is clear that affective measurement is becoming a more frequent component of state assessment programs. The trend here is matched by more emphasis upon affective measurement in preschool programs (*Phi Delta Kappan, News Note*, 1973, *54*, 568). Thus, more and more information is being collected about student reactions to their educational environment (more on this in Chapter 9). However, affective records are less likely to be collected in programs where the information is used for decision making at the state level.

Furthermore, it is worth noting that participation strongly tends to be voluntary in programs where the information is used for local decisions; whereas, in "state decision" programs, participation tends to be mandatory. Interestingly, though, norm-referenced data are more frequently collected in programs where data are used for local decision making. This is ironic because, as we shall see in Chapter 7, one of the advantages claimed for criterion-referenced testing is that it provides specific information about skills that have been directly influenced by instructional programs.

Other minor trends are evident in Table 6.8, but the main point here is to illustrate that the anticipated use of state assessment data exerts influence upon the type of information and the way that information is collected. Also, action in state accountability and state assessment programs is occurring very rapidly and the information presented in Tables 6.7 and 6.8 is provided only to suggest the diversity that exists in present programs (as of August 1973), no doubt the pattern of programs will be different when this book comes to press. However, information about the points where programs may differ will be of assistance in assimilating new information about state accountability and assessment.

Of special interest will be how state assessment data are used to improve educational programs. The perceived value of the data that states collect fluctuates widely in our opinion. In some states the information appears to be no more than expensive census data. We will need to have evaluations showing the way in which state assessment data are utilized and the *benefits* of such knowledge.

Beers and Campbell (1973) aptly summarize our feelings: "It is probably safe to say that statewide assessment will not produce any startling revelations about what can be done by teachers with pupils to help children learn more effectively. This conclusion is not meant to be as much an indictment of statewide assessment as it is a statement of its limitations. Revelations in teaching practices and methods can come only from intensive analysis within each school building and within each classroom. If statewide assessment data can whet the appetites of teachers and administrators for doing the evaluations only they can do for themselves, statewide assessment will serve its purpose well." (p. 7)

Accountability: An Old Idea

Accountability is not a new concept. Marland (1972) notes that in 1649 the Massachusetts Bay Colony required each town to teach children to read the scriptures. Furthermore, as Sciara and Jantz (1972) note, in Ontario from 1876–1882, high schools' financial budgets were dependent upon the number of students who passed the intermediate exam. Interestingly, they note that teachers centered their instructional efforts on the average or slightly below average student for getting maximum gains (on the assumption that lows couldn't learn and top students would pass the test no matter what the teacher did). The practice was abandoned in 1883 because teachers were fixed on preparing students for end of year tests, and other goals were abandoned.

TABLE 6.8

Information about Selected Features of State Accountability Programs[1]

Group 1	Group 2	Group 3
Program emphasis: Collecting information for decision-making at the state level. N = 17	Program emphasis: Collecting information for decision-making at the local level. N = 13	Emerging Programs. N = 24
1. Assessment is mandated by the state legislature in 9 states (52%).	1. Assessment is mandated by the state legislature in 1 state.	1. Assessment is mandated by the state legislature in 6 states (25%).
2. Assessment results are reported to the state legislature in 13 states (76%).	2. Assessment results are reported to the state legislature in 3 states (23%).	2. Reports are not yet compiled, but the focus for 20 (83%) of the programs is the collection of data for state-level decision-making.
3. The collection of data for PPBS and/ or a statewide MIS is specified for 7 programs (41%).	3. The collection of data for PPBS and/ or a statewide MIS is specified for 4 programs (30%).	3. The collection of data for PPBS and/ or a statewide MIS is planned for 9 programs (37%).
4. Assessment data are used to allocate state and federal funds in 8 states (47%).	4. Assessment data are not used to allocate state and federal funds in any state.	4. Assessment data will be used to allocate state and federal funds in 10 states (42%).
5. Participation is required in 10 states (59%).	5. Participation is voluntary in 12 states (92%).	5. All but 3 states report that participation will be voluntary.
6. Samples of students rather than all students in the target populations are tested in 12 states (70%).	6. All students in the target populations are tested in 12 states (92%).	6. Seventeen states (71%) plan to draw samples of students for testing.

138

7. Cognitive skills only are assessed in 11 states (65%).
8. Criterion-referenced tests are administered in 9 states (52%).
9. Assessment is financed by state funds only in 6 states (35%), federal funds only in 4 states (24%), a combination of state and federal funds in 5 states (29%), and a combination of local, state, and/or federal funds in 2 states (11%).

7. Both affective and cognitive skills are assessed in 9 states (69%).
8. Norm-referenced tests only are administered in 9 states (69%).
9. Assessment is financed by state funds only in 2 states (15%), federal funds only in 3 states (23%), a combination of state and federal funds in 4 states (31%), and a combination of local, state, and/or federal funds in 4 states (31%).

7. Thirteen states (59%) plan to assess both cognitive and affective skills.
8. Of the 17 states which specified whether norm-referenced or criterion-referenced tests will be used, 11 states plan to administer criterion-referenced tests.
9. Assessment is financed by state funds only in 5 states (21%), federal funds only in 14 states (58%), a combination of state and federal funds in 3 states (12%), and a combination of local, state, and/or federal funds in 2 states (8%).

[1] *Reprinted from Beers and Campbell (1973)*

However, we have made but little progress since 1883 in attempting to clarify goals other than standardized achievement or in developing techniques for measuring such goals. Hopefully this *cycle* of accountability will at least sharpen goal awareness and lead to the development of a research base that will help to establish ways in which such goals might be accomplished.

Summary

In this chapter the reasons "for" accountability have been traced, ironically, in part to a high level of public confidence that was "betrayed." Different plans for implementing accountability were discussed, but it was noted that none had a research base to show that it could work to improve *student learning* or *affective growth*. Further, it has been seen that present legislation is not very specific, and that the impact of accountability pressure (at least at the moment) lies in the hands of local educators. Accountability is a process, and like most process phenomena it is fundamentally neither useful nor harmful. Its utility will arise from its particular application, so that only later will it be possible to know the true impact of the accountability movement of the 70s on education in the United States. Present indicators do not look promising, in that there is no apparent input in state laws from lay citizens, or in some cases even from professional educators outside the state department of education.

The problem is that everyone wants simple formula data and quick answers when this is not realistic. To get real answers will take careful collection of data and careful research as well as the development of new instruments. But inappropriate simple formulas are available, and irrational pressures plus "job" anxiety of school officials may lead to their use. What school officials need is *not* pressure for an immediate solution but rather the demand for the creation of research-based alternatives that will improve upon the present level of school effectiveness. However, already there is some rampant movement in the country for more alternatives in education, but most of this flow (to open schools or whatever) stems from fadism rather than a careful articulation of priorities (see Chapter 8). Unfortunately, the accountability movement, to date, has not contributed to such goal clarification (see Chapter 5).

However, there does seem to be some "consensus" in American education that individualized "responsive" curricula are needed that will allow students to master specific subject matter in their own fashion and at their own pace. Specificity of learning goals and individualized milieus have become the current Zeitgeist. The research base that supports these two concepts will be reviewed in the next two chapters.

Chapter 7 Criterion-Referenced Testing

Independent of statewide accountability programs are narrower questions that may be raised by teachers themselves. How do I evaluate my classroom performance? Do I help students to master subject matter content to the best of their abilities? Did I do a better job this year than last? Have I helped pupils to improve their self-views and interpersonal skills? Should my classroom be more open? If I team-teach will students benefit?

The chapters in the latter part of this book are designed to help teachers develop strategies for dealing with "effectiveness" in their own classrooms. In this chapter, discussion will center on criterion-referenced testing. Many educators are now stressing the importance of grading students on the basis of the content they master rather than in comparison with other students. Their argument is that an emphasis on *helping students to learn by identifying specific learning criteria will allow more students to master basic concepts without having to worry about competing for grades with classmates.* This is the principle of criterion-referenced testing. Although evaluation of criterion-referenced and mastery learning (providing each student the necessary time to master explicit curriculum goals *before* moving on to a new unit) is far from complete, the literature is encouraging. However it is clear that they do not provide magical solutions for all educational problems. *Teachers* have been found to be a critically important factor in making mastery learning systems work. In particular, teachers' willingness to reteach material that was not mastered by some student is especially important.

However, before discussing the teacher's role and a variety of substantive issues involved in criterion-referenced testing, it will be useful to explain how criterion-referenced testing differs from norm-referenced testing (the traditional way in which student's academic progress has been assessed) and to explain the term "behavioral objective," which forms an integral part of a criterion-referenced testing program.

Norm-Referenced Testing

Teachers regularly collect information about students' classroom performance and assign marks on the basis of that information. Traditionally, the marks or scores teachers assign to students provide information only in comparison with scores received by other students. Examine the three statements that follow and think about what the scores mean (if anything): Bill received the highest mathematics score in the class; Mary scored in the middle on the same test on fractions; Sandy got a B.

Two of these three descriptions appear to make immediate sense. We know that Bill received the top mark and that Mary's performance on this fraction test was average in comparison with classroom peers. However, we do not know what Bill and Mary's performances would be if they were tested on similar material (fractions) by another teacher and/or with another group of students. Bill might retain his high rank; however, if the students in the other class were brighter and if the second teacher asked more difficult problems, his rank might fall. "Top grade" and "in the middle" only provide information about Bill's and Mary's *relative performance* compared with students in *their* room who have received roughly similar opportunity to learn the test material.

Sandy's B is even more difficult to react to, because we do not know how many of her peers performed more ably than she did. That is, if we wanted to know what her B meant we might ask how many A's, B's, C's, D's and F's did the teacher assign? If we learn that one-third of the class received a grade of A or B, we know that Sandy's performance exceeds two-thirds of her classmates.

Sometimes the distribution of letter grades is used mistakenly to indicate quality. Knowledge that one-third of one class received A's and B's cannot be used to infer that a "B" means more than in another class where three-fourths of the students received an A or B. The reverse claim is also unreasonable. Scarcity of A's and B's *per se* is unrelated to performance. For example, the teacher who gives 75 percent of his students an A or B may have all or most of his students outperforming students in the class that appears (superficially) to have higher standards. The grade "B" (with no other information) at best tells us that the student has achieved above minimal course demands. However, minimal demands vary widely, and students who receive a "C" in one class when they would have received a "B" from another teacher (had they been luckier when teachers were assigned) are numerous.

Knowledge of the distribution of assigned grades tells us absolutely nothing about the quality of instruction in a particular classroom. The only way the meaning of a course grade can be established is by examination of the levels of teacher assignments and of student achievement on such assignments. We stress this because on occasion, teachers or principals have suggested that their low numbers of A's or B's reflect their demands for excellence. Low frequency of high grades may just as easily mean that the teacher fails to communicate key ideas to students (after all, the goal of teaching is to facilitate learning) or arbitrary grading. In summary, the grade "B" only communicates a gross measure of a student's standing in a *particular* classroom or on a particular test. Classroom grades typically involve such *norm-referenced assessment*.

Norm-referenced testing provides meaning to a student's score only by comparing his test performance with the performance of others taking the same test. In norm-referenced testing, a score is not based directly upon the student's actual knowledge or skills (the quality of his work). For example, if student A masters 85 percent of course content but 90 percent of other students who take the test master at least 90 percent of the course content, then student A's performance is relatively "inferior." This is so because virtually all other students do better on the norm-referenced test. If on the same test student A masters 65 percent of the course content but 90 percent of other students master only 60 percent, then student A's performance is "good." Meaning on a norm-referenced test simply provides an answer to the question, How did student A do compared with other students?

Standardized Tests

Standardized testing also yields a norm-referenced comparison (Phil scored at the 99th percentile. Jewel had a standard score of 70. Jane, a third grade student, is reading at the fifth grade level). However, the norm or comparison group on a standardized test usually is much larger and more varied than the norm group for a classroom test. To reiterate, the comparison group for a student taking a classroom test is simply the other students taking the test in his class (unless several teachers teaching the same material have written a common test, thereby expanding the norm to all fifth grade teachers at Wilson School or all the fifth grade mathematics rooms in a particular school district).

Norm tables for a standardized test make it possible to compare a student's score (a rough estimate of his ability in a particular area) on a national basis.

Generally speaking, commonly used standard achievement tests have been adequately normed on a national basis such that Ted's score of "87" can be compared to the performance of *all* other third graders (within the limits of the norming sample). "Average" performance is a statistical definition that simply assigns the grade equivalent score of third grade, no months to the scores of students who fall in the middle of the distribution of scores from all beginning third graders on each subtest. For example, if the average or mean score for beginning third graders on the "paragraph meaning" test of a standardized achievement test is 60, all students who score 60 on this test (regardless of age and grade) would be assigned the score of "third grade, no months" as their "grade level equivalent" score. Similarly, third grade students who take the test in September and score 66 would be considered a bit above "average" on this particular test (say a grade level equivalent score of "third grade, three months").

The point is that "average" is a statistical term. It does *not* mean that the skills and factual knowledge needed for third grade work are represented in the score 60. Indeed, students may score a 60 in a variety of ways, so that identical scores on a standardized test may be based on a combination of weaknesses and strengths that may have little overlap among students. Diagnostic information identifying specific weaknesses and strengths of a student can be gained only by examining the types of skills regularly missed, etc.

Furthermore, since "average" as used in standardized testing situations is a statistical term, *50 percent of all students that take the test will be below grade level by definition.* Normative scores have no value independent of their comparative value. To talk about raising all students above grade level (nationwide) is absurd! Even if relative performance increases (scores of second graders in 1976 versus scores of second graders in 1966), normative tests guarantee that equal numbers of students will score above and below grade level (that is, when norms are revised, the base for "average" will be increased to obtain an even number of scores above and below grade level). The value of the standardized test is that it provides a broad background to use in judging the relative value of a student's performance. However, this advantage is negated when the standardized achievement test does not measure those curriculum objectives that the local school district and teachers emphasize. Ironically, some teachers are not allowed to see achievement tests—for fear that they might teach for the test. As a result, these teachers do not know whether the achievement measures are useful or not! To know that a student ranks in the 70th percentile on a particular subtest in mathematics is worthless information if test items are unrelated to the school's mathematics program.

Disadvantages of Norm-Referenced Testing

The advantage of the norm-referenced *classroom* score is that it ranks the students in terms of their performance on *local* goals. But, as noted above, both content and performance criteria vary so widely from classroom to classroom that a student's score has no meaning beyond his immediate classroom. Furthermore, use of a normative grading system guarantees that some students will be relatively "good" and others will be relatively "poor" (independent of their actual performance) by definition. In normative testing, the goal is to spread students' scores out as far as possible. Indeed, the best way to do this is to ask questions that roughly 50 percent of the students answer correctly and that are answered correctly more often by students who earn top scores on the test as a whole than by those who earn a *relatively* low total score. Clearly, no teacher can plan such a test with precision, in advance. But the task can be accomplished by asking a number of test questions of varying difficulty initially and retaining for subsequent testing only those questions that have good item difficulty (avoid extremely easy or hard questions that don't differentiate among students) and positive discrimination power (students who have high total scores answer the question correctly more frequently than students with low total scores).

However, one problem with such an approach to testing is that, systematically, the test progressively emphasizes those items that separate students and drops out significant questions (valid content) that all or most students *have mastered.* Thus, in time, the test does not assess what students know but instead functions like an IQ test that differentiates, not achievement *per se,* but the very bright from the very dull (Gagné, 1970).

Clearly, not all teachers continue to refine achievement tests to the point that items providing reasonable coverage of content goals are supplanted with esoteric items that discriminate student performance. Still, a persuasive argument can be made that norm-referenced testing *as utilized* too often only separates students for status purposes (the distribution of grades, awards, and so on) and rarely for instructional purposes (differential student assignments on the basis of test scores).

In summary, two major criticisms frequently have been leveled at norm-referenced testing: (1) it does not encourage the average or below average student nor provide direct feedback for improving instruction (i.e., it functions mainly as a system of status differentiation); (2) it emphasizes what students fail to master and does not provide a record of accomplishment. (That is, norm-referenced tests would not help a legislator obtain an answer to his questions: Specifically what have the students learned? What does achievement at the third grade, fifth month level mean? What skills must a student have to obtain this score?)

The first criticism is especially pervasive. If grades discourage or fail to help many students, how can they be justified? Clearly, grades influence students—bright and dull alike. The college coed needs a B+ average to retain her curator's scholarship. On her first round of hour exams, she receives an A in history, a B in Spanish, a B in biology, and a B in political science. She decides that she will get a B in Spanish with little work, but the extra time necessary for an A represents twice the amount of time she is presently putting in for the course. She doesn't have that much extra time, and hence an A in Spanish is out of the question. An A in biology is out of the question even though she enjoys the subject, had a good high school course, and finds the college text easy to read. The lectures are too vague and she can't anticipate what the instructor wants students to learn; hence, she can't use her time advantageously in studying for the test. Thus, she plans to maximize study time in history and political science in hopes of retaining her scholarship. Note that two of the basic criteria in her decision process were *time* and *knowledge of what to learn*. We will deal with both of these criteria later in the chapter. The second criterion is discussed below.

Behavioral Objectives

Some writers have contended that teachers and schools could improve their effectiveness if they would communicate their instructional expectations more clearly both to students and to themselves. Recently a plethora of books have been written explaining the need for explicit statements of expected learning outcomes (behavioral objectives). As Mager (1962), one of the more articulate behavioral objectives spokesmen, noted some time ago, teachers must ask three basic questions if they are to instruct effectively: (1) What am I teaching? (2) How will I know when students have learned it? (3) What materials and activities will be necessary? Behavioral objectives serve to help teachers answer these questions.

One might argue that behavioral objectives, even if not communicated to students, might help teachers to become more aware of their goals and to mobilize their resources and time so as to improve student performance on the test. However, those who stress the need for behavioral objectives seldom wish to stop with instructor awareness of goals; they want such awareness communicated to students. Typically, as Mager and others have stressed, writing behavioral objectives is a three-step process.

1. Name the terminal behavior. What proof would you accept that the learner has achieved the goal? (For example, must he build a house, or merely design a blueprint?)
2. Specify the conditions under which the behavior will be demonstrated. (Will he pick answers from a list or from memory? Will he recite for the entire class or only the teacher?)
3. Tell the student the criteria (how well he must perform) for acceptable performance (15 out of 20 for an A).

The aim of the behavioral objectives "game" is to remove the guessing from classroom testing. "Tell the learner what you want him to master and test him on that specific material." Student time, so the argument goes, can be directly applied to the study of relevant material rather than wasted in aimless anxiety-reducing activities. A behavioral objective in its simplest form is simply a written or oral statement that describes what the learner will do, how he will demonstrate the behavior (that is, how he will be tested), and how well he must perform.

Disagreement

There are numerous educators who feel that the use of behavioral objectives is not good instructional practice (for example, see Broudy, 1970, and Simon, 1973). However, if one merely counted the frequency of articles supporting or not supporting behavioral objectives, support would outweigh nonsupport. Thus, among educators (or editors who apply selection criteria) whose work appears in educational journals, behavioral objectives have become a "hot" concept, in part no doubt because a behavioral objective provides a measurable goal and this is necessary for accountability (however, nonenthusiasts would stress that instruction can also be evaluated other than by behavioral objectives).

Can a thousand "French" educators be wrong? Will behavioral objectives improve student learning or motivation? Before examining the data supporting the use of behavioral objectives, it will be useful to summarize some of the more frequently "alleged" advantages and disadvantages of behavioral objectives.

ADVANTAGES OF BEHAVIORAL OBJECTIVES:	DISADVANTAGES OF BEHAVIORAL OBJECTIVES:
1. They increase teacher awareness of what the student should be working for, and lead to more optimal planning; a wider range of objectives is included.	1. They increase teacher control at the expense of students' own objectives.
2. They provide a basis for assessing continuous progress (allowing students to proceed at their own rate) as specific skills are focused upon.	2. They unduly emphasize things that can be measured; only low level objectives are likely to be measured.
3. Students have a better blueprint for guiding their learning activity; hence, they learn more.	3. Once established (teacher invests the time to write objectives and set up a measurement system), the system perpetuates itself; objectives remain the same; spontaneity is reduced.
4. After reaching a criterion, students have more time to work on their own learning objectives.	4. A great deal of instructor time is used in writing behavioral objectives; such time could be utilized better in other ways (such as one-to-one conferences).

Do Behavioral Objectives Make a Difference?

Interestingly, some of the advantages and disadvantages listed above cite the same evidence! This fact in and of itself suggests that the data base or evidence is not there and/or that the presence or absence of explicit behavioral objectives *per se doesn't make a difference* but rather *the way in which the teacher uses them is the key*. An examination of the literature clearly supports the idea that little comprehensive classroom research has been conducted on the effectiveness of behavioral objectives.

There is some nonclassroom data from the work of David P. Ausubel (1963) to show that students who are provided with advance organizers (principles or labels that can be used to anchor or organize the material that follows) in experimental settings are able to master more of novel material than are subjects who do not receive the advance organizers. Also Rothkopf's (1965, 1967) work provides general support for the idea that questions embedded in the text will help students to retain more of the material than students who read the same material without the embedded questions. However, questions *per se* don't make a difference. Many findings suggest that the usefulness of such procedures is noticeably affected by a variety of contextual factors (see, for example, Sanders, 1973). The point here is simply that some data suggest that general features which help students to identify relevant content or relevant ways to organize material are useful aids to learning.

No Comprehensive Research

Numerous studies have been conducted in the attempt to assess the effects of behavioral objective usage on student learning and attitudes. When the research is reviewed in its entirety, the data for and against appears to be evenly matched. Such results suggest that usage *per se* is not associated with positive results. Apparently the usefulness of behavioral objectives is dependent upon factors not yet identified (teacher skill, type of content, learner characteristics, and so forth). The reader may want to consult Duchastel and Merrill (1973) for an expanded review of research on behavioral objectives.

A step that has not, so far, been taken is to conduct comprehensive studies to measure general teacher behavior and student performance on tests *prior* to training teachers in the use of behavioral objectives and to then see how usage effects the naturalistic classroom (teacher-student interaction, the type of homework assigned, the type of questions asked on exams, etc.). Thus, there is no definitive data to illustrate the effects of behavioral objectives on (a) instructor behavior, (b) student behavior, or (c) course outcomes. Even if we assume that the broad experimental findings cited above apply to the classroom, we are left only with evidence suggesting that "general understanding" is useful.

These assumptions are easy enough to test. Let's walk through one claim. For example, consider the argument that teachers' "awareness" will be improved by their use of behavioral objectives. A specific way to measure one dimension of awareness would be to see if the types of questions that teachers ask on exams change as a function of increased use of behavioral objectives. Studies consistently show that teachers' tests emphasize the recall of very specific facts, as high as 98 percent in one study (see for example, Lawrence, 1963; Pfeiffer and Davis, 1965; Scannell and Steelwagon, 1960).

Furthermore, teachers' use of low level cognitive questions is matched by their use of low level questions during class discussion (Rogers and Davis, 1970). Davis and Tinsley (1967) report that even questions embedded in textbooks are most likely to be based on recall of specific information. One suspects that such consistent demands cause students to focus on isolated specific facts, perhaps to the detriment of their general understanding.

The argument is that teachers writing out behavioral objectives would become more aware of the demands they are placing on students, and that the type of learning outcomes expected on exams would show more variety. The way to test this question is, of course, to study the actual exams that teachers use before and after the introduction of behavioral objectives. Ideally, such studies would also include information about the study habits of students. What do they study, how do they prepare for exams, and how much time do they expend? The effects of behavioral objectives upon the style or amount of student preparation would indeed be interesting data. Finally, one would want to know if students' immediate test scores were better than those of previous students in the courses taught by the experimental teachers, and how their retention scores compared several weeks after initial testing.

Similiar data could be collected on any pro or con claim for behavioral objectives. Interest in "system" effects could be tested by examining teachers' objectives and tests over a three-year period to determine if "behavioral objective" teachers are less prone to change than are other teachers (so behavioral objectives automatically become self-perpetuating once written). Spontaneity and teacher control variables could also be checked. One might find that teachers who teach with behavioral objectives are spontaneous (for instance, if one of their behavioral objectives is to leave 20 minutes unplanned each day to have time for "now" interests) and less controlling (they ask students to write their own objectives) than are teachers who don't use behavioral objectives.

However, we suspect that when such comprehensive research is done (if ever) there will be no simple differences between users and nonusers. This is so because the use of behavioral objectives is not a presence/absence variable: The effectiveness of behavioral objectives depends upon the way in which they are used, not the presence or frequency of their occurrence. For example, it is not variety of teacher questions that is important, but the selection of teacher questions that appropriately measure the desired learning goal (sometimes 100 percent factual questions are appropriate test content). Similarly, the desirability of objectives written by the students themselves depends upon a variety of contextual factors (goals, age of students, and so on).

The real questions for any teacher are: Does the use of behavioral objectives (or whatever) improve student learning? Am I more pleased with the performance of students now than before? Are there side costs as well as gains? (For more discussion of teacher-initiated evaluation see Chapter 10.)

Most educators would agree that teachers should communicate general learning objectives and the conditions of testing (Will it be an essay test?) to their students, and would agree that many teachers fail to communicate their objectives satisfactorily even at a general level. If some communication is good, can more explicit communication be anything but better? There are some (including the authors) who would suggest the following loose analogy: The car as a mode of transportation was basically a good idea; however, the evolution of that idea and its accompanying frills (bigger motors, excessive fuel, pollution) were dysfunctional steps. Could teacher-student communication function in the same way for some tasks?

As a case in point, consider the following teacher instructions and see which seems to be most adequate for fifth grade students.

A. Class, tomorrow each of you will be asked to stand before the class and repeat the Gettysburg Address, using the best speaking style you have and with no notes.
B. Class, tomorrow each of you will stand before the class and repeat the Gettysburg Address. You must use appropriate inflection (try to model your voice after the tape recording you will hear today). You can have no more than three false starts and you must complete the entire address within three minutes after your initial start. No pauses longer than 15 seconds will be allowed.
C. Know the Gettysburg Address by tomorrow.
D. Be able to recite the Gettysburg Address tomorrow.

From our preceding discussion of behavioral objectives, it's clear that B is a much more precise statement and comes closer to fulfilling the commonly assigned definition of a behavioral objective than any of the other instructions. Instruction C fails to communicate completely, and if the teacher has any standard or criterion in mind other than just repeating the words, statement D is inadequate. However, statement A has *psychological* meaning. Both communications A and B tell the student what he is to learn and how his learning will be demonstrated. But is B more effective than A? Clearly, B communicates more of the criteria and perhaps will guide student behavior more fully. But it can also be argued that some of the specificity in message B is dysfunctional.

For example, all or some students may be so stimulated and consumed by the training presentation that it takes more time to learn the address than in condition A. The anxious student may become so concerned over "false starts" such that a self-fulfilling prophecy is effected.

The case for the use of behavioral objectives which go beyond the communication of psychological understanding neither has been made or disproved. Much work is needed on the appropriate density (number of criterion elements) and specificity of behavioral objectives across a variety of subject matter areas, grade levels, and types of students.

Behavioral Expressions

It is possible to distinguish between at least two different types of behavioral statements. Above we discussed *behavioral objectives.* Behavioral objectives present a complete prescription of learning. (That is, a behavioral objective specifies what is to be learned and provides an explicit statement of how the learning will be tested and the acceptable level of performance.) Statements that specify learning outcomes but which do not provide tight guidelines for "how" to demonstrate the skill can be viewed as *behavioral expressions.*

We do not provide this distinction because behavioral expressions are *ipso facto* more effective than behavioral objectives. Instead, we do so to suggest a broader range of instructional possibilities and because we suspect that the desirable degree of "structure" varies widely depending upon the nature of the instructional task. For example, when teachers are interested in replicative knowledge (rote learning, recall), and perhaps some types of associative knowledge, they may find "tight" structure useful. In contrast, if the teacher is interested in associative, interpretive, or applicational knowledge, behavioral expressions may be more useful.

The term behavioral (behavioral expression) as we use it here suggests that the learning assignment presented to the student can be measured in a rather direct fashion. Furthermore, students and teachers have a shared agreement about what is expected. But the word behavioral does not demand that the teacher be able to state the low inference attributes (specific features) of the assignment.

For example, the assignment in a college course in fiction writing might be "have a short story published." Clearly the objective to have a story published is understandable without additional specification (density of sentence structure, style, manuscript length). The essential *communication* aspects are present. The student knows exactly what the assignment is, and he knows when he has successfully demonstrated the skill (article accepted for publication). Such assignments are, of course, rare but perhaps reasonable and appropriate for students intending to be writers.

True, there are ways in which the above directions might be improved, but the essential elements are there if the teacher is willing to accept publication in any journal. If not, the teacher should provide the students with a list of 200 (or whatever) appropriate publication sources and perhaps clarify the time students have to accomplish the goal. For example, can they take two or three semesters of deferred grades while working on the assignment?

Given the directions "publish a short story," students and teacher are aware of what the task is and each can become task oriented. The instructor implicitly is allowing students to pick the type of short story they will write (such as humorous or human interest) and subsequently he can begin to assign appropriate material and resources to students after their choice is made. Students now can react in a discriminating way to instructor material. They know their needs. If the material doesn't help them to clarify their thoughts, they can ask the instructor for different material. Furthermore, when they obtain instructor reactions to their rough draft, they can use the feedback selectively. They know that the goal is not to please the idiosyncratic demands of one judge, but to publish the story. Good advice can be acted upon, and ambiguous feedback can be clarified and/or rejected.

Choice of Behavioral Objectives

We suggest, then, that when students are encouraged to use their own initiative and ideas in reaching course goals, behavioral expressions may be more useful than behavioral objectives. Furthermore, we suggest that behavioral expressions are preferable when there is *no* single correct solution or predetermined set of responses. For example, how could a fifth grade teacher or a college instructor specify content criteria for essays entitled, "Meeting Energy Needs in the Year 2015" or "Man in Space: Economic Boondoggle or Wise Investment?" Only if teachers want to make *arbitrary* decisions can content criteria be supplied in these cases. At best, teachers can supply minimum standards of scholarship. "Use at least five references." "When you respond, discuss the following ten factors . . ." Clearly, however, such specifications are not (or should not be, in most cases) goals in themselves. That is, the *integration* of reference material and the *selective use* of material is fundamentally more important than the number of references.

However, if one wants to assess factual information, the best way to do it is through behavioral objectives. "Pages 116–134 discuss the five leading causes of pollution. Be able to identify *all* five causes, and for each cause be able to list two possible ways to reduce the problem." There are, of course, legitimate reasons for asking factual knowledge questions and demanding rote skill mastery (especially for students in the primary grades). When factual recall is wanted and/or precise demonstration of a skill is desirable, use *behavioral objectives*. In other cases, behavioral expressions may be more useful.

Again, behavioral expression as we define it means that students and teachers have a shared understanding of learning goals and that the student has some room for bringing his own meaning into the assignment. Unless teachers ask students to write their goals (either behavioral objectives or behavioral goals), the teacher is still controlling the learning goals. However, behavioral expressions allow teachers to assign students increasing opportunities for self-direction within the limits of the student's capacity (that is, maturity) and within the structural limits placed upon the instructor.

For example, another instructor of fiction might be allowed to delay grades only one semester. Hence, his assignment might be: "Write and submit a short story for publication. Selection of topic and general scope are your own decision. Submit the article for publication to any journal on the 'approved 300' list. Your project is satisfactorily completed when the article is accepted for publication or tentative publication. If rejected, the final article you submit should be rewritten to accommodate the criticism of myself and your classmates. Not all criticisms need be reacted to, but do explain your reasons for not responding when you choose not to. Grades will be assigned thusly. Papers that are accepted for publication receive an A (criterion-referenced grading). Papers not accepted for publication will be graded next semester by Professor Hoop's fiction writing course at the University of Missouri. His students will rate independently each of the stories on its own communicative power, interest capacity, and style. Those papers that receive the top four rankings will receive an A. All other papers that are judged by at least six of his students to have achieved minimal effectiveness will receive a B, and all others a C (norm-referenced grading)."

The above example illustrates how *time* effects the learning process. Initially the assignment to publish a story is straightforward, if demanding. However, the pressure of time forced both the student and the teacher to terminate the course assignment before the student achieved his goal. Whether the teacher gives instructions vaguely, or uses behavioral expressions or objectives is largely irrelevant to this time problem (except in those cases where students could have achieved the goals if he had given clearer instructions).

Restraints

Thus, we see again that the *use* of behavioral objectives or behavioral expressions *per se* (even high quality ones appropriately used) may not necessarily be related to student goal attainment. In dealing with the time problem, the teacher must either structure goals that can be achieved in the specified time period or ignore goal failure.

Teachers face this problem everyday. Teacher A gives a mathematics test. Some students do well, others get average scores, and still others fail to master the basic skills. Yet, the next day all students move on to the next unit even though many haven't mastered the past unit. Clearly, the prognosis is poor for students who have only partially mastered a unit that is even marginally basic to the following unit. Teacher B gives a similar test, and the student scores are similar to those of Teacher A. However, Teacher B assigns only those students who demonstrated minimal skill proficiency to the next unit. The other students are retaught the unit and will start the next unit later in the week.

Clearly, Teacher A ignored the goal failure of some students, and appears to be using the evaluation system more for differentiating achievement than for providing developmental feedback to help learners achieve teacher- or self-selected goals. Teacher B doesn't ignore the problem and is allowing (forcing!) students to work until they achieve the goal.

But has Teacher B solved the problem? Probably not. Time is still a relevant factor. Teacher B has temporarily brushed aside the issue, but eventually the year runs out and the students of A are promoted to C's room and the students of B go to D's room. Now the relatively slower students in B's room have fully mastered many more units than the relatively slower students in A's room, but B's students have been exposed to fewer units.

Are the relatively slower students from B's room better off than those from A's? At the end of the year in room A and B, it would seem that B's students would be much better off because they have truly mastered the content. But come September their advantage may become a disadvantage. If Teacher D assumes that these students are ready for unit 15 when they are only ready for unit 11, and if Teacher D proceeds with units 15, 16, 17, and the rest (ignoring goal failure feedback), the students might be better off with partial understanding of all units than with mastery of most but not all. However, if D plays the classroom game the same way as Teacher B, these students will come out ahead (at least until the next year).

The important point is that an individual teacher's freedom to individualize is limited by the teachers in the next grade level. Thus, the second strategy for dealing with time is to manipulate the system so that students can achieve full mastery of at least key concepts, skills, and information. Teachers and schools can do this through the formal adoption of an individualized curriculum or through communication of information. We'll return to this point later in the chapter.

We have seen that behavioral statements are but one of the forces at work on the learning process, and we have suggested that independent of the use of clear learning assignments, time, and other teachers have important effects. So, too, do teachers' marks. The point here is to make clear that the use of behavioral statements *per se* does not dictate the use of a norm-referenced or criterion-referenced grading system. Recall the grading procedure that the fiction instructor used to assign grades to those students who did not have their papers published. A's went to the four students who received the highest ranking from off-campus students. Thus an A was determined by the relative value of papers. Clearly this is an example of *normative* grading. However, B students were graded on the basis of an absolute scale (although in this instance the scale was ill-defined). All students could get a B. Further-more, all students could get a C. The grade was based upon achieving a standard (in this case, six students agreeing that the paper achieved minimum communication standards). Thus, one could use behavioral expressions and still grade on either a norm- or criterion-referenced scale.

Criterion-Referenced Testing

Criterion-referenced grading simply means that a student is graded in com-parison to an absolute standard (criterion) rather than in comparison to other students taking the test. However, unlike our college instructor's vague criteria for assigning B's, good criterion-referenced tests, as described by the popular and scientific press, have specific criteria of acceptability. For example, consider these two statements: "The student will work *8* out of *10* correctly." "You will be able to use *all* the 100 addition facts."

The most useful feature of criterion-referenced testing is that it provides a measure of what the student has achieved. Teachers who make heavy use of criterion-referenced testing will have a well-documented record of the skills each student has demonstrated. Part of the mathematics report card used in in one school system can be seen in Table 7.1. Clearly this report form communicates much more than the traditional labels of Good, Average, and so forth. Specificity of performance standards is of course one of the major advantages of criterion systems. However, teachers may impose differential grading practices upon a criterion-referenced system. For example, one per-formance called for in Table 7.1 is to tell time. One teacher may demand that a child correctly identify the correct time 25 out of 25 times, whereas, another teacher may accept 23 out of 25. Similarly one teacher may require 7 out of 10. One teacher may require 7 out of 10 spelling words each week, while another may demand all 10. Criterion-referenced tests tell the student what level of work he must attain to receive an A, but the grade of A *per se* com-municates nothing to the parent or others. An A in one room may stand for the same level of skill mastery that is represented by a B in another room. Thus, grades (or Pass/Fail designations) cannot be used for comparing stu-dent progress in different classrooms. To assess student growth one would still have to know the criterion level demanded by the teacher and the various skills taught in the room.

Two immediate advantages come about from the use of criterion-referenced testing: (1) specific skills are identified and *must* be mastered to "criterion"

TABLE 7.1

Sample Performance Skills from the Mathematics Record Card
of the Winnetka Public Schools

Recognizes number groups up to 5	_____
Recognizes patterns of objects to 10	_____
Can count objects to 100	_____
Recognizes numbers to 100	_____
Can read and write numerals to 50	_____
Recognizes addition and subtraction symbols	_____
Understands meaning of the equality sign	_____
Understands meaning of the inequality signs	_____
Can count objects:	_____
by 2's to 20	_____
by 5's to 100	_____
by 10's to 100	_____
Addition combinations 10 and under (automatic response)	_____
Subtraction combinations 10 and under (automatic response)	_____
Can count to 200	_____
Can understand zero as a number	_____
Can understand place value to tens	_____
Can read and write numerals to 200	_____
Can read and write number words to 20	_____
Use facts in 2-digit column addition (no carrying)	_____
Roman numerals to XII	_____
Can tell time	_____
1. Hour	_____
2. Half hour	_____
3. Quarter hour	_____

before the student works on the next skill area, and (2) the success of some students does not automatically mean that others will do poorly. Students simply work until they achieve criterion and then begin the next unit. Obviously, the use of criterion-referenced testing assumes (demands) that teachers will not teach the class as a class, but instead will work with students as individuals or in small groups.

The use of criterion-referenced testing has maximum potential in a school where subject matter goals are agreed upon and where students can move flexibly from one learning area to another. Essentially, this means that the organizational pattern for placing children in learning groups is based on mastery of subject material rather than age.

Nongradedness and Criterion Testing

Ellison (1972) has suggested that the popular term "grade level" has little meaning. What, for example, does "third grade" reading or social studies mean? Ellison reports data showing that more children from grades three to seven measure above or below a one-year spread around the grade norm than fall within it. Looking at achievement scores from fourth to seventh grade, he reports that more children at each grade level score outside a two-year spread around the grade norm than fall within it! Clearly, the fourth grade teacher who has "age grouped" students faces an extraordinary range of ability. The use of criterion-referenced testing is one way to deal with this wide achievement spread.

Some schools are now set up on an individualized basis such that students' progress through the school is not slowed by other students. Both bright and slow students are hampered by the teacher who teaches the class as a class. Bright students reach criterion but have to wait until the class instruction ends on the unit. Slow students go to the next unit when the class moves on even though they haven't mastered the material.

Individualized schools (sometimes called nongraded) are so called because the individual student proceeds at his own pace. Students are organized for instruction on the basis of content mastery, and it is common for three teachers (usually) to be in charge of 100 students with about a three-year chronological age range. When students master unit material they move on to a new unit. Unfortunately, however, when third graders master "third grade material," they usually are held back from "fourth grade" work until the next September when they enter the fourth grade, even in these schools. We'll have more to say about the individualized school in the following chapter. School organization is briefly discussed here to suggest again that the presence or absence of any variable is affected by other variables. Criterion-referenced testing *per se* is neither good nor bad. Its effectiveness depends upon how it matches with other school elements. It would seem that criterion-referenced testing makes most sense when students are allowed to demonstrate learning when they are ready and are allowed to advance as soon as they demonstrate mastery. An elementary school teacher who administers criterion-referenced tests every three weeks may be unduly restraining a child who is ready to move on and be inadvertently teaching the child to wait to study until the night before the mastery tests. Similarly, a teacher who uses criterion tests, but moves all children on independent of test scores will *not* make a difference (and there are teachers who function this way).

Clearly, the heart of a criterion-referenced test is the behavioral objective. While it is true that behavioral objectives can be utilized in either a norm- or criterion-referenced assessment program, they are mandatory in the criterion-referenced program. Thus, criterion-referenced tests are subject to the same strengths and weaknesses of behavioral objectives. The chief advantage is their potential for providing the learner with immediate feedback about his performance in relation to expected performance.

There are two major criticisms. The first is that much learning (knowledge) that occurs in schools does not come in the form of small, specific units. One example noted above occurs when several solutions, especially unknown ones, may apply to questions. Also, behavioral objectives may be inappropriate when student expression is wanted. This is not to suggest that one cannot write behavioral objectives for the entire range of cognitive outcomes on Bloom's Taxonomy or in the terms of Broudy (1970) for replicative, associative, interpretative, and applicational uses of knowledge. However, behavioral objectives at the higher levels measure such a small range of skill that it would take countless criterion-referenced measures to be sure that an area was fully sampled. Thus, a given objective may be a legitimate instance of the skill, but it is highly arbitrary given the large number of alternatives. We agree with Ebel (1971) that criterion-referenced measures are more useful when applied to basic skills that all students need to master, and with Gronlund (1973) that it is much easier (and appropriate) to use criterion-referenced measurement (a) when instruction is divided into relatively small units, (b) where the domain of learning tasks is clearly defined, and (c) where specific steps are taken to obtain an adequate sample. Further, we agree with Broudy (1970) that a complete emphasis upon behavioral objectives *per se* tends to result in too much stress on replicative use of knowledge. (But still we strongly acknowledge the need for wholeheartedly encouraged research on these statements.)

Our conclusion is that *criterion-referenced measures are ideally useful for instruction in kindergarten and the early elementary grades where agreement exists on many common goals and where it is possible to break down content into small instructional units so all students can master a commonly agreed upon set of behavioral skills and factual information.* We would hope such a system would be utilized in an environment where grades are used as descriptive feedback rather than status differentiators. This will help students not only to develop cognitive skills but also to become more fully aware and respectful of their own achievement potential. Criterion-referenced testing has notable potential for contributing positively to desirable student outcomes when learning systems are marked by individual pacing, flexible grouping, and the use of test results for feedback.

A second problem with criterion-referenced testing is that even when one does know how to divide the learning task into small instructional steps, one does not know automatically how to set the criterion level. This situation is totally unlike the norm-referenced situation, where there are clear principles. In norm-referenced situations, the idea is to get the greatest spread of scores possible, that is, to differentiate among students. Therefore, the difficulty level of questions is used as a criterion for retaining or deleting test items. But in criterion-referenced testing situations, item difficulty is a useless concept. This is so because the item difficulty is set by the domain of instructional tasks that one wants to measure.

One solution to the problem of setting criterion level has been the use of *mastery learning* as a standard. John Carroll, Ben Bloom, and James Block have been the chief proponents of this point of view. The essential argument is that virtually all students (often estimated at 90 percent) can reach the same level of mastery if given enough time. Thus, in a mastery learning program, the student keeps working until the cognitive task is mastered, and he then goes on to the next level. There is no such animal as failure to master; the student recycles until mastery is demonstrated.

Mastery Learning: Some Data

Ben Bloom and others have documented the pervasive influence of amount of instructional time upon student achievement. When students are allowed the same amount of time to learn a set of material, the correlation between student aptitude and achievement consistently appears to be about .70. Thus we know that brighter children, as a group, learn more quickly than lower aptitude children. The critical question is what happens to achievement levels when students are allowed to work until they achieve mastery?

It is beyond our purpose to review all the mastery learning literature, but it will be useful to summarize Bloom's reaction to recent and comprehensive review papers (Bloom, 1973a; 1973b). The striking conclusion he reaches is that 80 percent of students under mastery conditions attain an achievement level which less than 20 percent attain under nonmastery conditions. Interestingly, such notable achievement gains come only at the additional expense of 10 to 20 percent of instructional time.

Simply put, by spending an extra 10 to 20 percent of instructional time on units, 80 percent of the students reach a proficiency level that less than 20 percent achieve if that extra time is not spent. This conclusion appears to be a consistent finding supported by several studies. Furthermore, several studies suggest that *cooperation* (students help other students to master basic material) and an improved self-view are important by-products of mastery learning. (More discussion will appear in Chapter 9 about the relationship between achievement and self-view.)

However, Bloom notes the existence of many studies (including many that have not been published) in which mastery learning strategies have *not* proven to be very effective in influencing student achievement. Bloom reports that the chief reason for failure appears to be that the teacher has not corrected learning difficulties. Thus, even though specific performance levels are set up and frequent tests are administered to identify student errors . . . it is still necessary for the *teacher* to react to such information and actively help students to acquire the information. It would seem that if students do not receive appropriate help WHEN they need it, the potential motivational advantages of mastery learning will be eroded.

That is, in addition to increased time students need appropriate help if they are to use time efficiently, although teachers do not have to apply this assistance directly. Bloom and others have noted that student tutors are an especially useful way to improve the amount of on-task behavior and achievement of students who need help. Clearly, the mastery system depends upon more than criterion-referenced specifications and increased time . . . in particular it depends upon a teacher who is willing and capable of reacting to test results and providing direct, appropriate help to students when they need it.

Again, it exceeds our purpose to review the extensive body of mastery learning research that has been completed at various grade levels, in several foreign countries, and so on. But we did want to illustrate that specification of learning performance and providing appropriate learning conditions (especially sufficient time to learn the material) can help to alter the excessively low performance of many students. However, it appears that mastery approaches will reach their potential only in the hands of motivated, competent teachers.

Mastery learning is an attractive strategy; however, as we noted above measuring mastery of certain complex skills may be an impossible task. Even within narrower skill areas where it *is* possible to design an instructional sequence, it may be unreasonable and undesirable to set mastery as a goal. Again, the difficulty is that there is no known way *at present* to establish the criterion level for many instructional units because the necessary research has not been conducted.

Consider some of the practical questions involved in setting mastery as a goal. The teacher gives a ten-item fraction test on Monday and 15 of 30 students get all items correct. Fifteen students start the next unit and 15 recycle (receive new instructions designed to help them master the material). On Wednesday these students take a new unit test and 6 of the 15 correctly answer all 10 problems, and 5 students score 9, 3 score 8, and the other student scores a 7.

Now does a score of 10, 9, 8, or 7 really make a difference? Should students repeat the unit a third, fourth, or fifth time until they demonstrate mastery? Logic suggests that there are some skills that are so basic that they should be overlearned and that students should drill until they reach complete mastery, but that other skills are less essential to the units that follow and that a 7 may be as good as a 10. The problem is that "key" skills are not always known.

But how could a 7 be as good as a 10? If one finds that students who are allowed to move on to the next unit with a 7 score do as well on retention tests and on subsequent units as do students with a score of 10, then a 7 *is* as good as a 10. However, the research base on such questions is just beginning to be collected, and no doubt it will be years before clear answers are provided on *key skills* and the appropriate criterion level for various skills.

Why not demand complete mastery of *all skills* that can be placed into specific sequential units? It is possible to do this, and as a general strategy, "near" mastery performance may be useful for very young children. However, at a certain point the hypothesized motivation role of mastery learning may disappear. The reader will recall that we began the discussion of mastery learning with the assumption that 90 percent of students can master the material at a level exhibited by top students *if given enough time.*

If fifth graders were suddenly placed into a nongraded, mastery learning environment, we really don't believe this hypothesis would hold at present. Theoretically, if they worked long enough, low achievers could match high achievers' performance on a particular body of content. But after five years spent in a self-contained classroom learning that they are relatively inferior to other students, learning strategies for saving face (such as not making an effort), we suspect that students' motivation and persistence levels would not support their achievement potential.

The viable immediate goal of doing away with the age graded curriculum is *not* to transform the school population into learners where all are as incisive and competent as the best student in the self-contained classroom. This is impossible. However, *it is possible to create a situation where most students achieve up to their potential by doing away with structural features* that force students to move to new content areas prematurely and where consistent invidious comparisons cause some students to give up and/or become emotionally detached from school-related activities. Another realistic goal of such curriculum efforts is to produce an affective environment where children have at least minimum acceptance and satisfaction with school life (see Chapter 9).

But back to the immediate issue. A reasonable-sounding goal for kindergarten students and first graders who come into a mastery curriculum is that they will achieve up to their potential since they have not already developed bad attitudes such as negative expectations. It is conceivable, though, that a student who regularly has to retake a unit test several times before passing to the next level may find his motivation eroded, so that some mastery learning "concepts" (such as age-graded curriculums have) may have undesirable side effects on student motivation. Thus, we suspect that if a 7 is as good as a 10, the student should move on, if for no other reason than that the literature *systematically* suggests that children who are promoted in the self-contained system do better than those having similar achievement records but who repeat the grade.

However, much of the stigma of failure can be reduced in the mastery level curriculum by teachers who react to the student's score as a piece of information and who do not show overreactive levels of concern or joy with low or high scores. If teachers model positive learning expectations and respond appropriately to student difficulty (and we suspect that there is considerable variance on this teacher skill), then some of the potential debilitating effects of recycling on student motivation will be dissipated. Teachers remain a key variable.

There is still the question of *time*. If students repeatedly are forced to stay too long on units due to unnecessarily high criterion levels, time will be wasted and progress will be slowed. The point is that no one knows at what levels to set the criterion. Those who produce curriculum packages for the most part have not researched the effects of different criterion levels. At best they can predict the performance of students at one criterion level. Hopefully more of this important decision-making research will be conducted to help teachers to select the appropriate pacing level of performance.

Sensitive Usage

At present, the safest strategy for the classroom teacher is to use the criterion level suggested by the curriculum materials but to judge its effects on students. Do many students have to repeat? How many students have to recycle more than once? If many students are having difficulty, the materials, especially remedial ones, and the remedial skills of the teacher need to be examined. Perhaps the criterion is set too high. Perhaps not enough instruction time precedes the mastery test. Perhaps the teacher doesn't have needed diagnostic and remediation skills. When large numbers of students have difficulty any or all of the above possibilities could be at work. All must be checked out. Teachers who can manipulate learning conditions and discover the causes of problems for individual students will help to make mastery systems work. Mechanical teaching, on the other hand, will be associated with an unresponsive, stultifying school system.

If the curriculum materials have no suggested criterion level, the initial strategy on basic skills and concepts is to require mastery or near mastery and to communicate to students that scores are simply information and that students will and should proceed at different paces. Teachers then need to carefully monitor student progress. Monitoring can be thought of as a series of questions. What happens to the work behavior of students who fail two consecutive mastery tests? Is there a drop in motivation? If so, perhaps the student will benefit from more frequent testing covering less material and/or lower mastery levels. Does such intervention work; that is, do work behavior, mastery test scores, and end of unit retention test scores improve? Are many students failing mastery tests? If so, perhaps the criterion level is too high. Do students who proceed slowly become the subject of peer hostility? If so, strategies for helping students to expect and accept differential productivity are needed. Teachers, schools, and school districts should manipulate criterion levels (even those suggested by curriculum writers) to see if different criterion levels are related to different retention scores and attitudes toward the subject. It would probably be best in these situations to set the criterion conservatively high, since the real utility of a mastery-criterion-referenced approach is to ensure that all students achieve mastery. Thus, the question might be: Is a criterion level of 90 percent necessary, or is 80 percent just as effective (rather than 90 percent versus 50 percent)? Such questions are especially important when many students are regularly achieving below 90 percent on the first test.

The work on criterion-referenced testing is just beginning, and its ultimate utility will be proved or disproved on the basis of how it is applied and its resultant effect on learners (the test of any school variable). It appears to offer teachers a way of emphasizing basic skills and would seem to be a good strategy for helping to teach young elementary school children necessary skills. These children can use in their own way as they explore self-defined objectives or work on teacher-defined objectives requiring the student's original thinking in later grades.

As students become older and develop strongly differentiated interests, it is impossible to predict the learning content that is maximally appropriate to them. For example, the tenth grade literature teacher may have some skills that are deemed essential, and such skills may be usefully taught with a criterion-referenced system. However, there also are many situations where content or skills can be identified in an *arbitrary* way. That is, the student can demonstrate the skill in a variety of ways, and although the teacher can write rigid objectives to measure the skill, it seems self-defeating to do so because it denies the student the chance to exercise his capacity for self-expression and to assume responsibility for his own learning.

At most levels of schooling, then, students might be assessed in the same course on both criterion-referenced tests and broader tests scored on a normative basis, at least in those cases where it is important to differentiate student performance and where there are fixed time periods (for instance, the tenth grade biology class ends at the end of the semester; some students have no opportunity to master all criterion goals). Also, of course, it would be possible to use both criterion-referenced measures and behavioral expressions in the same course and grade on a combination scale.

Gronlund (1973) distinguishes between mastery objectives and developmental objectives. In his framework, mastery objectives correspond to specific, criterion-referenced objectives, and development objectives to those where it is impossible or undesirable to specify low inference descriptions of the learning goals. In such "combination" courses when grades are necessary, he suggests the following plan:

1. Achieved all mastery objectives and high on developmental objectives
2. Achieved all mastery objectives, but low on developmental objectives
3. Achieved all mastery objectives only

Students continue to cycle through units or courses until they achieve mastery objectives. After reaching a C level, students could continue to work on higher levels of attainment (if the material was of high interest to them or deemed critically important by school officials) or begin new instructional units or courses. If a continuous progress system is not desired or possible, then grades of D or F could be assigned to students. Similarly, other combination plans can be used effectively. Effective here means that students learn required material of importance, but have time to pursue successfully material of interest on an acceptable grading plan. For example, history teachers might expect all students to obtain (recall) mastery of key points from all periods of American history (and grade such knowledge on a criterion-referenced basis), but then allow students to take integrative tests (norm-referenced) or to write a behavioral expression and conduct an intensive study of a particular historical period (graded on a pass/fail basis).

Other Uses of Criterion-Referenced Tests

Criterion-referenced testing is not limited to the measurement of cognitive performance of students. For example, developers at the Instructional Objectives Exchange in Los Angeles, California, have been attempting to develop criterion-referenced tests to measure affective objectives for *groups* of students. Such measures attempt to provide information about the general reaction of students to the educational environment. Examples of these measures appear in Chapter 9.

Also, many teacher education institutions are using performance based criteria as a way of training teachers. Teachers in training master explicit skills rather than information about skills. Many good training materials have been produced through the Protocol Materials Project sponsored by the U. S. Office of Education. The Far West Regional Laboratory has been especially productive in developing materials that can produce specified teaching behaviors. However, the problem we mentioned in Chapter 3 remains: the ability of the field to design training materials that change teacher behavior far exceeds the ability of the field to identify what teaching behaviors are most appropriate in specific situations.

Simply put, criterion-referenced measures of teaching behavior cannot be used to identify good teachers. However, such measurement practice may be useful in gathering research data about teacher behavior and its effect upon student achievement and to help train teachers to perform new behavior (the effects of such behaviors, of course, needs to be verified in experimental testing). Many of the promising variables discussed in Chapter 4 have been translated into training packages which involve criterion performance standards. For example, Kounin's management variables (with-it-ness, accountability, and so forth) have been developed in a Protocol Materials Project by Walter Borg and others at the University of Utah. Other examples could be cited but the point here is simply to suggest that criterion-referenced training materials do exist and hold forth much promise if the research base for such materials is expanded and verified in classroom research.

Summary

In this chapter we have differentiated between the two terms, criterion- and norm-referenced grading. We have seen that both have an appropriate place in school measurement programs. Norm-referenced tests are especially useful when it is desirable to differentiate student progress. (Does John learn *quickly enough* to be a surgeon? How does Ruth's mechanical aptitude *compare* with other entering freshmen at the University of Illinois who also aspire to be mechanical engineers?) However, it has been argued that needless and continuous comparisons with others may have debilitating effects on some students, and that specific targeting of *minimum* objectives (criterion-referenced tests) and a system that supports individual pacing is useful for helping students to achieve mastery of *some* goals. Also, such systems may help to develop positive learner expectations. Still, teachers will be a relevant factor in determining whether or not continuous learning systems have salubrious effects on students. Dynamic teachers are necessary if school systems are to be responsive to the needs of individual students. In particular, it was noted that mastery systems are especially dependent upon teachers' ability to react appropriately to student failure and success and to assess the effects of recycling on student motivation.

Further, it has been contended that communication of learning goals is a useful teacher behavior that facilitates student learning. However, overly rigid use of behavioral objectives may have harmful effects on learners, so that in cases calling for more than minimum mastery of skills and ideas it may be more appropriate to use *behavioral expressions*. Behavioral expressions focus on learning outcomes and help both teachers and students to mobilize their time in goal-related activities. However, if specific learner outcomes are known, the use of behavioral objectives is more appropriate, in our opinion.

We have seen that there are some complex problems behind "attractive" ideas such as the use of criterion referenced testing and that only research will resolve these problems. The point is that behavioral objectives, behavioral expressions, or criterion-referenced testing programs are not necessarily good or bad. They are merely tools that teachers can utilize. If overused or used mechanically, they may do more harm than good.

We have introduced the general notion of continuous learning environments (such as individualized schools and mastery systems). In the following chapter, we'll explore the existing data that support the efficacy of such ideas, and explain more fully the teacher's role in such systems.

Chapter 8 Individualization and Open Education

In the mid-sixties, as the pressure to raise standards of American schools increased, school officials started to search for responses to growing criticism. "Individualization" was the Zeitgeist at first, and now the "open classroom" has become the password. The purposes of this chapter are to define these two concepts and to review the research base describing the effects of these structural changes on the educational lives of children. Have efforts to make schools more responsive by implementing these changes been successful? This is the question we shall deal with in this chapter. Obviously, given our focus on teachers, we also will want to see how teachers behave in open and individualized programs. Furthermore, it will be important to learn if programs have general effects independent of the teachers who implement them.

Unfortunately, research design problems described in Chapter 3 frequently appear in "openness" studies, and at this time it is impossible to present definitive conclusions about their effects. But certain findings appear with regularity and it will be important to stress these trends. Obviously it is impossible to review all of the literature in a short chapter; thus what follows is a selective but representative review of the literature.

Individualization: A Definition

In the previous chapter it was noted that the major disadvantage of grouping children by age is that it tends either to depress the learning speed of high achieving students by forcing them to continue work on a topic beyond the point of mastery or to force slower students to move on before they achieve mastery. Educators realized that the age-graded curriculum systematically "depressed" cognitive gains and had undesirable side effects (boredom for many high achievers; frustration and alienation for many low achievers), so they began to take corrective action. If indeed the term grade level has no meaning (that is, as many third graders work at the second and fourth grade level as the third), then it should be possible to do away with the notion of grade level and to group children on the basis of skill level independent of age and to allow students to be in multi-age groups.

For example, instead of working with "third graders," teachers would work on the skills normally taught in third grade arithmetic class but would teach children of varying ages who were working on these skills. Depending upon teacher skills and preferences and upon school district policies, the age-graded curriculum was replaced in various ways by schools that opted for individualized plans. For example, teachers might team teach all subjects for a group of students, or, teachers might teach just one or two subjects in a relatively self-contained fashion and team teach the others. The only general meaning to the term "individualization" was that students would advance as fast as they could in distinct subject areas (poor mathematics performance, within limits, would not hinder advanced work in social studies).

Some teachers or groups of teachers have regularly swapped students *within* grade levels for instructional purposes in some subjects (usually reading or math). That is, one teacher takes the highest readers, another takes the middles, while another takes the slowest readers. Here students are heterogeneously grouped for much of the day (so that the social gains of working with diverse student groups are achieved), but are allowed to make maximum progress in one or two skill areas. Furthermore, by supplementing such programs with peer tutoring opportunities and learning centers for independent study, teachers can achieve an individualized program in a system where grade grouping is still operative. (For a full discussion of how to achieve individualization in a traditional system, see Good and Brophy, 1973.)

Thus, for some time teachers have been developing strategies to make more time to spend with individual students in order to determine their needs and to set up relevant learning exercises. What was *new* in the individualization efforts of the 1960s was the willingness of school systems to *break up age assignments* and to develop other ways of grouping children for instruction that allowed them to have a full range of resources and opportunities for progressing as fast as they could in a subject. Initially, it was popular to call these programs *nongraded,* since children were not grouped on the basis of age. It has become increasingly more popular to use the term "individualization."

Individualization helps reduce time pressures ("students in the third grade must be prepared for fourth grade work"), and the associated pressures of teaching the class as a class. Furthermore, the potential for reducing self-damaging comparisons, which are so evident in self-contained classrooms, was established by allowing students to proceed at their own pace, theoretically guaranteeing that successful mastery would come in time.

Subsequently, we shall review the literature describing how individualized programs have influenced cognitive achievement and students' attitudes (respect for self and others). However, before reviewing these results, it is necessary to stress that there is no such thing as "the" individualized program. Previously, we have noted that the format of an individualized program can vary widely (such as teachers specializing in one subject, team teaching with/without subject specialization).

The specific methods used to reach broad goals also vary. For example, as Quirk (1971) notes, sometimes the term "individualization" means that *all* students are taught the *same* curriculum with the *same* methods, although they progress at different rates. In other cases, the same curriculum is presented to students through *different* instructional activities. In still other cases, different curricula are offered, so that each student works toward the instructional objectives that best fit his interests and abilities.

We have seen three different process goal definitions of individualization (and there are others, of course). These definitions can operate with various formats for division of labor (team teaching, etc.). Thus, the meaning of individualization depends upon how it operates in a particular situation. The only common universal attached to the term is that students generally will be able to proceed at their own pace in some areas (most likely using the same curriculum at different rates, with but *minor* differences in learning activities).

There is at least one more distinction important enough to discuss. In addition to a variety of models of individualization that one might mount within the resources of a school system (such as sharing instructional materials, writing objectives for independent learning stations, team teaching), there are packaged programs that provide materials and/or strategies for helping school districts to identify goals and prepare relevant materials. Three of these packaged opportunities are discussed below.

Project PLAN

Project *PLAN* is a program of individualized instruction in language arts, mathematics, social studies, and science. It is being developed by the American Institutes for Research in the Behavioral Sciences (AIR), the Westinghouse Learning Corporation, and several school systems. Professional personnel from AIR worked with teachers to identify instructional objectives and construct teaching units, and then scanned available published materials for potential use. "Best fit" materials were then ordered and made available in PLAN rooms. Thus, each unit specifies both the learning goal and the materials that the student is to use in meeting it. An example of a "materials-specific unit" for tenth grade social studies is shown in Table 8.1.

Students in PLAN classroooms have some opportunity to select unique

TABLE 8.1

Early Civilizations

Step 6   Objective: DEVELOP A PLAN AND MAKE TENTATIVE WORK ASSIGNMENTS FOR A STAFF OF FIVE ARCHAEOLOGICAL ASSISTANTS WHO, UNDER YOUR DIRECTION, MIGHT EXCAVATE AND INTERPRET THE SIGNIFICANCE OF AN ARCHAEOLOGICAL SITE YOU MAY CHOOSE.

Example: "The map attached to his report illustrates the surface features of SITE X, the remains of the ancient civilization of _____. . . .

"My plans indicate the need for the following materials. . . .

"Duties of five staff members are specified below. . . .

"Among my reasons for selecting this site were. . . ."

Use	Do
National Geographic magazine.	(a) Select any real or potentially productive site. Choose a site in your area. A nearby college department of anthropology or archaeology may be able to include you in their field work. If no local anthropological site can be found, you can find descriptions of productive sites in back issues of *National Geographic* and *Scientific American* magazines.
Scientific American magazine.	
Library references:	(b) Map the site and surrounding region.
anthropology archaeology	(c) List the materials which will be needed in an excavation at this site.
Encyclopedia.	(d) Write a description of the system you will use for storing artifacts which are found.
	(e) List the duties or functions of each of five staff members on your expedition.
	(f) Write three or more paragraphs in which you explain at least three reasons for selecting this site.

An excerpt from a materials-specific Teaching-Learning Unit

objectives, to develop instructional procedures, and to establish schedules for meeting those objectives. Students are gradually trained to plan and schedule learning activities. Primary students plan only a portion of one day. Eventually, students plan a few days, then a few units, and ultimately they work independently of adult supervision.

Our purpose here is not to describe PLAN in detail (for a good description, see Quirk, 1971), but to illustrate that systematic programs exist for packaging objectives and materials as well as for training students to develop independent study skills. Furthermore, it should be clear that PLAN concepts could be used by teachers in a traditional system to individualize instruction so that the pace is generally comfortable for most students and so that student abilities and interests are built upon at least some of the time. Clearly, though, breaking up the age-graded curriculum makes possible flexible planning that truly allows students to proceed at their own pace.

Individually Guided Education

Another system of individualization has been developed (and continues to be refined) by the Wisconsin Research and Development Center for Cognitive Learning (for extended descriptions, see Klausmeier, et al., 1971a, and Klausmeier, et al., 1971b). The IGE concept has been systematized and packaged for school usage by the Institute for Development of Educational Activities, Inc., the educational affiliate of the Charles F. Kettering Foundation.

Here, too, emphasis is placed upon helping students to develop, ultimately, self-direction and prosocial behavior. But direct teacher instruction is stressed as a legitimate activity (especially for younger children who read poorly and who do not possess needed basic concepts and self-starting skills). Thus, the attempt in the Individually Guided Education (IGE) program has been to develop a system of education to help students learn at their own pace in a variety of instructional modes, and not just to produce a variety of self-instructional materials. Furthermore, basic learning goals are set in the IGE model, and criterion-referenced tests are used to determine whether students are making satisfactory progress. If a child scores low in certain conceptual skill areas, the major instructional objectives for this child then are based on his particular pattern of deficiencies. Comparatively, then, IGE seemingly places more emphasis on articulating a support system of teacher "control" and on establishing priorities (the basic skills come first). However, the IGE model provides opportunity for individual goal setting and the expression of self-direction, although planning opportunities lie largely within the existing curriculum structure. In many ways, then, the structure for attaining important common goals is clearer in the IGE model than in some of the models that school officials might choose from when implementing individualized education.

IPI and PEP

Other viable models are *IPI* and *PEP*. Individually Prescribed Instruction (IPI) is somewhat similar to the two educational systems discussed above. It was designed by the Learning Research and Development Center at the University of Pittsburgh. The system specifies a fixed minimum set of goals for all students but allows for varying times (and techniques) to reach these goals. In general, the role of the teacher is expressed in three major ways: (1) evaluation, (2) diagnosis, and (3) guidance with individual students. Curricular materials are sequential such that students can manage the curriculum at their own pace. The Primary Education Project (PEP) is very similar to the IPI curriculum. The major difference is that in PEP, some managerial arrangements involving teaching or using the class as a whole still exist. In general, the system has been carefully built, and developmental work continues.

Even the use of a known program does not guarantee a standardized curriculum. Teachers and school officials can and do apply their own "twists" to any curriculum model, so that the "paper" version and the actual classroom usage are often quite discrepant. Hence, it is virtually impossible to know how much of a variable such as "structure" is present in a particular program without collecting observation data in the classrooms.

Questioning the Assumptions

There can be no quarrel (from our point of view) that the age-graded curriculum is an obstacle that puts too many restraints on student learning and that individualization is a viable staffing principle (students whose individual needs overlap are the organizing focus), but one wonders if individualization doesn't become an end in itself in some programs. Are there times when students should read *common* books so that they can be discussed and debated? How do students learn that others reach different conclusions from the same data, or learn "how to learn" from others, except through interaction with others?

Achieving a balance between individual learning (self-pacing) and group work or even whole-class work (learning a song, discussing the moral issues involved in certain forms of playground behavior) is a delicate task. How teachers balance these demands is the key question. Will teachers overlook meaningful opportunities for whole class learning, especially the type of learning that stems from social cooperation, because they *are* individualizing? Similarly, because the "local" definition of individualization includes self-selection of goals, will teachers allow students to go through series of fragmented learning episodes? Or, will a student's learning style be catered to in such a way that his strengths are built upon but his weaknesses avoided completely?

Only research will answer such questions. However, it should be understood that individualization only provides the *potential* for achieving personal goals. It does *not* guarantee that such goals will be reached, and indeed, individualization may make some goals more difficult to achieve. We suspect that some teachers will achieve a good balance between individuality and group learning, so that both cognitive and affective growth occur. Furthermore, we suspect that students' preference for a work/learning style (for instance, working alone) would be catered to by some teachers in such a way that building a curriculum around a student's preferred learning style would be self-defeating (in other words, it might prevent him from developing the ability to learn from and with others). Thus, individual programs will vary widely in their effects on students in part as a function of how teachers and students implement them. Our purpose here is merely to raise questions so the reader will want to look carefully at the data that will be discussed later.

Open Classrooms: A Definition

There is no common definition of "open" that is widely accepted. We have seen that the term individualized is "loose," but "open classrooms" is even more elusive. The best way to describe the concept is to specify the features that are often used as comparison points between open and traditional classrooms. For example, Traub, Weiss, Fisher, and Musella (1973) utilized ten characteristics in an attempt to differentiate "open" and "closed" classrooms.

1. *Setting instructional objectives* (here the argument is not on goals *per se* but the way in which they are set. In the open class, objectives must refer to individuals—the more the student is free to set his own objectives, the more open the class)
2. *Materials and activities* (the more diverse, the more open)
3. *Physical environment* (flexible use of space in open classes)
4. *Structure for decision-making* (students decide which teacher they will work with—move from activity to activity)
5. *Time scheduling* (flow of events dependent upon motivation of students)
6. *Individualization of instruction* (little or no large group instruction in which students learn the same thing in the same way; less large group instruction: more open)
7. *Composition of classes* (not grouped by age or achievement, but by interest; more "interest" grouping: more open)
8. *Role of teacher* (little or no time presenting planned lesson—class members develop new materials, etc.)

9. *Student evaluation* (information collected *for students*: the more
   so, the more open)
10. *Evaluation by students* (students participate in rule-making)

These characteristics of open education were drawn from the writings
of Barth (1969, 1971), who had attempted to spell out explicitly the assumptions made by open educators. Using these general characteristics, Traub, *et
al.* (1973) developed a questionnaire called the Dimensions of Schooling
(DISC) to measure openness. Others too have produced instruments for
classifying the degree and *type* of openness that exist in schools.

Such instruments are valuable research tools because it is difficult to interpret the results of an open program unless one knows the specific com-
ponents of the open program. For example, assume that open school 1
emphasizes student goal selection and student evaluation; whereas, open school
2 emphasizes flexibility in use of building and curriculum material to reach
teacher-selected goals. We might find that school 1 increased the percentage
of on-task student behavior, while school 2 raised achievement. However, in
comparisons with traditional schools, it might appear that no gains had taken
place. This is because the increased amount of time that students in school 1
were spending in work on self-selected goals would be offset by the low
frequency of such behavior in school 2. Similarly, the achievement gains
in school 2 could be offset by the lack of achievement gain in type 1 schools,
so that the open type schools (1 and 2) would have no better achievement
records than traditional schools.

"Openness" is best viewed as a continuous set of variables. Schools may
be open on some characteristics but closed on others. Some advocates of
open education would not require that all 10 of the characteristics mentioned
above be present in a school for it to be "good" (many would, however).
Thus, an openness score *per se* is not necessarily an expression of goodness,
but rather an empirical score whose meaning needs to be clarified. For
example, the "open" advocates would be willing to accept moderate openness scores if such scores were related to the accomplishment of humanistic
goals.

The classification scheme used by Traub, *et al.*, implicitly suggests that
teachers in a traditional system could not have an "open" classroom because
of the individualization and nongradedness dimensions (students move to
next unit whenever their performance allows). However, other definitions
would allow the classification of teachers who "individualize" within a traditional system to be classified as "open."

Katz (1972) presents another useful attempt to provide a way of looking
at openness (shown in Table 8.2).

Which of these two schemes is the more useful for defining openness?
We don't know, because both have their advantages. The Traub model

TABLE 8.2

Comparison of Open and Traditional Classrooms

Space	Flexible, Variable	O–I	T–F	Routinized, Fixed
Activities of Children	Wide Range	O–I	T–F	Narrow Range
Origin of Activity	Children's Spontaneous Interests	O–I	T–F	Teacher or School Prescribed
Content or Topics	Wide Range	O–I	T–F	Limited Range
Use of Time	Flexible, Variable	O–I	T–F	Routinized, Fixed
Initiation of Teacher–Child Interaction	Child	O–I	T–F	Teacher
Teaching Target	Individual Child	O–I	T–F	Large or Whole Group
Child–Child Interaction	Unrestricted	O–I	T–F	Restricted

O–I = Open–Informal Classes; T–F = Traditional–Formal Classes

has empirical assessment behind it and allows direct measurement in questionnaire form. The Katz model suggests some of the same properties but would allow for the identification of relatively open teachers within the traditional system.

In general, individualization stemmed from the interest in freeing teachers and students from the lock-step curriculum, although other goals were acknowledged as well. Openness is an attempt to free students from unnecessary institutional demands and to allow students to project their own structure on the learning situation, thus having more positive opportunities for self-expression and affective growth.

Given the data described in Chapter 4 suggesting that teacher and school variables do not share simple one-to-one relationships with student outcome measures and that too much of a "good" behavior may be as harmful as too little, one would predict that the desirability of an individualized or open plan would vary with the nature of the plan, the type of students, the outcome measures, and other factors. However, when writing about open class-rooms, researchers frequently do not specify any information other than grade level (leaving to the imagination what "open" meant in the schools under study, the SES level of students, and so on). This of course is un-fortunate, because this lack of information makes it impossible to specify those "open" features present when programs apparently worked or failed or the contextual conditions operating in successful or unsuccessful ventures.

Questions about the Assumptions of Openness

There are no data to refute or to support the assumption that openness creates humanistic, responsive systems of education where students simul-taneously register greater gains in creativity, morality, and appreciation of self and others, enjoy school, and achieve mastery of skills at least as well as children in self-contained classes. Our goal is not to debate these assump-tions here, but to stress that *data* should be used in seeking the truth. How-ever, we do feel that it is useful to raise a few questions for the reader to consider before we consider the data.

What data exist to support the assumption that largely unrestricted choice of learning leads to happiness or productivity?

Can't satisfaction stem from completing an externally imposed demand that has a definite beginning and end such that the student knows he has achieved well on an important task?

Why shouldn't a student be expected to help other students answer *their* questions rather than single-mindedly pursuing his own unique interests?

Teacher structuring may provide children with invaluable modeling for diverse types of learning. Why do we assume that children learn more when teachers are silent? (It would seem that the "situations" are more important than the frequency of teacher talk!).

In self-selected activities, what percent of the time do children need to finish their project? It would seem that self-concept is more related to selective persistence and successful resolution than to freedom to choose *per se.*

Do students spend more time dealing with aesthetic and musical experiences or affective interaction of substance with others, or does openness as it is typically operationalized mean only independent study?

Research on Individualization

In reporting data on the effects of individualization and openness on learners, it must be noted again that extremely loose terms are being used, and that the descriptions of many research projects fail to define openness or report on contextual variables of interest. However, in the following section we shall provide a selective but representative review of the field.

Thompson (1973) conducted a study to test two goals of PLAN: (a) more individualization, (b) shift in teacher role from direction to facilitation. Twelve PLAN and twelve control classes were drawn from grades 1, 2, 3, and 10. Pupils from each class (5 boys and 5 girls) were selected for attitude testing. Futhermore, PLAN classes were divided into *open* (specially designed architectural features built to facilitate free movement) and semi-open (traditional rooms with movable partitions) schools.

Teachers' scores on the Minnesota Teacher Attitude Inventory showed no mean differences between PLAN and control teachers. To measure the effects of the program on teacher behavior, an observation system was used to collect data on the PLAN and control teachers while they were teaching. The observation schedule coded several *types* of teacher behavior: questioning; directing; explaining; informing; managing; monitoring; attending; nonrelevant; rewarding; and giving feedback. Furthermore, the *focus* of teacher behavior was coded: (a) individuals working alone, (b) individuals working in the company of others, (c) a group, (d) the whole class. Also, some attempt was made to code the *appropriateness of pupil behavior*.

Roughly 7½ hours of observational data were collected in each room over a two-week period. The observational measures provide two ways of looking at the effects of PLAN: (a) changes in pupil behavior, (b) changes in teacher behavior. In addition, the effects of PLAN on student attitudes were measured by two subtests of the Coopersmith Self-Esteem Inventory.

Findings in the Thompson study showed that PLAN pupils spent more time working alone in a group, and more time as a member of group, than control pupils, and that PLAN pupils spent most of their time *working alone on their own individual projects*. Control students spent most of their time in whole-class activities (time spent in groups was roughly equal in PLAN and control classrooms).

However, grade level differences were pronounced. In both PLAN *and* control first grade rooms, students spent much time working alone on individual activities. Progressively, in second grade and especially in third grade, PLAN students began to spend relatively *more* time in individual work, while control students spent more time in whole class activities.

No differences were noted in the *types* of behaviors that teachers engaged in (for example, the ratios of instructional/managerial behaviors were similar). However, the *focus* of teacher behavior (except at the first grade level) was markedly different, with PLAN teachers more often dealing with individual students or small groups.

Analysis of variance tests on the two subscales of the Coopersmith Self-Esteem Inventory revealed that *control students* were more favorable than

PLAN students, and that third graders as a whole were more satisfied than second graders.

Two additional questions were also administered to control and PLAN students. Children were to respond (most of the time, some of the time, hardly ever) to the following questions:

"Do you think you are able to pick the work you want to do in school?"

"Are you able to finish your schoolwork on time?"

The first question was answered significantly differently by PLAN and control students, with 40 percent of PLAN students indicating "most of the time" but only 20 percent of the controls responding this way. However, the second question was answered this way by control and PLAN students:

	Most of the Time	Hardly Ever
Control	71%	0%
PLAN	43%	17%

Thus, students who are assigned similar unit after similar unit may need more reinforcement at selected points to make them aware of their progress and indeed to notch "bench marks" in their progress. Ironically, students may be freed from a teacher-dominated system only to be controlled or at least bored by another system: sameness. Clearly, there are dangers in interpreting individual questions (as opposed to groups of questions), but nonetheless we find the results interesting. They suggest a potential problem that teachers should guard against.

Separate analysis on open and semi-open schools showed few differences. The semi-open facilities functioned as well as the architecturally planned open facility. Thus, openness is more a *program* and a *philosophy* than it is a building type.

These data did show that an individualization program was successful in changing the whole class focus so evident in control classes, but one wonders if vast amounts of time working alone is a better system if students are exposed to one cognitive module after another. Furthermore, it is noteworthy that individualization *per se* was *not* associated with more favorable attitudes toward school, self, or others, at least in this program.

Although the study reviewed above showed mixed results, individualized schools (whatever they are) usually compare well with control schools. Pavan (1973) reviewed the literature on nongradedness from 1961–1968, and noted several major trends:

1. More positive labels are being used now in preference to the term nongradedness (individualization, for example).
2. Most studies now include affective measures and/or a variety of outcome measures.

3. Fewer children are retained.
4. Much more individualized and small-group work takes place than in control classes.
5. Individualized instruction seems relatively more beneficial for blacks, boys, and underachievers.

Goodlad (1970) had noted that most early studies found individualized programs on a par with graded ones, even though only standard achievement test results were used as criteria. Pavan expands upon this point of view, and reviews data to show that the achievement of students in recently studied individualized programs is generally as good or better than the achievement of students in control-traditional classes. However, the problem with such box scores is that one is apt to conclude that "individualization works" rather than "individualization *often* works." The problem is that studies (whether negative, mixed, or positive results were obtained) often do not provide information beyond the degree of program success. For example, often we do not know the nature of the individual program or the contextual range in which it operated. It is too bad that more studies have not reported differential effects on students of different age, sex, race, SES level, or aptitude.

In general, we agree with Pavan—research suggests that participation in an individualized program does not hurt student academic progress (and is more likely to have a positive effect than a negative effect). Furthermore, the conclusion that boys in particular are helped by individualized programs draws support from three separate studies. In addition, the conclusion that more individual work takes place in individualized classes is fully supported by the literature. However, the "argument" for the benefits of individualization to blacks is built upon only one study (Case, 1971), and, although it is an interesting hypothesis, more data are needed. The notion that fewer children are retained in nongraded programs also is supported by only one study, but this proposition seems to be true by definition (McLaughlin, 1970).

The behavioral data on individualized programs are mixed, and often the way they are interpreted is shaped by the values of the authors. Consider the results that Myers (1971) obtained when he asked Canadian children to respond to a 74-item teacher checklist. The most prevalent responses of open space and self-contained students are noted below:

OPEN-SPACE	SELF-CONTAINED
1. Makes interesting assignments.	1. Gives everyone a chance to express himself.
2. Trusts his students.	2. Administers punishment fairly.
3. Is eager to help when I need it.	3. Thinks all pupils are important.
4. Will admit his mistakes.	4. Knows the subjects.

In general we would agree that responses of the open-space children suggest striving for autonomy, while children in self-contained classes were concerned wth fair treatment. However, if one stresses cooperative behavior these attitudes may be seen favorably, and if one believes that respect for individual differences is an important goal, he may be encouraged to find that self-contained teachers are modeling a view that *all* pupils are important. Perhaps a more appropriate question is how do these measures relate to important outcome measures? At this point, no one knows.

The review by Pavan is a useful summary of the data relevant to the effects of nongraded instruction on pupil performance in the 60s. Weaknesses in the review are really weaknesses in the field. For example, the fact that average student achievement does not differ greatly in individualized or traditional classrooms may hide as much information as it reveals. Perhaps the gains of some students are offset by the losses of passive students who cannot use the teacher as a resource and hence, spend much of their time worrying about how to complete assignments or just "fooling around" without learning very much. Such questions are important to answer, because they may identify and lead to the elimination of obstacles that prevent individualized programs from achieving their full potential.

In general, however, relevant data do *not* suggest that individualized programs have undesirable effects of a general nature (although there may be hidden costs for some students), and the affective reactions of students seem to be somewhat higher in *some* individualized schools. As programs have time to develop, they will probably become more interesting to students *if* student feedback is used in program improvement.

More Individualization Data

Data to suggst that the IGE "structured" form of individualization can positively influence student attitudes and classroom climate is provided in a recent study by Nelson (1973). Approximately 1000 students (grades 9–12) selected from 13 IGE and 12 control schools were administered the School Morale Scale and the Semantic Differential or Self-Concept as a Learner. Differences, when they occurred, favored the IGE schools: attitudes toward fellow pupils; higher general attitude toward school; and higher pupil attitudes toward the community. Some of the findings showing *no* differences included: pupils attitudes toward teachers, attitudes toward school plant, and attitudes toward school administration. Furthermore, there were *no* differences between control and IGE schools in attendance and tardiness rates.

Finally, it should be noted that an analysis of individual schools showed that, with but few exceptions, means for all scales and subscales were higher for pupils in individualized programs than in traditional schools. Clearly, the "team teaching approach" characteristic of IGE may strengthen pupil–pupil relationships without impairing teacher–student relationships. Furthermore, the generally high morale scores for the IGE pupils suggest that the program worked well for *most* of the students.

Such improved learning climates did not appear in *all* IGE schools. Still, the data are very encouraging and serve as a concrete example that well-developed individualized programs can influence student *attitudes*. Hopefully, subsequent work in IGE schools will reveal the behaviors and arrangements that are (are not) present when IGE schools do (or do not) improve student attitudes.

Furthermore one wonders if subgroups of students (introverted girls or boys, low achievers) respond somewhat differently from one another. We can hope that subsequent research will deal more comprehensively with the effects of different types of individualization and examine the data for possible differential effects on students.

Shimron (1973) conducted an interesting study to test the adaptability of the IPI curriculum to student individual differences. Students in the IPI program follow a set sequence but control their own pace, so that it is possible for individual difference variables to emerge. If the curriculum really is as adaptable as the designers claim, then (1) slow and fast students should not differ in the time they spend in on task behavior, and (2) there should not be differences in the availability of the teacher (at least when students want help). Subjects were eight second-grade students. Four students were labeled "fast" because they had mastered the most curriculum units, and the four students who had mastered the fewest units were labeled "slow." Each of the target students was observed during five 20-minute periods. Some of the more interesting observations found in this pilot study include:

1. In general, faster students spent *twice* as much time working on assignments than slower ones;
2. Slower students spent *twice* as much time in off-task behavior;
3. The number of waiting occurrences (frequencies, not actual time) was significantly higher for fast students (waiting to get permission to go on to the next unit, to ask questions, and so on. However, waiting is *active* in the sense that the student is not engaging in off-task behavior. Rather, he is seeking the teacher out);
4. With on-task (work-related) activity, student-teacher interaction occurred a much higher percentage of the time for faster students;
5. Virtually *no* peer–peer work-related contacts were taking place among any of the students.

Reacting to his data, Shimron suggests that the individualized program is not fully adaptable to the slower students or that the curriculum does not hold their attention. He notes several reasons why slower students might engage in off-task behavior, including:

1. Need for more gradual sequencing;
2. Some prerequisite tasks may not be fully mastered;
3. Units do not have interest for them.

He further suggests that teachers' higher rates of work-related interactions with faster students may be a function of student requests for help, so that teacher behavior is under the control of students. However, we suspect that, when a wider number of teachers have been observed, teacher susceptibility to differential press from students will prove to be an individual difference variable on which teachers vary considerably. Previous research in traditional classrooms (Brophy and Good, 1974) has shown that some teachers are largely controlled by student characteristics; whereas other teachers are more able to retain the initiative through proactive behavior (for example, he will call or approach a student who doesn't have his hand up).

Nevertheless, much student time appears to be *controlled by students* themselves, and Shimron's data would suggest that variance in the behavior of students is due to the fact that faster students spend more time working than slower students. His pilot study has provided some very striking data and illustrates a useful methodological way of viewing the process dynamics in individual classrooms. The extent to which these data generalize to other settings is, of course, unknown, and will be answered only by more data.

However, the notion that student work habits and perseverance in mastery learning environments are of critical importance is gaining wide recognition. For example, a recent study by McAvoy, Franklin, and Kalin (1973) concluded that *aptitude* was not significantly related to the time it took a student to reach criterion level in a self-instructional setting. However, personality variables (as measured by the Sixteen Personality Factor Questionnaire) collected on 178 sophomore subjects did relate significantly to learning time. Clearly, personality and work styles will influence the amount of time students take to finish assignments, and information about the precise mechanisms involved is needed. We suspect, though, that such research, when conducted, will show that teachers and/or teaching teams vary widely in their ability to motivate certain types of students, and in their ability to monitor events occurring simultaneously in complex individualized programs. We conclude that program effectiveness will be influenced by the participating teachers.

Research in Open Schools

We have been discussing results for nongraded or individualized schools. Let us now turn our attention to open schools. As we shall see, research results are mixed. Some studies show that openness makes a positive difference; whereas, other results suggest that student progress is better in more conventional classrooms. Although there are some supporting data the "openness" literature does not appear to be as promising as does the individualization literature.

There are some data to suggest that students in open classrooms are developing positive self-views and perhaps gaining greater respect for individual differences. Four studies in the Pavan review were conducted in open space classrooms: Purkey, *et al.* (1970), Jeffreys (1971), Warner (1971), and Meyers (1971). Rather consistently, it is found that greater individualization is occurring in open classrooms (teachers are found to work more frequently with individuals or small groups and to allow more student-to-student interaction). However, bear in mind that the opportunity for an individual to work on his own does not necessarily mean that new and exciting learning forms will be introduced in the curriculum. For example, Jeffreys (1971) found more paper and pencil work in open space classrooms. Obviously, the *substance* of what individuals or small groups work on is as important as solitude.

The Purkey, Groves, and Zellner (1970) study provides evidence that one experimental open school was more conducive to the enhancement of self-concept than was a comparison traditional school. The physical plant was new, built for team teaching and an ungraded curriculum, and pupils were continually regrouped on the basis of their progress. Furthermore, teacher aides were available to help teachers with noninstructional tasks, freeing teacher time for individual contacts with children; students participated in setting their own learning goals.

A neighborhood school that used conventional grade levels and self-contained classrooms was picked as a contrast school. Both the experimental and the contrast school served similar populations.

The test instrument used to assess self-concept development was the 25-item form of the Coopersmith Self-Esteem Inventory. The mean scores by grade level are noted in Table 8.3. Analysis of variance tests revealed that the general difference between schools was significant, and so were the differences between the schools at *each* grade level.

In general, pupils in the experimental school were scoring significantly higher than students in the traditional school. The exception at the third

TABLE 8.3

Mean Self-Concept Scores across Grade Levels
in Experimental and Traditional Groupings

	Grade 3	Grade 4	Grade 5	Grade 6	Total
Experimental	15.36	15.03	15.01	16.58	15.49
Traditional	15.70	14.59	13.94	13.95	14.54
TOTAL	15.53	14.81	14.48	15.16	15.02

grade level, even though statistically significant, is not really important. This small difference is *statistically* significant because a large number of students were tested, but a difference of 0.34 points is of no practical significance.

The trend for differences between the open and traditional schools to increase with the grade level is of greater interest and it is important to see that really large and important differences separate fifth and sixth grades in the two schools. Unfortunately since the length of time that pupils had been in the open school was not controlled for, it is difficult to interpret the meaning of this finding. (Do the results imply a cumulative school impact or only different effects on students of different ages?)

The study does not contain any *process* information about the classroom behavior of teachers and students. Also, the study provides no information about the effect of the experimental school on students who differ in sex, aptitude, or other variables. Thus the possibility that the school was especially useful or detrimental to some students remains untested. We realize that this point has been raised before, if sweeping curriculum patterns are to be institutionalized, we need to know how they affect *all* students.

The Purkey, *et al.* study is a useful attempt to document differences between models. A similar strategy could be applied profitably to several open schools to identify those that are having positive effects on student self-esteem scores (or any other variables) and to select from these a number of schools for intensive study (see Chapter 3).

Comprehensive Studies of Openness

Two recent studies have mounted a reasonably comprehensive study of openness. An especially notable effort was reported in symposium form at the 1973 meeting of the American Educational Research Association meeting by Traub, Weiss, Fisher, and Musella. These researchers used the DISC instrument to select schools which differed in *openness* and architectural form. Thirty elementary schools were chosen from 43 within one school district in a Canadian city.

Eighteen type I schools (schools having less than 15 percent of students coming from homes where English was the second language) and twelve type II schools (schools where more than 30 percent of the students came from homes where English was the second language) were identified. Type II schools draw their population from a lower socioeconomic level.

Observation data in some schools supported the fact that in a very general way, openness scores on the DISC were associated with differential forms of teacher and student behavior. For example, teachers were more mobile in open classrooms, spent more time *observing* students, and engaged in recitation activities with students less often than teachers in less open programs. Furthermore, teachers in open classrooms were more likely to mark seatwork and to consult with small groups of students. Students in open classes were observed to walk and "stand" more frequently. However, open students were *unengaged* more often (watching and listening less often), and higher noise and activity levels were observed in open classrooms.

Weiss (1973) stressed that past studies of openness had concentrated on cognitive skills and that no research had attempted to come to grips with the wide range of outcomes necessary to assess open classrooms fairly. Researchers at the Ontario Institute for Studies in Education thus mounted an impressive effort to determine the effects of openness on a variety of student outcome measures. Eight- and eleven-year-old students in the target schools were tested.

Dependent measures to provide information about the differential effects of open and traditional schools were collected on a variety of cognitive, expressive, and affective instruments. Cognitive achievement was measured by the Canadian Tests of Basic Skills (CTBS) and the modern mathematics supplement to the CTBS.

For type I schools, there was no consistent or important relationship between achievement scores on the CTBS and either program openness or architectural type. *But for the 12 type II schools, at each age level, more open programs were associated with notably lower achievement in all CTBS measures.* The data suggest that students in type II schools (mostly children who live in the inner city and/or who have language difficulties) may need more structure than the open classroom arrangement provided for them.

For affective variables, data were available in two age groups (8, 11) in type I schools only. The affective data were more encouraging than the cognitive data. Openness was associated with more positive student attitudes. In both architecturally open and mixed-open program schools, eight-year-old students had more positive attitudes toward school, teacher, and self and felt more independent than peers in closed schools. But these positive attitudes did *not* translate into achievement or creativity gains. Also it is important to note that more positive attitudes were found only in high SES schools.

Differences were more pronounced for eleven-year-olds. More open students scored higher in all areas, but significantly so on self-report measures of initiative, autonomy, and responsibility to self. Also, eleven-year-old students in open architectural schools reported more independence, responsibility to self, and autonomy.

In general, to the extent that good things were happening in open programs, the architectural plan *per se* did not seem to be a critical factor even though some higher self-report indices were associated with architectural type (but such results are confounded by the fact that architecturally open buildings were also new and students could be responding to that dimension).

However, other tests yielded no support for the efficacy of openness. A test of situational curiosity suggested that students from mixed schools registered higher curiosity scores, but this is hard to interpret because students in two mixed architectural schools had different "treatments." Eleven-year-olds in one school were housed in the open area addition, but in the other school they were housed in the original closed area.

The Torrence tests of creative thinking yielded no consistent pattern for the four figural scales, but the three tests of verbal creativity results favored schools *with less open programs and architecture.* Furthermore, the Day Specific Curiosity Inventory yielded no consistent differences. This was an unexpected finding, because facilitating curiosity is a key objective in open education. Clearly, the open schools in this study did not influence creativity or curiosity. Furthermore, the Russell Sage Social Pattern Test did not indicate that the programs were having different effects on students.

In general, then, research data indicate that the achievement of cognitive skills, group problem solving, creativity, and curiosity remain basically the same across different types of schools. How do we interpret these findings? Do we draw the conclusion that different school plans make *no* difference? . . . the *same* difference? Unfortunately, the most useful information would be the amount of variance *within* school types. Perhaps open schools in general make no difference because the good effects of some schools are washed away by the ineffectiveness of others when open schools as a group are compared to traditional schools. Data describing the range of outcomes within open and traditional classrooms would be interesting. Similarly, perhaps gains are dissipated because subgroups of students find such assets as their creativity dramatically stifled in the open school. Furthermore, in a normative sense, one wonders what similar achievement in cognitive areas in open and closed schools means in comparison to other schools serving students of similar characteristics. Were the comparison schools getting better than expected results?

If subsequent analyses of the data reveal that some schools (either open or closed) showed extremely disordinal results on creativity, affect, and so on, these schools should be subjected to careful scrutiny via intensive observational studies. Traub, Weiss, Fisher, and Musella have collected a rich data pool on student outcome measures. The lack of support for either open or closed classrooms strongly suggests that the particular mechanisms involved in operationalizing a program are important (but as yet unidentified), and that different degrees of openness will be called for to facilitate different goals and the needs of different students.

It has been noted previously that inner city students benefitted (on cognitive measures) from the structure in traditional schools. Clearly, structure *per se* is not necessarily bad! Such a finding is not only important in itself but again it reminds us that differential program effects on students are likely to be found if investigators look for them.

Encouragingly, the impressive attempt by this Canadian research team to discover the effects of openness is to be extended in a long-term study. The researchers plan to draw a random sample of schools (although we would suggest a pool of classes or schools who have disordinal DISC scores and differential effects on students) and to collect data for three years to see if schools are stable in their effects on students over time.

The lack of positive influence of open schools upon achievement and creativity scores found in the Canadian study have been reported by others as well. For example Owen, Froman, and Calchera (1974) report no differences in self-concept, locus of control, creativity, or cognitive achievement among white middle class students who had been assigned to a regular or open program within a middle school. The absence of affective gains or achievement gains underlines the fact that "openness" *per se* has no positive, consistent influence upon student performance.

Tuckman, Cochran, and Travers (1973) also have conducted a fairly comprehensive study of openness in three schools in New Jersey. The purpose of this study, Project Open Classroom (POC) was to develop a model for changeover from formal to informal methods. A treatment designed to facilitate this was applied and evaluated. The POC treatment consisted of a three-week trip to England to study British Infant Schools, a summer workshop, consultant visits during the year, and a few inservice workshops.

Two randomly selected classrooms were observed at each grade in each school, and student outcome data also were collected in these 30 classrooms. Classrooms were observed on two occasions for at least 20 minutes after the teachers had been in Project POC for close to a year. Given the small amount of observation, the condensed time period in which it was collected, and low reliability on two of the measures, it is difficult to generalize from the data (which the authors, to their credit, do not do).

Results on process measures did not yield consistently *strong* differences between POC and control classrooms. However, in grades 1 through 3 open rooms were associated with significantly higher activity levels, more flexible use of space, greater teacher warmth and acceptance, and more teacher responding and reacting.

At grades 4 and 5, more simultaneous diverse student activity and more diverse student grouping patterns were observed in POC rooms than in control rooms, but teachers responded to students' questions more frequently in control classrooms. However, control teachers in grades 4 and 5 talked significantly more and their pupils significantly less.

Without precise information about how these process measures relate to student outcomes, it is hard to assess their value. For example, one goal of opennesss is to allow the student to ask more questions and to use the teachers as a resource. Whether this happens in a positive way cannot be determined without finer process measures that go beyond frequency counts and provide qualitative data. For example, are the more frequent student questions in the grade 4 and 5 control classrooms a function of greater inquisitiveness, or do the questions signify greater student dependence? (Am I doing what you want?) To answer such questions, finer process measures are necessary. However, the data in the Tuckman, *et al.* study provide general support for the notion that teachers *were* playing different roles in POC and control classes, and that teachers were more active in POC classes.

A variety of student outcome measures was collected by Tuckman, Cochran, and Travers. Overall, standardized achievement was *unaffected* by the switch to open classrooms. *However, students in all instances were performing above grade level*; thus, it would be hard to show favorable effects for openness in such a study. The small number of schools proved to be a handicap, as it allowed only for the study of high achieving classrooms. However, the study still shows that high levels of achievement are possible in open classrooms and that striving for other goals does not necessarily preclude academic achievement.

The authors did not present first grade data in explicit form because the teachers reported extreme difficulty in administering the test. However, the authors report that *control classrooms significantly* outperformed POC classes in two of four areas. But, given the administration problems, it is impossible to see if this apparent support of "structure" for young children is a reliable finding. In grades one through three, POC classroom children had more positive attitudes toward self in *one* of two treatment schools, but there was no effect in grades four through five. With regard to attitudes toward school, children in POC classrooms were more positive. There was more of a positive trend at grades 4 and 5 than at 1 through 3.

Once again, the results tell the old story of differential effects. Why one school was more effective than another is unknown, but we see that school effects do occur. Of value here would be information about the degree of openness in the two schools (DISC scores, for example). The fact that openness is perceived more favorably by older elementary students than by younger ones is evident, and has been reported above in several other studies.

What accounts for the more favorable attitudes toward schools when they do occur? The authors suggest that the use of small groups and individual contacts allows the teacher to be more personable, and that it is this dimension to which students are responding. However only more research will answer the question. In any case, whatever causes the improved student attitudes does not in the short run influence cognitive achievement.

Creativity and Structure

Corlis and Weiss (1973) note that Barth (1969) put forth three assumptions relevant to curiosity and openness: (1) children are innately curious and display curiosity behavior independent of adult intervention; (2) exploratory behavior is self-perpetuating; and (3) active exploration in an environment providing a wide array of manipulative materials will facilitate children's learning.

Corlis and Weiss (1973) conducted a study to test these assumptions and to verify the relationship of openness and curiosity. This study was conducted within the broader framework of the Traub, *et al.* (1973) study. Thus, openness was defined two ways: programmatically (by a DISC score) and architecturally. Curiosity was defined in a way consistent with Berlyne's (1954) definition of specific curiosity, that is, as behavior resulting from the need to extend one's knowledge into unusual, novel, or complex aspects of the environment in the absence of clearly defined goals.

To measure specific curiosity, the authors created a performance test of nonverbal curiosity (NVC). The NVC consists of six pairs of tasks. One member of the pair (if chosen by the student) requires curiosity behavior; the other does not. The curiosity task in each pair was a novel, strange task with little instruction and no statement of expected outcome. The noncuriosity task was a rote task with clear instructions and a clear expected outcome. To compensate for the intrinsic reward value of the novel tasks, noncuriosity tasks carried a small reward (penny, piece of bubble gum).

The results indicate that *curiosity was not associated with openness* (at least not in a general way). Interestingly, curiosity behavior scores as measured by the NVC, in relationship with openness, form an inverted-U distribution. At the *lowest* points on a graph were the most extreme schools: *open architecture-high open program* and *closed architecture-low open program*. Thus, in this study, *higher curiosity* is associated with *moderate* amounts of program openness.

In reviewing their results, the authors note that *too* high a level of conflict may inhibit exploratory behavior (as Berlyne had pointed out in 1960). Further, they suggest that open classes may provide a child with more alternatives than he is ready to handle or provide tasks that are too complex; whereas, in closed classes there may be too few alternatives or the alternatives are not sufficiently stimulating. Interesting indeed would be a detailed study of the curriculum effects of openness: for instance, what tasks, specifically, are assigned in open rooms; how many and what type of alternatives exist? The study should determine if openness presents activities that make cognitive demands on students that are not made on them in control classes.

Corlis and Weiss themselves offer two suggestions for improving curiosity and for subsequent testing: (1) Provide fewer materials but select the materials carefully (as opposed to having a vast array of materials that are randomly presented); (2) Provide guidance for the child as he explores new materials so that *goals* will emerge for the child (as opposed to providing new materials with but relatively little guidance from the teacher).

Kohler (1973) examined the effects of private open schools and private traditional schools on upper middle class students ranging in age from nine to thirteen. Data were collected in three open schools (126 students) and three traditional schools (153 students). The openness of each teacher in the participating schools was rated on the *Walberg-Thomas Observation Scale* and a *Teacher Questionnaire*. Both the questionnaire and observation instruments showed a significant difference between the two groups of schools. The *Sears Self-Concept Inventory* was also used.

In general, self-concept scores for students did not differ as a function of being in an open or traditional classroom. However, boys in open classrooms were found to register higher self-concept than girls. Furthermore, these boys' self-concept scores exceeded those of boys enrolled in the traditional program.

The findings fit in nicely with data reported previously, that boys may be helped by programs of individualization. However, what is not clear is whether or not such gains come at the expense of depressed self-concept scores of girls.

Furthermore, significant differences on total self-concept score were found to exist *among* open schools and *among* traditional schools. Again, it is clear that open schools vary widely in their programs and in their effects on children.

After identifying the two schools (one traditional, one open) where the highest self-concept scores were found, Kohler attempted to identify the processes relevant to self-concept development by analyzing the observed process measures, comparing these effective schools with the less effective ones.

The author reports his findings in a verbal (no data) form, as follows: the most notable characteristics present in both the open and traditional classrooms in the effective schools were *appropriate expectations* for the children and *clearly defined and enforced rules* for what should not be done. In contrast, rules in other schools seemed to indicate what could be done. The minimum and open-rule arrangement seemed to curb needless managerial conversations, so that teachers and children had more time for general conversation. The other three characteristics that marked both the open and traditional effective schools were mutual respect and acceptance, honesty of relationships, and a demand for excellence. These observational findings are interesting but hard to evaluate without data. However, they are consistent with Coopersmith's (1967) work indicating that home environments associated with the development of high self-concepts have the following characteristics: clear *structure* and enforced *limits; freedom* to explore and to improvise within the limits; and an overarching expression of *respect* and *encouragement.* Perhaps appropriate structure, respect, and high expectations are associated with students who develop healthy self-concepts. However, more detailed *process* studies will be needed to verify these assumptions, and of course data reporting the effects on student self-concept scores when teacher expression of structure, respect, and expectations are altered will be most useful.

What then do the data in the Kohler study suggest? First it seems apparent that schools serving upper middle class students differ in their impact on students' self-concept scores. Openness as such has no influence on the self-concept scores of students in general, but boys appear to benefit from participation in open education more than girls. However, open schools differ from one another (as do traditional schools), and there were considerable differences in self-concept scores *among* open schools. Finally, it has been suggested that four characteristics mark schools that are effective (as measured by student self-concept): structure, respect, authenticity, and high academic expectations. Apparently these four qualities *can* be exhibited in either *traditional* or *open* arrangements. Kohler's idea to study schools which had similar high effects on students but which differed in educational philosophy was an exciting effort. Such work may eventually lead to the identification of *core* teacher behaviors and attitudes that have impact on students across varied teaching situations.

Conclusion

We have seen that the terms *individualized* and *open* mean different things. Thus, it is important to determine the precise qualities of "openness" if data are to be interpreted correctly. This is especially so because results show that individualized programs and open programs are neither universally successful nor unsuccessful. If those features of openness that correlate with student gains are to be discovered, greater attention must be focused on defining the particular operating features of open programs and on the use of more sophisticated observational systems. Observational systems must go beyond simple frequency counts to provide qualitative data on interaction variables and describe task demands in detail.

In general, studies of individualization have been found to be associated with greater cognitive gain and affective growth (when there are differences) than control classrooms. Unfortunately, such studies have seldom been examined for possible effects on subgroups of students or to see the effects of special contextual circumstances. However there are several studies to suggest that boys are especially likely to benefit from individualized arrangements.

The results reported in the individualization literature fit in nicely with the research on effective teaching that was reviewed in Chapter 4. In particular, individualized systems appear to present teachers with the opportunity to vary instructional style and to have more time to work with individuals or small groups of students. As was noted in Chapter 4, more teacher time with individual students is often found to correlate with student achievement *if* teachers use the time to focus on academic tasks in their private contacts with students and can give children their undivided attention when they interact with them. Clearly, teachers need managerial skills if they are to create a situation that allows them time for sustained personalized contacts with individual students. The fact that some individual programs show more effects than others is probably due to differential teacher capacity for articulating a basic curriculum structure, focusing upon academic tasks with small groups of students, and providing students with appropriate, responsive feedback.

We suggest that individualization carried to the extreme may do more harm than good. As Lipson (1974) has argued, *group* lessons, activity, and responsibility often give a learning activity importance. Students who continue to do their own unique lesson plan day after day may do more poorly than students who receive a balance of unique and shared assignments. We offer this conclusion as hypothesis; not fact. However, the fact that individualized programs have had but moderate effects may reside in the fact that an optimum balance between individual and group activity has not been achieved. Only intensive studies of *effective* individualized classrooms will provide detailed information about desirable process behaviors.

Also needed are detailed process studies of students who do and do not use open environments effectively. The few data that are available suggest that student personality variables may be as important in predicting their success as their aptitudes. Clearly if this is the case, teachers may need to work more frequently with some students than others.

Openness has not had as impressive a "box score" as individualization. (Recall that individualization is but one index of openness.) Here, too, researchers have tended to study openness without dimensionalizing the concept. No doubt, some aspects of openness (like student evaluation of his own work) will be correlated with some outcome measures, but not others. Student characteristics and contextual systems will vary with openness in complex ways, such that openness *per se* is neither good nor bad. Especially important are fuller descriptions of the student population in open schools. For example, Newton and Hall (1974) note that there are at least two types of students whose parents seek out open settings: achievement-oriented and students who have had previous problems in school. Information about the motivations and expectations of students as well as their sex, aptitude, and personality are important if we are to sort out those students who are most likely to benefit from particular open programs.

It also has been noted that architecturally open programs do not appear to be superior to open programs that are mounted in converted traditional schools. Indeed, some critics have suggested that architecturally open schools may make it difficult for moderate-sized instructional groups to meet even when it is desirable to do so. *Thus, there are no data to support the billions of dollars that no doubt will be spent on architecturally open classrooms.*

Furthermore, we see that structure does not prevent the expression of curiosity, and indeed it may be necessary if children are to feel free to be creative. For some time, educators have been discussing the need for a "match" between task demand and ability. Perhaps structural balance is needed if affective and self-assertive growth are to be maintained. Moderate demands on student planning and curriculum design seem much more appropriate than schools that force students to make too many decisions.

We have also noticed that the affective responses of older elementary children appear to be more favorable than those of younger elementary children. Perhaps the needs (both affective and cognitive) are such that moderate levels of adult supervision and goal setting are both preferable and necessary. Indeed, there are some data to show that the absence of structure is correlated positively with fatigue levels for young children. Whatever the cause, there is some tendency for younger children to be less satisfied with open programs than older elementary students.

Here, too, the findings fit in nicely with the literature reviewed in Chapter 4. Indirect teaching seems more appropriate to students who have mastered basic skills and who are capable of assuming responsibility for their own learning. This responsibility is learned by exposure to situations that gradually demand more self-assertion and direction. Contact with an individual teacher or teachers who carefully monitor children's progress on these dimensions is essential if the appropriate structure as well as appropriate content are to be identified. Indirectness, openness, and other student-centered forms of instruction assume implicitly that students possess tool skills and independent work habits. Until students possess these qualities, direct teaching and some degree of structuring appear to be necessary and desirable.

Many educational critics have argued that a fundamental problem with public schooling in America is that it sorts children into losers and winners. Furthermore, such branding is so pervasive that it needlessly reduces cognitive and affective (for instance, self-esteem) potential of many children. Mastery learning and criterion-referenced systems have been constructed, partly in the attempt to "humanize" schools (among other things, to de-emphasize invidious comparisons between children). In the next chapter we will take up the general topic of affective development, examine data describing the noncognitive effects of schools on pupils, and discuss general problems in measuring noncognitive variables.

Chapter 9 Measuring Noncognitive Variables

Much of the criticism directed toward schools in the late 1960s and early 1970s dealt with their lack of responsiveness to the day-to-day psychological needs of students. In addition to their failure to meet the cognitive needs of *some* students, it was charged that schools were boring, uninspiring places where the affective needs of *all* students went unsatisfied.

Schools coerced and controlled student behavior, denying the expression of free will, said some critics. Other critics emphasized the fact that the evaluation system guaranteed that some students would be rejected by classmates as inferior, ultimately setting up caste systems. In sum, schools were labeled as inhuman.

Descriptive criticism was soon followed by prescriptive comments: "Schools *should* help children to gain respect for individual differences." "Schools *should* allow students to do as they please." "Children *should* have the right to make errors and learn from such errors." The fact that some goals might be incompatible (e.g. children learn from errors more easily and quickly through adult intervention; young children naturalistically expect everyone to be similar and *don't* respect differences) was seldom considered, and the fact that no research base existed for these recommendations was ignored.

It was widely assured that the *now qualities* of schooling (schools should be fun, interesting), greater *social growth* (communicative skills, tolerance for individual differences) and unique *expressiveness* (creativity, problem solving) would be accomplished in individualized classrooms *or* open classrooms (depending upon the critic).

Interest in the noncognitive dimensions of classrooms became popular in the early 1970s. For example, many more papers dealing with affective aspects of education were read at meetings of the American Educational Research Association (AERA) during the 1970s than at meetings in the mid-1960s.

Others, too, have noted this interest in affective growth. Coopersmith and Feldman (1974) report that, in the past 10 years, over 500 studies have been completed on self-concept and self-esteem variables in educational settings. Furthermore, interest in affective measurement also has mushroomed at the preschool level (*Phi Delta Kappan*, News Note, 1973, *54*, 568). Yet another signal of interest is the fact that states are beginning to include affective measures in state assessment programs (see Chapter 6). To illustrate the breadth of affective topics being studied by educational researchers, a few of the topics presented at the 1973 AERA meeting appear below:

Teacher genuineness
Teacher-offered conditions of respect
Vocational expectations of preschool children
Effect of feedback on aesthetic judgment
Experimental curriculum to modify sex role perception and aspiration
Criteria used by children to justify their affective responses to art experiences
Effects of interpersonal skill-training on the social climates of elementary school classes
Effects of student-centered curriculum upon racial attitudes
Participation in student activities
New measures of noncognitive performance
Psychosocial and moral elements in curriculum theory
Social behavior in preschoolers
Self-concept enhancement of preschool children
Use of nonverbal warmth to increase learning
Modification of low self-concept

The precise cause of the wide interest in open education is impossible to fix, but the growing awareness of open education in Britain was no doubt a major factor, as was the simmering dissatisfaction with traditional schooling.

The *search* for ways to improve schooling is always a necessary, useful process. However, in the early 1970s prescriptions were written in some instances without complete diagnoses. Openness was indiscriminately and widely applied, but without a carefully articulated program of research and development. As we saw in the preceding chapter, openness has not brought about sweeping changes in student achievement or attitudes toward school. Open schools no doubt are a viable alternative for students, but research to date has *not* provided information about what teacher behaviors and instructional patterns maximize cognitive or affective growth in open settings.

We do not mean to suggest that the schools' emphasis upon affective education was or is inappropriate. Indeed, we too suspect that some schools are filled with needless frustration, failure, and boredom. But our point is that a research base should precede widespread innovations, so that "progress" can be planned and evaluated meaningfully and so that we can learn when and how classrooms (open or traditional) improve school learning for different types of students.

The purpose of this chapter is to describe what is known about noncognitive variables in schools. Were the critics right? Do students experience different feelings toward school or class in different schools or classrooms? Do positive feelings improve classroom achievement? Are teachers aware of how students feel about school? What measures are available for looking at affective growth? How can a school or teacher learn more about its (his) effects upon students' affective growth? What type of research needs to be done if we are to identify the types of environments that will support both affective and cognitive growth?

Are Schools Inhuman?

There are distressing, documented reports to show some of the problems that exist in schools. For example, Hamachek (1972) reminds us that one-third of the students who enter first grade do not complete the eleventh grade. Surely for many of these students, school cannot be a fulfilling enterprise. Branan (1972) asked college students to recall their most negative life experiences, and found that students most frequently recalled unpleasant *school* experiences, such as humiliation. However, when one considers the vast amounts of time that students spend in school, perhaps Branan's study is not so disturbing. How frequently do such experiences occur? For example, if he had asked students to recount the moment when they were most proud or satisfied, would school have been mentioned with similar frequency?

There are some data to suggest that students on opposite ends of the achievement scale report divergent teacher attitudes toward them. Morrison and McIntyre (1969) state that 73 percent of low achievers feel that teachers think poorly of them, whereas only 10 percent of high achievers report such feelings.

Perhaps the best description of student attitudes toward school appears in Philip Jackson's (1968) book *Life in Classrooms*. He concludes that students do not feel strongly (either positively or negatively) about schools. When students respond to global questions about school, they generally indicate an underlying *passive acceptance* of school.

Others, too, have reached that conclusion. For example, Tenenbaum (1940) asked students to describe their attitudes toward school in anonymous essays, and only 20 percent of the students indicated dislike for school. Boys were more likely than girls to express dissatisfaction. However, Tenenbaum noted that most of the positive essays lacked gusto. Although students accepted school, there was no consistent sign of intense satisfaction or involvement.

Jackson notes that results similar to Tenenbaum's appear with regularity across different student age groups and across varying socioeconomic levels. Data drawn from different time periods also yield similar patterns. Thus, until the dawn of "openness," only 20 percent of students in the schools sampled by investigators expressed dissatisfaction, and these students were more likely to be male. (For a full discussion of sex differences in behavior and attitudes toward school, see Brophy and Good, 1974.)

Jackson makes the point that a student could dislike *many* aspects of school, but still use a positive rather than a neutral or negative descriptor if forced to describe his *overall* feelings toward school. For example, Jackson and Getzels (1959) administered a 60-item version of the *Student Opinion Poll* in an affluent private school, and found the mean score to be 37.3 with a standard deviation of 9.57. On the average, students expressed dissatisfaction on almost 40 percent of the items. Thus, students who have a generally positive orientation toward school can and do have specific complaints about schooling.

Teacher differences were also noted in the Jackson review. Of most interest is the fact that teachers vary in their ability to "satisfy" students. For example, Jackson reports that administration of a 47-item version of the *Student Opinion Poll* in 10 sixth grade classrooms in a suburban school yielded a wide range of scores. Classroom means ranged from 21.44 to 31.00 on the attitude instrument, despite the homogeneous student sample.

Others, too, have noted that teachers have different effects. Tschechtelin, Kipskind and Remmers (1940) report highly significant differences among individual teachers. Also, recent studies of classroom climates (as perceived by students) show large differences between schools (Sadker, Sadker, and Cooper, 1973; Walker, 1971). Thus, *teachers are perceived differently by students*. It seems safe to conclude that all schools were not as barren as many critics claimed. Indeed some schools consistently have worked well. We believe that comprehensive study of such schools and classrooms would have been more helpful than the indiscriminant call for sweeping changes in the organization pattern of schooling. To reiterate, data collected at various times in various school settings during the last thirty years suggest that students in general see schooling experience as "O.K." (with most exceptions arising from *some* low achievement students and *some* inner city schools), but students do see differences in their teachers (large differences in some cases).

Beyond this point, there are few data. For example, little is known about how teachers achieve highly positive scores (more on this later) or about whether or not a teacher's ability to produce high affect scores is a stable characteristic across years. Also, the stability of students' attitudes across consecutive years (with different teachers) is unknown. Do students form a rigid view toward school? At present some research is being conducted on the stability of teacher influence on affective scores over consecutive years and on the general relationship between cognitive and affective effects (Good and Grouws, 1974; Peck and Veldman, 1973).

It would seem that some teachers, especially those who are rated very high or very low in general rapport by their students, are stable in their effects (students' reaction to the teacher and the classroom environment) over consecutive years. However, many teachers (and the classroom environment) appear to vary widely from year to year in the eyes of their students (Good and Grouws, 1974). Clearly, much more work is needed to identify the characteristics of teachers who have stable high and low rapport and to understand factors that cause such scores to fluctuate.

Attitudes and Achievement: Any Necessary Connection?

Simple one-to-one relationships between global attitudes that students hold toward school and achievement on standardized achievement tests do not appear to exist. Jackson reviews a variety of studies showing (with but one exception) little or no relationship between achievement and global attitudes. This 1968 review is augmented by a recent, nicely controlled study of teachers teaching the same subject matter in experimental short courses. Here, the relationship between achievement and student ratings was found to be very weak (Potter, Nalin, and Lewandowski, 1973).

Jackson suggests one possible explanation in an attempt to explain the lack of relationship: Students don't hold strong reactions to schools, so that attitudes would have to be extreme to interact with achievement. However, an additional explanation comes to mind. Perhaps global attitudes are simply too diffuse to serve as predictors.

This possibility is a simple, straightforward idea. For example, a global attitude of "Hostility Toward Minority Group Members" may not predict a hotel manager's behavior when he meets a clean shaven "minority group member" face to face. Similarly, the global and accurate student attitude "I dislike school" may not predict student achievement; the student learns because he dislikes losing his allowance or to spite the teacher. But, perhaps more to the point, there are many reasons to like school (opportunity to meet girls, chance to letter in a sport, and so on), so that liking school or liking a particular subject may not be related to the achievement aspects of schooling (for instance, liking for a particular class may be due to easy tests, no homework). Similarly, students may dislike school because they are called eggheads or worse, or because school work does not challenge them, but still may pull good marks.

It is clear that a simple relationship does not exist between global measures of school attitude (general like or dislike) and school achievement. Will specific attitudes predict achievement? We now turn to an examination of this question.

Attitudes: Another Look

Gable and Roberts (1973) reviewed Jackson's summary and other research. They, too, were perplexed by the lack of strong relationships between student attitudes and achievement, and they devised a study to see if more specific attitudes would be associated with school grades. It revealed that motivation toward school work correlated significantly with grades. In this study, then, a favorable predisposition toward the academic, work-related dimensions of schooling was associated with grades.

Some promise for the possibility of using student work attitudes as a predictor of grades is suggested in the Gable and Roberts study. Several standardized study-habit inventories exist, but, as Mehrens and Lehmann (1973) note, such inventories seldom have demonstrated that the study habit score in combination with previous grades predicts grades any better than previous grades alone. Nevertheless, the Gable and Roberts study suggests that study habits or work attitudes may be associated with good school performance. Expansions and replications of this research are needed, particularly to see if intervention with teachers and/or students could raise attitude scores (and then to see if the quality of student work rises concomitantly).

This is not to suggest that attitudes *per se* are important only if they predict or correlate positively with achievement. Indeed, we feel that student attitudes are important goals in and of themselves. Students should feel that school is an "O.K." place to be and that teachers respect them. However, this does not necessarily mean that students should perceive school as more fun than after-school activities! Indeed, high levels of student satisfaction may even be incompatible with the development of cognitive and affective skills that depend upon perseverance and occasional frustration. More information is needed about the general relationship between attitudes and achievement, especially to see whether there is a core of common teacher behaviors or structural characteristics of the classroom (for self-pacing, etc.) which supports both goals, or if, instead, choices and compromises between these two goals have to be made.

Other Affective Variables and Achievement

Some affective feelings other than attitudes toward school (either global or specific) have been found to relate to achievement. A study by Kifer (1973) is a good illustration of this point. Kifer designed his study to test Bloom's (1972) argument that students who meet school expectations develop healthy personalities, while those who fail exhibit signs of emotional difficulty. That is, he asked whether students who are regularly successful in school come to view themselves as competent and capable *because* they successfully meet schools demands.

Kifer identified success in terms of school grades, and identified groups of male and female students who had distinctly successful or unsuccessful school records. Students were selected from second, fourth, sixth, and eighth grade classrooms. Student affective characteristics measured included self-esteem, self-concept, and locus of control.

The point of this design was to see if consistent patterns of success (or failure) have a cumulative effect on the affective traits of learners. The data show that more positive affect scores are associated with higher achievement, and that other differences (in general) *increase over age levels*. Thus, affective measures other than general attitudes toward school (self-value, "can do" feelings, and a realistic self-view) are associated with school success.

Interestingly, Kifer selected from grades five and seven a sample of students who varied across the full achievement range (rather than just highly successful or unsuccessful students) to test for positive relationships between school achievement and affective scores. Positive relationships were generally observed, and there were stronger relationships among seventh grade students than fifth graders. These results are consistent with findings reviewed earlier suggesting that affective variables may be more closely associated with the achievement of older than younger children.

Positive self-esteem, self-concept of ability, and internal locus of control were all associated with successful achievement. The work of Kifer needs to be replicated in longitudinal research, but nonetheless his study strongly suggests that good affective self-views are the products of successful mastery of school tasks. Some longitudinal research following preschool graduates into elementary schools suggests a similar pattern: positive affective feelings about *self* were found to be the products of successful academic experiences (Weikart, 1971). However, there is also reason to believe that positive self-views, once established, exert influence upon achievement patterns. For example, Wattenburg and Clifford (1964) found that self-concept scores of kindergarten children were a better predictor of reading achievement performance (measured two-and-a-half years later) than were intelligence tests.

Of additional interest in the Kifer study is that parental concern (as reported by the students) was positively related to students' affective responses at all achievement levels. Similar data have been reported elsewhere. For example, Sears (1970) noted that self-concept scores of twelve-year-old students were related to home events present when the students were five years old. A great deal of data have been collected, largely self-report, describing the behaviors of parents of children who subsequently develop realistic, healthy levels of self-esteem. McCandless and Evans (1973) summarize the data this way: "High self-esteem seems to result when parents are concerned, warm, set clear limits, employ praise as a major control technique, and allow wide latitude to the child as he pursues approved goals." (p. 420)

The above statement is based upon a variety of correlational research, and hence cannot be viewed as an experimentally established fact. However, the sheer repetition of these findings by investigators differing in theoretical and methodological orientation is impressive (Brophy, Good, and Nedler, 1975). Much less is known about the behaviors of teachers or the characteristics of classrooms or schools that correlate with student self-esteem.

A Note on Affective Development

Affective development apparently proceeds in the same fashion as cognitive development. That is, initially we learn about ourselves through concrete experiences and feedback from others. Gradually we form a concept of what we are, what we can and cannot do, and, ultimately, our general worth. The initial self-view is highly dependent upon the quality of early life experiences.

For example, infants who are constantly prevented from exploring their surroundings will implicitly learn to look for others to sanction or initiate behavior. Similarly children who are unduly impressed by their parents' preoccupation with "what others think" are also likely to be excessively concerned about pleasing others.

Children develop attitudes about their ability to achieve generally in similar fashion, and if these initial feelings are reinforced by school success or failure, then a reciprocal pattern of confidence and achievement is initiated. Such patterns are difficult to change once established.

Interestingly, as we noted above, several different researchers attempting to study the home conditions that produce successful children (children who feel good about themselves and others) have reached highly similar conclusions. To reiterate, these studies target the following parent behaviors as important: (1) complete acceptance of the child, (2) clear standards and expectations for the child, (3) respect and latitude for child initiative within defined limits. Possible implications of these findings for classroom behavior will be discussed later in the chapter.

However, here we would like to express two relevant general assumptions. First, an emphasis upon affective development does not necessarily mean time away from curriculum content. Factors that influence affective growth (appropriate structure, feedback, and so on) also influence or at least are not incompatible with cognitive development. Second, affective growth, like cognitive growth, depends upon a sensible blending of what an individual can do and the new demands that are placed upon him. Few teachers would assign a story demanding a seventh grade reading ability to a child reading at the second grade level. However, teachers often provide students with too much or too little structure in learning assignments. Too little or too much direction diminishes progress. Thus, we suspect that in any school arrangement students will show wide differences in their ability to evaluate their own efforts, to design self-study units, to use the teacher as a resource person, just as students differ in their achievement level.

We suggest that, in the absence of new evidence, a reasonable hypothesis for the preschool and early elementary school years is that behaviors similar to those observed in parents of high self-esteem children will be most conducive to growth. Individualization allowing for structured progress, *coupled* with warm teacher-child relationships, appear to be prerequisite for *both* affective and achievement growth.

School Influence

Kifer's study would suggest that schools can influence certain affective variables (self-concept, internality). More support for the notion that school experience can influence self-concept development is provided by Torshen's (1973) finding that grades correlate with self-concept scores independent of achievement scores. Hence grades seem to communicate a sense of self-worth. More direct evidence is provided by Tuta and Baker's (1973) study of preschool children from varying socioeconomic backgrounds who did or did not attend nursery school. They found that students who attended nursery school had higher self-concept scores at the end of the year than students who did not attend nursery school. Thus, there is some fragmentary evidence that at some levels schools may be able to enhance self-concept development. Such evidence is of clear importance in the sense that it seems necessary to show that schools can and do influence the particular affective variable of interest *before* it becomes a standard school goal. For a broader discussion of how the teacher can attempt to influence students' self-esteem, see Coopersmith and Feldman (1974).

Teacher Behavior and Noncognitive Student Gain

Little definitive research on the relationship between teacher behavior and noncognitive student gain is available. The reasons for the lack of useful information in this area (and in any attempt to relate teaching behavior to student outcome measures) have been set forth in Chapter 3. A chief problem is that teachers, classrooms, or schools have not been picked because of their ability to produce high scores on various noncognitive measures. Thus, in the typical study there is no good reason to believe that the teachers under study were highly effective in producing noncognitive gains. An additional problem is that many noncognitive outcome variables have not been collected in the same design in which comprehensive measures of teacher–student interaction were also collected. One of the few noncognitive areas that has often been studied with accompanying information about teacher and/or student behavior is student attitude toward school. Unfortunately we have already seen that global attitudes of students do not predict achievement. Let's see what is known about the relationship between teacher behavior and student attitudes.

Rosenshine (1973) does a reanalysis of five studies previously reported by Flanders (1969), and shows that in these separate studies, the unadjusted post-scores of student attitudes consistently and moderately correlated with teacher indirectness and warmth. In one of these studies three sets of student attitude data were available. In general, the original findings of Flanders and the secondary analysis by Rosenshine suggest that teacher indirectness and praise were positively associated with student attitudes and critical teacher statements were negatively correlated with student attitudes across all three administrations. However, Dunkin and Biddle (1974) caution that higher indirectness scores are not correlated with higher student attitudes *ipso facto*.

The Dunkin and Biddle review provides independent support for the positive effects of teacher praise and the damaging effects of criticism on student attitudes. However, they note that *frequency* of praise does not consistently correlate with high student attitudes. Instead it is the *appropriate use* of praise (effectively delivered reinforcing teacher behavior after students have performed an appropriate behavior) and the absence of excessive or abusive use of criticism that seems to make a difference. These results also remind us of the Brophy and Evertson (1973b) and Soar (1972) results: Too much or too little praise is ineffective in promoting cognitive achievement. Thus, to promote both cognitive and affective growth, an appropriate *hypothesis* would seem to suggest *moderate* and *appropriate* use of praise as a reinforcer.

Another variable that appears central to both attitude development and achievement is the interchangeable teacher comment (see Chapter 4 or Aspy, 1973). Hearing what students have to say (and expressing interest to students) is no doubt a direct way of expressing to students that "I accept you," and acceptance by others appears to be a fundamental prerequisite to self-acceptance. The effect of interchangeable teacher comments upon student achievement was reviewed in Chapter 4. There is indirect evidence that such teacher behavior may be related to student attitudes as well. For example, DeCharms (1968) provides data to show that students in experimental settings have more positive attitudes toward teachers when they incorporate student suggestions. We'll expand these points below.

Some Hypotheses about Affective Development

More is known about the teacher's role in promoting cognitive than affective development. Little has been learned about classroom practice and the affective growth of students because there have been few *comprehensive* attempts to study these two classes of variables simultaneously. Even when substantial amounts of teacher–student interaction data are collected, typically only teacher interaction with the entire class is coded (rather than the behavior extended to individual students or subgroups of students). This practice makes it impossible to relate affective student responses to the teacher behavior students actually receive (or perceive) in the classroom.

However there is much indirect evidence (for example, from studies of parent-child interaction) to suggest that teachers can make a difference in the affective development of their students. It is beyond the scope of this chapter to provide an extended discussion of these promising variables (for extended discussions see Good and Brophy, 1973; Brophy and Good, 1974; Coopersmith and Feldman, 1974), but we do want to make a few statements here to convey the "flavor" of this literature.

Structure in the Classroom

For inexplicable reasons, many educators automatically associate creativity, affective growth, self-confidence, and so on with discovery, and student centered and/or structureless learning. As we noted above, reasonable structure appears to be necessary for substantial growth, either affective or cognitive. Reasonable structure depends upon the capabilities of the individual student. For instance, the student who cannot design and complete a one-day unit is *not* going to design a successful one-week unit.

Given the vast individual differences that exist among students, there is ample need for direct teaching in open settings and for indirect teaching in traditional settings.

Student completion of an assignment suggested by the teacher is of no more or less value *per se* than the completion of a student selected assignment, although in individual cases it may be possible to make distinctions concerning the value of work assignments. But the point here is that the *form* of a learning activity (student selected versus teacher selected, individual versus group, written report versus oral report) does *not* provide a measure of *quality.*

Expectations control behavior and may lead to self-defeating patterns of classroom behavior. We feel the *appropriate* expectation is that varying degrees of structure are needed in the same classroom. To strike the appropriate balance for students or groups of students, it will be necessary to observe, to listen, and to examine their progress (more on this later).

Affective Growth and Achievement

We have seen that global attitudes of students do not predict their school achievement. However, there is some evidence to suggest that students' views of themselves as *learners* are intimately related to school progress. Hence, individual feelings of mastery, "can do" attitudes, and willingness to share and work with others can be achieved without loss to cognitive goals. Other affective areas (school as fun, attitudes toward drugs, sex education) may come only at the expense of cognitive gains.

However, the basic affective dimensions discussed above may not be well achieved, and may even impede cognitive progress if they are taught independently of day-to-day life in the clasroom. Events that students see and experience daily (as opposed to special teaching exercises and the like) are most likely to influence their affective progress.

Teacher Behavior and Student Performance

It has been pointed out that acceptance of self is at least partially dependent upon acceptance by others (Coopersmith and Feldman, 1974). As was mentioned in Chapter 4, teachers' ability to *listen* (interchangeable responses) and to *communicate* what they have heard to the student is an important skill. Such behavior explicitly demonstrates that the teacher cares, and this is one form of acceptance. Other basic ways in which the teacher may communicate interest in and acceptance of students are: *private conversations; solicitation of student ideas; integrating student ideas into the curriculum; explaining why suggestions are rejected or delayed;* and generally *modeling respect for individuals and interest in learning.*

Teachers who consistently model the expectation that all individuals learn in their own unique way and at their own pace will be more likely to have students *look* at their performance and accept it than teachers who stress relative comparisons between students. However, mere verbalizations will not be effective: Teacher statements have to be linked with teacher behavior. For example, teachers who leave students in the same group for the entire year or who never give individualized assignments will do little to promote the idea that individuals can proceed in their own way.

Teacher reaction to student performance is an especially powerful influence on student behavior. Overreaction (positive or negative) will lead some students to focus on pleasing or avoiding the teacher. Teachers who hope to encourage students to *look* at their behavior openly and undefensively must consistently communicate the fact that feedback (whether about classroom behavior or work productivity) is simply information that the teacher and student use jointly in planning for optional growth. Teachers who consistently react to students and their performance in this manner will do much to create an atmosphere in which students can look at their own behavior without invidious comparisons between their performance and the performance of others.

Simply put, the call is for teacher behavior that says *I see you and you're okay* (and then "you can do better" statements). Students who have experienced much failure often get feedback (from parents and teachers) that say *you can do better* (and when you do I'll be proud of you). Statements which do not communicate acceptance, or which delay it, are likely to backfire by encouraging students to develop complex strategies for looking good in the classroom. Much student time that could be better utilized in the active study of course material goes into avoiding being "caught."

Thus, with these students, teachers need to demonstrate that they *see* their behavior and implicitly to suggest that it does not frighten, annoy, or disappoint them, thereby encouraging the students to look at their behavior rather than attempt to cover it up. If students are to focus on their behavior, teachers must help them by providing objective feedback coupled with positive attempts to engage the student in thought and action to improve. For example, the teacher might say "I've noticed that on the last two spelling tests your scores have been 40 percent and 45 percent. Clearly you're getting some of the words right and making progress, but what can we do to get the percentage up to 60?" Such discussion might lead to the student keeping a record of study time, to changes in teacher behavior, and so on.

Too often, teacher feedback discourages students from self-examination. Statements such as "If only you would try" are likely to encourage the student to continue feigning indifference, because at a minimum such behaviors *protect him from failure,* and they may be very reinforcing (implicitly the teacher is saying "You're really very bright"). Teachers who model their acceptance of student performance (I see you. I know where you are at. It's not good, but it *can* and needs to be improved), model behavior for attacking a problem, help students set goals, and *actively* help students to work out procedures for accomplishing these goals, will do much to help students look at themselves and ultimately accept themselves. This requires a combination of acceptance and the communication of performance expectations. Both acceptance and demandingness are essential for student growth, but acceptance must precede demandingness.

Similarly, teachers who exhort the value of learning with others will extend their credibility by showing that they learn from others too. (They can ask another teacher to teach a unit, make reference to a recently read article, or ask students for information.) Finally, by providing *all* students the chance to learn from others (peer tutoring, group learning assignments), they can help students to gain respect for fellow classmates; to succeed, they must help students to *see* one another. Typically, this can be accomplished in normal classroom activities (students interview classmates for articles in the class paper, and so on).

Contact with other students is a necessary condition if respect is to be developed for students who differ in sex, ethnicity, aptitude, or personality. However, contact alone is unlikely to change attitudes. Much experimental (nonclassroom) literature suggests that *shared responsibility* is a necessary condition for changing attitudes. When people depend upon others and joint responsibilities are successfully performed, attitudes change. Students who have the chance to engage in joint tutoring or learning activities have the opportunity to broaden their respect for others. Interestingly, peer tutoring provides two additional advantages: First, the literature on peer tutoring consistently suggests that both tutor and tutee make more cognitive gains in the subject under study than do control students; second, teachers can spend time with selected individual students while most class members participate in tutoring or group activities. Again, we see that it is possible to tie certain affective goals directly to the curriculum.

Indeed, we would argue that if two critical affective goals are to be accomplished (belief and acceptance of self as a learner and respect for others) it must be by integrating these two goals into the curriculum. Teachers help to "teach" respect for self through the continual display of *genuine* and appropriate behavior toward students in normal, routine activities. So too, mutual respect grows by exposure to conditions that demand trust and allow responsibility to be reciprocally fulfilled.

Again, the notion of structure or teacher involvement is important. Students who are placed in situations where joint responsibilities are not fulfilled may show reduced rather than enhanced respect for others. Students benefit from a teacher *modeling* (for instance the teacher demonstrates tutoring behavior, solving problems, and so on, with a student while the class watches) and from direct supervision in their attempts to establish group goals and procedures. Progressively, of course, teacher involvement is reduced as students develop the capacities for directing their own behavior.

The behaviors called for here are complex and impossible to plan without reference to a particular group of students. For example, teachers are called upon to individualize parts of the curriculum but at the same time to provide for meaningful group experiences. Overemphasis upon one form of learning will depress gains in the other area. Furthermore, the balance changes as children grow older (during the same year as well as in subsequent years) and develop more self-supervision skills. However, if teachers are to err, it probably is better to have too much rather than too little structure, especially for younger children. Still, as children demonstrate ability to manage aspects of their environment, they need the opportunity to expand and to grow. However, these are our inferences from a sketchy data base, and they need to be tested systematically through appropriate research.

Are Any Teachers Outstanding in All Aspects of Teaching?

Cromack (1973) describes one of the few studies attempting to look at effective teaching, using, simultaneously, both cognitive and affective student measures as criteria. Cromack noted that Gage (1963) had listed criteria for evaluating the immediate consequences of teaching, and that the first two were (1) pupil achievement of current educational objectives and (2) pupil satisfaction with the teacher. Cromack employed these two criteria for classifying the effectiveness of 17 public school teachers who had presented 20-minute micro-lessons to public school students in an experimental situation. Teachers' effectiveness in producing cognitive gain was defined by rank-ordering class mean scores on the five-item achievement test that was administered at the end of the unit. Teachers' affective effectiveness was defined by rank-ordering mean student satisfaction scores. Student satisfaction scores were obtained by asking students to rate 12 dimensions of teacher behavior by responding "yes," "sometimes," or "no" to items such as: gives directions that are clear and easy to understand; shames and embarrasses some students; spends time helping each of us with his special problems; tries to find things that we are "good at" rather than "poor at"; causes us to be afraid to ask and to answer questions, and so forth.

In this study teacher effectiveness was defined as the ability to promote student achievement and to satisfy students. Teachers who were high on one ranking (among the top six) and high or at least in the middle on the other ranking were classified as effective teachers. Thus, effectiveness in the study was a multidimensional but *relative* concept. The extent to which these teachers were effective in an absolute sense is unknown.

The purpose of defining relatively effective teachers in the study was to see if teachers who were effective on both criteria taught the videotaped units differently from teachers who were relatively low on the combined rankings. The strongest process variable was *positive reinforcement* behavior (*p* less than .10). Teachers who were high on one dimension and at least moderate on the other used praise more frequently than the others. Again, we see some evidence that effective praise is a teacher behavior related to both cognitive and affective gains.

Interestingly, the correlation between achievement and satisfaction ranks was not reported. Our own analysis of the two sets of rankings reveal a Spearman Rho correlation of .04. Thus, in this study there was no relationship between a teacher's ability to produce cognitive and affective gains. But despite these low correlations there is some evidence in the Cromack data to support the belief that high affective and cognitive gains can co-occur (although his data also strongly suggest that such co-occurrence, without training, may be rare). An examination of the rankings revealed that two of the teachers were in the "top six" on both rankings. Separate analyses of these two teachers' *behavior* would be useful. Cromack's idea is a good one, and hopefully other investigators will apply similar strategies to the study of classroom teachers in real settings.

However, given that global measures of student attitude correlate weakly or not at all with student achievement, it may be useful to use other affective criteria for identifying teachers for intensive observation. Perhaps some *combination of gross process measures* (attendance, breakage) coupled with student reports by former pupils (teacher comparisons that have been adjusted for subject-matter popularity) and *student performance records* (improved self-concept *re* school skills) would yield an interesting sample of teachers with sufficient and interesting variance to justify an intensive observational study. It is possible that *direct questioning* of students about teachers' reputations and performance will yield better measures of teachers than has the traditional pattern of measuring students to infer teacher effects.

Other Affective or Expressive Variables

Given that direct research in classroom settings has not identified those teacher behaviors and/or classroom environments that facilitate the affective growth of students, it is *impossible* to hold teachers accountable for the affective growth of their students. To highlight the problem we remind the reader of the Turner-Thompson study discussed in Chapter 4 which showed that the achievement gains of college students and their affective response to the learning environment were negatively correlated! Thus, the present state of research does not provide support for a definitive set of effective teaching behaviors that enhance affective development.

We have presented a few *hypotheses* about affective development and promising teacher behaviors. We have done so because we feel that many of the popular descriptions (structureless learning) are at odds with literature that has been collected outside the classroom (such as infant–parent literature). However these are presented as hypotheses and not facts.

We feel that two basic affective goals (belief and acceptance of self as learner and acceptance of others), as well as minimal acceptance of school, can occur without depressing cognitive gains. Other affective variables probably can be accomplished as well, but we suspect that some (or inclusion of too many) affective goals may depress cognitive gains, because there is only so much time in the curriculum. The relative advantage of selected cognitive or affective gains is a value choice, but a choice we would like to see educators make explicitly with data rather than implicitly without data.

There are numerous affective aspects of schooling, other than student attitudes of satisfaction toward school and self-concepts, that are of potential interest to some teachers, principals, or parents. A few representative "demands" on school are:

> to influence attitudes toward drugs,
> to make better citizens,
> to develop moral behavior,
> to enhance aesthetic appreciation,
> to foster creativity,
> to stimulate curiosity,
> to improve social/communicative skills, and
> to develop vocational awareness and/or job skills.

It is hard to discuss the types of noncognitive variables listed above because little systematic (including detailed measures of *process* behavior) research has been done with any of them. Perhaps the most useful way to proceed with the point would be to raise a series of questions that should be answered about each outcome area before a school is assigned (or assumes!) responsibility for any of the above. It would of course be possible for schools to provide different mixes and allow children and parents to choose their brands.

1. Is the outcome top priority or one of only moderate interest (dropped if it takes resources or time needed for more important goals)?
2. Do instruments exist to measure the outcome variable?
3. Can scores be interpreted in a normative sense?
4. Do schools or classrooms naturalistically show stable *variance* on the outcome measure?
5. If so, what teacher behaviors and/or classroom arrangements are necessary for the development of the behavior? Can teachers perform these behaviors without special training?
6. If schools and/or classrooms naturalistically show little variance on the outcome measure, can schools influence the outcome? If so, by what behaviors? Can teachers perform these behaviors?
7. What is the time required to achieve the outcome?

8. How compatible are the "necessary behaviors" and time and expense associated with achievement of the top three or four goals?

To achieve step one, value clarification would have to take place within the school staff, and preferably within the broader community it serves. Step two was an impossible problem several years ago, when few noncognitive instruments were available, but now it is possible to measure virtually all of the noncognitive variables listed above (more on this later). However, problems similar to those in achievement testing exist. Namely, a school district may not be satisfied with the way curiosity or morality is defined on a test. Probably the biggest test deficiencies today are in higher-order measures of skills being taught in the curriculum and in *refined* noncognitive measures. Many promising noncognitive instruments exist, but few have been fully developed.

Step three is an especially vexing problem in affective measurement. Assume that a teacher or school administers a self-concept test to the students. Reasonable questions to ask include how the students' scores compare with those of students of similar age, socioeconomic status, sex, aptitude, personality. Such instruments have not been utilized in school programs until recently (in contrast to achievement tests), so that good, complete norms do not exist.

In addition to the lack of normative data, it is difficult to interpret the absolute value of a score on an affective measure. In using cognitive tests, we know that the higher the score the better. But this is not necessarily the case with affective instruments. For example, Crier and Carpenter (1973) report that second graders' responses to school are more favorable than those of fifth graders. This does not necessarily mean that schools have failed students, as such results could be interpreted. Crier and Carpenter note that fifth graders are not as enthusiastic to visit friends or go to parties as second graders, either, although it is true that "excitement" for school declines more than for parties or friends.

Noncognitive measures present complex interpretation problems. For example, one would expect students to become more negative towards school as they become older as a natural consequence of greater cognitive differentiation. Parents and other aspects of society also become subject to more criticism. But how much decline is "expected?" When is it excessively low?

Other affective variables show the same problem. In terms of vocational awareness, perhaps schools (or some of them) are better off if they motivate *fewer* students to go on to higher education. Again, the problem is that high scores and goodness are not automatically associated, as they clearly are in the cognitive area.

This is not to discourage the administration of noncognitive measures in school. We feel that the administration of such tests is both necessary and desirable. However, it might be wise to discourage the emphasis upon immediate interpretation of *all* measures. Given the relative newness of many instruments and the lack of norms and information about how various instruments and outcomes interact, it will be some time before the meaning and value of various instruments can be established.

Step four is of course difficult to achieve until instruments are refined (more on this later) but some instruments, for instance, self-concept, school attitudes, and creativity, could be administered reasonably in a schoolwide, systemwide, or statewide testing program. The idea, of course, is not to identify "good" or "bad" schools at this level, but to see if desirable outcomes are occurring in some schools and if these are stable characteristics. Do some schools "outperform" similar schools over consecutive years? If such high-performing schools exist, it would be worth the money to mount intensive observational studies to learn how they achieve such outcomes and then to see if teachers in other systems can perform those behaviors (and, of course, to see if outcome scores then increase in these schools).

If schools do not show naturalistic variance of sufficient magnitude for effective research, planned experimentation will be necessary to see if outcome variables can be influenced (question #6). If such influence is proven to be impossible, schools obviously can't be asked to effect the outcome.

The seventh question is relatively straightforward: How frequently must the behavior or activity be scheduled if outcomes are to be influenced?

Question eight makes the point that if different goals require different or incompatible responses, then school goals must be evaluated and assigned priorities.

Ultimately, through systematic record keeping, a school district could reach a position where (1) specific outcome priorities are known; (2) effective instruments exist for measuring desirable outcomes; (3) a knowledge base exists to explain how outcomes may be influenced and how to manipulate time restraints so that congruent goal outcomes may be attained simultaneously.

Historically, in the course of educational movements, *implementation* almost always *precedes experimentation,* and evaluation research follows. Collecting data in schools and informing the public, school staffs, and the research community about what is happening to the affective growth of students is appropriate and important. Unfortunately, these results *per se* will probably be used to justify program and budget alterations without the second generation of studies (how do teachers get these results?) necessary for building appropriate strategies. We would argue that directors of school system testing programs should demand that a knowledge base be built prior to the implementation of accountability plans, and that professional research organizations and research and development centers help in the process of building such a knowledge base.

Signs of Encouragement

There are some notable signs of growth in measuring noncognitive instruments. Many instruments have been developed in the last five years or so. Now studies are needed to discriminate among existing instruments and develop "best bet" tests into polished instruments with known properties (mean, standard deviation, standard error, and reliability across varying population groups) and predictive validity. Emmerich's (1973) study is an excellent example of the type of synthesizing work that needs to be done. He reports the relative psychometric and administrative merits of a variety of cognitive and noncognitive measures that are being considered for inclusion in the National Follow-Through Evaluation Battery. Extension of this work beyond the first, second, or third grade levels would be desirable.

Researchers at the American Institute for Research have produced some extremely interesting *performance* measures of citizenship. For example, rather than measuring student growth in citizenship with the typical pen and paper test of knowledge, efforts have been made to see if students will demonstrate certain skills and/or values. For example, when a student is placed in group situations with students who hold varying opinions, will he express his opinion? In general, the work seems to be headed toward developing important and useful tests of school effects. After all the appropriate criterion in citizenship and general moral behavior "training" is: "Does it influence behavior?"

Furthermore, richer ways of describing classroom environments continue to be developed. To take but one example, Sadker (1973) reports the development of the Elementary School Environment Survey (ESES), which has passed through several stages, stemming back to the work that Pace (1963) had done at the college level in describing environmental differences between schools. Sadker collected data from 54 elementary schools selected randomly in Massachusetts. Six factors were derived from student responses: alienation, humanism, autonomy, morale, opportunism, and resources.

Thus, ways exist to describe differences in elementary classrooms that could not be distinguished previously. Others, too, have produced or are working on environmental description (see Walker, 1971) for example. And, such developments seem to have substantive value. For example, Sadker (1973) notes the uniqueness of the elementary school level (in contrast to the previous measures of school environment obtained from college students) and the wide variance among schools. Elsewhere, Sadker, Sadker, and Cooper (1973) describe some of the differences between schools (for instance, what happens to school space when the last bell rings . . . immediately closed, used as detention hall, used as extracurricular center?), as well as some of the similarities across schools. For example, 85 percent of pupils feel teachers will raise grades if students work hard, and 85 percent find school to be a friendly place with warm teachers. Recall that this was a representative sample of schools in Massachusetts (only two schools refused to participate).

However, one wonders if high scores on particular factors have identifiable consequences. Do some student "types" enjoy certain environments more than others? Are factor scores stable over time for a particular class or a particular teacher? Are some outcomes more likely to be achieved than others in certain environments? It is only when such questions as these are answered that environmental instruments will have direct application value. At present, such instruments are of use primarily for describing what attitudes and environments do exist in school.

Another example of the attempt to measure the classroom environment through the eyes of students is the Learning Environment Inventory (LEI). The LEI, like other environment instruments, attempts to obtain student reaction to a number of relatively *specific* dimensions in the classroom, not just a global like–dislike score. Interestingly, in several studies LEI scores have been found to be better predictors of student achievement than were intelligence scores! (See Anderson and Walberg, 1974.) A few items from the LEI are presented below to illustrate the types of information that may be useful barometers of classroom life.

> The objectives of the class are specific.
> Class decisions tend to be made by all the students.
> Members of the class don't care what the class does.
> The class is disorganized.
> The class has difficulty keeping up with its assigned work.

The findings reported by Sadker, Sadker, and Cooper above bring us back to where we started this chapter. Large numbers of students (at least at the elementary level) do not hate school and most find it at least an "O.K." experience. However, we also know that variance exists between teachers and schools. Some schools and teachers are described as warmer or friendlier than others. How can a teacher go about finding out the attitudes of his students? We now address this question.

Assessment in the Classroom

Tests to measure student creativity and/or curiosity, student self-concept, and attitudes toward school are available for teachers' usage. If teachers want to know about creativity, curiosity, self-concept, or general attitudes, it is necessary only to administer an existing inventory, after obtaining permission from the principal and permission for use of copyrighted tests. However, in many ways such instruments are more similar at their present stage of development to *standardized survey* achievement tests than they are to *diagnostic* achievement tests. They provide a general score, but they do not specify the mechanisms (that teachers can alter) that underlie the score. Hence, such tests may be appropriate as part of an overall assessment program to find out what attitudes exist, but they do not prescribe teacher behavior.

We have argued that criterion-referenced tests of achievement provide direct information to the teacher about student progress on immediate curriculum-related goals. So, too, may teacher- or school-specific questions yield appropriate survey and diagnostic information. That is, attitude data collected in a teacher's room on specific program dimensions have the potential for providing information that can be used to *improve* the program. For example, it was noted in Chapter 8 that students in one individualized program reported lower attitudes toward school than did control subjects. Furthermore, students in the individualized program reported that they felt they never had time to finish their work. Using these two pieces of information, the researchers hypothesized that the "sameness" of the units was responsible for depressed attitudes.

After reaching this conclusion, two options are now possible. Program officials can (1) alter the program and see if attitudes improve, or (2) collect more information to identify the problem more closely before proceeding with sweeping changes. Remember, it was only *hypothesized* that the sameness of the physical appearance of the units was the problem. Perhaps it was the content *per se,* and providing points of closure. ("You've finished one-third of the unit *program,* congratulations! Today is yours to use in free activity.") would not help. Perhaps social isolation or too much group work is the difficulty; or, more likely, perhaps too much group work is the problem for some students but too little group work is the problem for others. Perhaps the assignments are too long or too difficult.

Given the plethora of possible "causes" for the problem, we suspect that the collection of more information would be a preferable response. That is, it would be useful to ask students in writing and/or in conversation about their reactions to *specific* aspects of the program and their suggestions for improving it. Representative questions could be asked at this point to gather information with regard to the following areas:

Isolation	Do students feel free to approach the teacher and/or other students to ask questions? Do students want to work with groups either more or less than the present ratio? Whom would the students like to work with? etc.
Pacing	Do students want to do more work on some units beyond the mastery level? Are we moving too fast?

Closure: Feedback Does the student want more conferences with teacher to evaluate work or set goals? How does the student gauge a successful/unsuccessful day? How satisfied/dissatisfied is the student with his general progress?

Appropriateness of Curriculum Gather student reaction to specific subjects and units, and especially to the *mode* of the units (answering specific or general questions, summarizing information, listening, etc.). What interesting content has been neglected?

The particular questions asked would of course depend upon the nature of the particular program and the characteristics of the students. However, the general idea would be to get detailed reactions from students and to use those ideas as a vehicle for improving the program. But the responses from students are not answers in and of themselves—students may not know what will make them happy or what they need to learn more effectively, and students' responses may be incompatible in the short run. (They all want to see the teacher more frequently!)

Student feedback is simply one way of judging the effectiveness of a program and gathering improvement ideas. Collection of student information does not always yield solutions. Ultimately, the only "solutions" are the ones that lead to effective change: improved learning and/or satisfaction scores. That is, analysis of student information may lead to systematic suggestions that certain changes may benefit students or subgroups of students. The role of such feedback, then, is to narrow the list of possible changes to a few "best bets" that the teacher can implement, and then see if the changes are helpful.

In review, then, we have suggested that teachers and/or schools interested in surveying general attitudes and other noncognitive variables may do so with any of a number of tests that are on the market. Normal care in choosing instruments of known and adequate reliability must be exercised, and the instrument should measure concepts that relate to local goals. However, given the general stage of development of these tests, they tell little about the *distance* between present and desired outcomes. They simply describe student attitudes. "Problems" have to be identified in terms of local goals. There are no simple answers. The issue is similar to that of setting the criterion level in cognitive tests. But instead of questions such as "What percent of material should be mastered?" questions like "How satisfied should students be?" are raised.

One especially useful source of affective instrumentation is being produced by the Instructional Objectives Exchange. Using subject matter specialists, educational evaluators, and teachers as collaborators, development workers have attempted to develop *criterion-referenced* measures of affective development (see Chapter 7 for a complete discussion of criterion referenced testing). Affective objectives presumed to be important and appropriate are identified and items are written to measure the student's attainment of the objective. Attitude toward school (including specific questions about willingness to study, interest in problem solving, and so on) and self-concept inventories have been prepared that appear to be quite useful for assessment in a variety of school settings. Some representative items from the School Sentiment Index (one of the many instruments available from the Instructional Objectives Exchange) include:

> My teacher doesn't explain things very well.
> When I do something wrong at school, I know I will get a second chance.
> I like doing my homework.
> My teacher would let the class plan an event alone.
> My teacher usually explains things too slowly.
> I would rather do almost anything else than study.
> I don't do very much reading on my own.

It would seem that information obtained from such questions would be useful information for teachers or schools to use as one index of school effects—"customer perception." Also, perhaps with slight adaptation, the above questions would seem useful for any school setting, from mid-elementary through secondary.

However, if decision making information is desired, teachers may need to write their own instrument. A study of available instruments will help teachers to develop a style for obtaining information, but the trick is to write items that students can respond to and that provide accurate feedback. No one can write items that are uniquely suitable for program evaluation in a particular classroom other than the teacher or someone working closely with the teacher. Examples of possible substantive questions and formats for students follow:

I. If there were three things I could change about individual study units, I would change
   1.
   2.
   3.

I. The two assignments I have most (least) enjoyed this year are:
   1.
   2.

I. The part of the school day I most like (dislike) is:
   1.

I. If I could change any two things about chemistry they would be:
   1.
   2.

I. If you could spend more time on one school subject or activity what would it be?

II. Compared to other art projects I have done this year I like landscape design   Better—1—2—3—4—5—6—less

II. Compared to individual work I like group work (on science or other particular areas)   Better—1—2—3—4—5—6—less

II. Compared to written work I prefer to present oral summaries of my work to small groups   Better—1—2—3—4—5—6—less

III. On the next science unit
   a. I want to work alone.
   b. I want to work with the teacher.
   c. I want to work with one or two friends.
   d. I want to work with a group.

III. 40 minutes in math class each day is
   a. Too much
   b. About right
   c. Not enough

	Always	*Sometimes*	*Never*
IV. Does time go quickly in school?	_____	_____	_____
Do most of your classmates like you?	_____	_____	_____
Do you feel free to say what you feel in class?	_____	_____	_____
Do you like to talk in class discussions?	_____	_____	_____
Do you have enough time to finish school work?	_____	_____	_____
Does the teacher listen when you have a problem?	_____	_____	_____
Does the teacher give clear directions?	_____	_____	_____
Does the teacher give help when you need it?	_____	_____	_____
Do you feel embarrased when you give a wrong answer?	_____	_____	_____

In general the questions raised here would provide an accurate survey account of how children respond to certain aspects of schooling. Some of the questions would provide ideas for immediate change, whereas others simply would signify the need for teachers to collect more information. The degree of specificity in the items would vary with the teacher's reason for collecting the information.

Each of the format types illustrated above has advantages and disadvantages. Type IV questions can be completed by very young students and yield a good survey of student attitudes. Type I questions are more likely to yield decision-making information, however, and they may be used as a natural sequence to "problems" identified by Type IV questions. Type II and Type III formats have both diagnostic and survey value. Clearly, the best format depends upon program goals and the age of the children. The content of questions is determined by what the classroom teacher feels to be important goals.

The collection of student information will give teachers at least a glimpse of how students see their classroom world. To get accurate and useful information, teachers are advised to collect it in completely *anonymous* ways. If information is frequently collected, the teacher should demonstrate to students the usefulness of their feedback, that is, he should call to their attention program changes that have been made. However, under most circumstances, sampling elementary children's attitudes more than once a month or so would be unnecessary. Indeed, a program of attitude assessment that collected relevant student information at the beginning, middle, and end of the year could be a source of effective information about progress on selected affective goals. Furthermore, such information would provide teachers with an accurate record of students' noncognitive progress, and would provide useful baseline information for comparing subsequent efforts that teachers undertake to improve the classroom learning environment in subsequent years.

Process Measures

Just as teachers may make decisions with the help of student attitude data, so too may teachers benefit from process records of student behavior (what students actually do in a situation). The trick again is knowing what you want to occur and finding a simple way to get the necessary information. For example, if the goal is to facilitate communicative skills in a group setting, the teacher might record the number of false starts that students make, the extent to which students indicate that they have heard the previous speaker, the number of times a student speaks during a group conversation, whether or not (and how) a student responds when other students challenge his opinion, frequency of attempts to summarize or provide solutions for the group, and so on. Information, whether collected by the teacher, student coders, or even target students themselves, is useful for discussing goals with individual students or for assessing the impact that the program has had on student *behavior*.

A teacher interested in creating respect for individual differences would be interested in different types of process measures. How often do high and low aptitude students come into contact? What prejudices, if any, do lunchroom seating patterns and playground grouping reveal? On what basis do students select other students for interest group work (when aptitude is not a prerequisite)? How long can effective work go on in small group arrangements? Such information would help teachers to assess the extent to which their goals generally were being accomplished. Teachers working toward affective goals will find process measures (if they are specific and related to important goals) a useful way of finding out about their impact on students.

Summary

Much criticism has been directed recently at the school's lack of sensitivity to the noncognitive needs of students. However, data (reported as early as 1940 and as recently as 1975) reviewed in this chapter illustrates that students as a group do *not* find schools emotionally barren. But neither do students as a group find school lively and/or intensively interesting. It seems that, for most students, school is accepted somewhat passively as an "O.K." institution.

Nevertheless, schools appear to be distressingly uncomfortable for some (15–20 percent?) elementary school students. (The figure may be higher in inner city schools for secondary students; most of the recent data reported in this chapter were collected in elementary schools.) For these students, efforts to improve their day-to-day experiences in schools would seem an important goal. There is no reason to expect that students at *all* levels should find school a joyful "high." We believe this because we suspect the time and "patterning" of resources needed to achieve this goal would interfere with progress on other goals, and because, as Jackson (1973) has noted, other institutions are better able to provide entertainment and fun experiences than are schools. But we do see as reasonable the goal that most students will accept and become minimally involved in school, such that school is judged to be an acceptable place to spend time. Hunches about how teachers might obtain such involvement were advanced, based upon parent-behavior literature and other nonclassroom sources.

It has been noted that a number of instruments are available for measuring noncognitive outcomes. However, few normative data are available, and interpretation, in an immediate sense, of most pen-and-paper measures is difficult. Some development work in describing the appropriateness of various noncognitive tests is going on. Work on criterion-referenced affective tests and attempts to measure students' perception of the classroom environment appear to be especially useful.

The lack of knowledge about the relationship between affective and cognitive achievement of students was stressed, as was the lack of information about *process* teaching behaviors and environmental conditions associated with noncognitive outcome measures. No one knows how to influence student progress on noncognitive variables, or if teaching behaviors effective for the realization of one affective goal impede progress towards another affective goal. Only through the systematic study of teachers and schools will we find out *how* teachers and schools can maximize students' affective growth. Designs that combine rich contextual information about students and teachers with detailed process observation and comprehensive assessments of student perceptions and various measures of affective growth are needed.

Finally, a few suggestions were made describing how a teacher could gather information about the affective attitudes of his students. Such information has value not only as a record of what *exists* but also as a reference point for comparing how *subsequent* modifications in the classroom affect students or how successive classrooms of the teacher compare over time. Such information in time would help teachers to understand the reactions of their students and to form impressions or plans suggesting how they might attempt to improve their instructional efforts.

In the chapter that follows, more emphasis will be placed upon how information can be used by teachers, schools, school systems, and other educational agencies in order to guide and ultimately improve educational practice. The chapter that follows will also pinpoint some of the difficulties (primarily attitudinal) that often work to prevent such action.

Chapter 10 Toward Effectiveness

We have seen that schools and teachers *do* have differential effects upon cognitive and noncognitive student growth, even when relevant student characteristics such as IQ, SES or previous performance level are controlled. There are even limited stability data to show that some teachers retain their relative effectiveness during consecutive years. Clearly, some schools and teachers *do* make a measurable difference. Thus, the conclusion that schools or teachers have no effect on student growth is a fallacious overreaction to inappropriate data.

Unfortunately, however, there is no simple way to identify good and bad schools or teachers. Program definitions or simple frequency counts of teaching behavior do not predict student growth. For example, there are both good and bad traditional classrooms and both good and bad open and/or individualized instructional arrangements. There are weak teachers in good schools, and good teachers in poor schools. Accountability on the basis of teacher behavior is not technically feasible at present; hence it is undesirable. However, we shall argue in this chapter that feedback to the teacher about his behavior and the behavior of his students has the potential for improving classroom life.

In addition to the fact that some schools and teachers have differential impact upon learners, it is known that teachers exhibit stable individual differences in some aspects of classroom behavior. For example, teachers vary widely in the percentage of time that they will repeat or rephrase questions after a student responds incorrectly (Brophy and Good, 1974). Such information is useful, because much research has emphasized the similarity of teaching behavior. It is true that the role of teacher exerts pressure such that some teacher reactions are quite predictable. Nonetheless, recent research suggests that behavioral variance exists and therefore that such process variance can be linked to differential student progress potentially.

Recent research marked by increased methodological sophistication has begun to link variance in teaching behavior with variance in student performance. Process-product research studying teachers of known effectiveness in naturalistic classrooms has already identified a number of interesting process-product relationships. In time, as this research matures and is clarified by experimental studies conducted in classrooms, a pool of dependable knowledge will be established.

In addition to a research base, schools need a value system that orders educational priorities. Value systems are essential if answers are to be found to such questions as: Is a pattern of high achievement, low internality, and moderate vocational awareness better than moderate scores in all three areas? We suspect that schools cannot simultaneously be effective in all areas of responsibility that have been assigned to them (the list runs from drug education to producing rocket scientists). A system for clarifying goals and resolving conflicts about the role of schooling (and perhaps the appearance of schools that represent different combinations of values) is needed to guide research activity. Without such a value base, schools and teachers are likely to remain prime targets for fadism.

The point was made in Chapter 4 that the knowledge base for *how* to train teachers exceeds knowledge about *what* to train teachers to do. Let's hope that in ten years we do not develop refined information about selected process-product relationships only to discover that we do not know how to choose among product outcomes even though we can specify how to achieve some of them!

We have argued that the proper type of research information can be a very useful and powerful force. So, too, we feel that the teacher or principal who collects information about his behavior and its effects will be able to improve his day-to-day performance. However, prior to discussing specific ways in which this might be accomplished, it will be useful to discuss problems that operate to prevent the effective utilization of information at all levels (government organizations, researchers, state educational workers, teachers . . . all of us are affected!).

"Nowness"

Americans, perhaps more so than any other nationality, have a marked capacity for "*nowness,*" the willingness and courage to attend to problems in an immediate context. "Nowness" is often an admirable quality, but not in situations where the information needed to make an appropriate decision does not exist. When needed information does not exist, immediate "tunnel vision" towards reaching a goal may be self-defeating. That is, a solution that precedes (and unduly delays) collection of needed information is not likely to be productive. Such a willingness to act historically has had a marked influence on the way we do research. In our urgency to solve problems *"now"* and to come up with *needed* alternatives, research characteristically has *followed* innovation.

This has proved to be a poor strategy because "pilot" innovations tend to become standardized rather quickly, allowing only a few aspects of the model to be tested. For example, language laboratories, despite limited and inconclusive evidence, became the instructional Zeitgeist, and every high school and college "had to" have one. Millions of dollars were spent on a bad bet, and research on relevant questions was impeded. (What is the role of the language instructor? What skills cannot be taught in a lab setting?) Questions that could have been answered relatively cheaply went unanswered because of the premature belief that language laboratories were good for all students in virtually all settings.

This educational vulnerability to plausible sounding but untested ideas (fadism) is compounded by a "now" approach to evaluation. Comprehensive process measures are too costly and time consuming to collect in evaluation studies, because results have to be published immediately (no time to examine program results for differential effects, etc.)—now!

These observations are not offered as moralistic reactions to the work that others have conducted. We, too, have been consumed by "now" demands from time to time. The point is that vast expenditures of monies on program innovations has not been effective in solving educational problems. Pumping vast amounts of money into school will not by itself guarantee desirable improvements, as the Ford Foundation recently spelled out in its own publication, *A Foundation Goes to School* (Ford Foundation, 1972).

Unfortunately, funding agencies tend to be most interested in groundbreaking new ideas that propose to "solve" significant education problems in three years! Little interest is shown in proposals designed to *answer* old questions definitively in ten years. This is not because such agencies are disinterested in effective educational research, but because they too are affected by "now" pressures.

In the last fifteen years, an exceedingly small percentage of the educational dollar has been spent on research, and an even smaller percentage on basic research *preceding* planned change. Some of the process-product results reviewed in Chapter 4 are very encouraging, illustrating that dependable information can be collected in classrooms. An especially good sign is that several results have been replicated in independent investigations. However, these studies are costly, and will become more costly when treatment studies are mounted to see if teacher effectiveness can be improved when teaching behavior is modified.

One hopes that the drive for quick results will not erode the small amounts of money available for basic research. This might happen if the monies that are presently available for research are diverted by premature application of process-product results.

Clearly, process-product results need to be validated in experimental settings; however, our suggestion is that such experimentation should not be implemented on a wide (and expensive) basis until experimental studies have shown such behaviors to be of value. Testing the results of process-product correlational studies in controlled classrooms experiments is needed. Not only is such research more likely to come up with better problem solutions; it is considerably *cheaper* than the mounting of ineffective treatment innovation activity. What is not needed are massive programs that are widely implemented *before* they are *researched*. That is, every teacher behavior training program in the country does *not* have to be modified *now*.

Short-cut methods do not produce definitive research, and fragmentary research results will not provide much useful direction. Once a knowledge base is established, solutions come relatively quickly (for instance, man on the moon, a successful vaccine for polio). But without an adequate knowledge base, problem solutions can be partly successful at best (for instance, combating cancer, stimulating cognitive growth in schools). In the long run, we will save time in designing effective school environments by taking time now to establish such a research base.

This plea is not an indiscriminate call for more research. Unless it embodies many of the design features presented in Chapter 3, research is of little, if any, value. The obvious exception for the legitimate use of case studies involving small samples and few dependent measures occurs in groundbreaking research in areas where so little is known that investment in large-scale research is unjustified. Our suggestion is for systematic, programmatic plans of research that provide an attack upon a defined problem area.

Large-scale research marked by comprehensive instrumentation should clarify profitable research directions and guide subsequent research. For example, where outcome measures do *not* show large or important naturalistic variation, it seems foolish to devote money to continued process-product research in naturalistic settings. Here, it would be more appropriate to design carefully controlled small-scale studies to see how student performance in these areas could be improved. Presumably, such experimentation would provide for experiences that are not present or are minimally present in the typical classroom. Participation in the design and execution of carefully controlled studies at this level is possible for the independent investigator who has little research support. However, testing the generality of his positive results when they do occur is beyond his means. Such positive results would call for controlled experimentation (*not massive implementation*) by larger research groups (or teams of "managerially" independent investigators who voluntarily decide to work together) to test the applicability of process-product relationships across a variety of school contexts.

However, where product measures have marked naturalistic variance, it seems desirable to spend large sums of money on commissioned observational studies to identify the process characteristics associated with student gains. Eventually, when clear relationships have been demonstrated, it would again be profitable to call for planned variation studies to determine how such results might best be taught in training programs, and other uses be made of them.

Clearly, complex studies by both large teams and simpler ones by independent investigators are needed for programmatic attacks on problem areas. However, it would seem that the relative advantages of the "systematic testing" and "wide range of ideas" associated respectively with large team research and with research by independent investigators needs to be a *conscious* decision by those who allocate funds. Random, diverse attacks on broad problem areas are ineffective as a general strategy. The use of large scale team research on process investigations when target teachers' effects on students are not known in advance is an equally dubious strategy.

Thus, we have qualified our call for more research and our plea for more sophisticated research, stressing that research should be conducted within an overarching programmatic structure, so that judicious problem-relevant decisions can be made to plan effectively the sequences of studies and types of research necessary at each level. But just as important as the willingness to provide money and a structure for guiding research is the concomitant supporting willingness to *delay* massive implementation, accountability plans that prescribe specified arrangements, and so on. Such restraint is desirable until established sets of process-product relationships emerge and are tied together in some coherent conceptual arrangement such that teachers have information not only about desirable behaviors but also about how they fit into an operating instructional program. *We repeat: Premature advocacy can and does have undesirable consequences.*

Teacher education programs, in their zeal to teach behavioral competencies, may communicate surplus meanings that impede rather than enhance teacher performance in the field. For example, the program may teach that learning how to ask questions at all levels of cognitive complexity means that good teachers "ask a full range of questions." Such training is deficient. Learning how to ask questions that pose different types of cognitive demands on students is important, and it is also desirable to acquire concrete skills for responding to students when they fail to answer or provide wrong answers.

However, the belief that the presence *per se* of higher-order cognitive questions (or a full range of cognitive questions) will automatically be associated with higher student achievement is inappropriate. The appropriate cognitive level of a question depends upon learning goals, the type of material being discussed, the learning arrangement, and learner aptitude or mastery level. In some situations, such as small groups of students working on similar assignments, teachers' use of a single but appropriate type of question may be most advantageous.

We could continue to cite examples, but the general point has been made: No teacher behavior has been shown, unequivocally, to have desirable effects on all learners in all situations. The development of refined teaching skills is important, but it requires a conceptual base that specifies the conditions under which various skills can be used profitably. In the absence of such conceptual information to guide teacher behavior, teachers in training need to know that the behaviors they learn are likely to have different effects in different situations, and that teaching behaviors are effective only if they have desirable effects upon students. Thus, the skills and behaviors they learn are *alternatives* that can be used in planned ways based on student performance and feedback.

However, this does not mean that teachers are operating in the dark. Results of process-product research describing useful teaching behaviors and classroom arrangements have been reported in Chapters 4 and 8, and to some extent in 9. Such indices provide a wealth of information that teachers and other school personnel can use as sources of *ideas* for attempting to improve instructional behavior. Such information is tentative and suggestive, but not yet prescriptive. Nevertheless, recent research has been promising. It is not our purpose to review these findings here. These chapters do not lend themselves to simple summaries, and we prefer that readers digest the findings in full context and remain aware of the fact that the process-product relationships reported will be clarified and expanded as more data emerge.

Until Tomorrow

But most of us have teaching responsibilities or are in one way or another responsible for training, employing, or supervising teachers. What then can we do *now* before a research base has been established? How can educators at all levels help to move the system toward effectiveness? Perhaps the place to begin is by posing some basic questions. An appropriate initial set of questions for educators at all levels would include: (1) What are my goals? (2) How well am I progressing on these goals? What effects am I having? (3) How can I set up a programmatic structure to learn more? (4) How do I have time to get information for future use in the face of constant day-to-day pressures? Eventually another series of questions can be raised related to the general question, how might present effectiveness be improved?

Specific questions that are raised at any decision level vary somewhat but can be subsumed under the general questions listed above. For example, policy makers at the National Institute of Education have to determine both proximal (now, immediate) goals and distal goals. Immediate goals include a variety of political needs that center upon "maintenance-survival" issues. For example, how do we get money for educational research? Obviously this question and similar ones demand a "now" response. However, sometimes "now" responses, as noted above, prevent needed research. Decisions to spread money around and grant a number of $100,000 contracts may be political coinage; however, a complex problem requiring a coordinated research effort will not be solved by giving ten diffuse projects $100,000. Similarly, commitment of funds for two years is not enough if the project requires five years. Yet, the National Institute of Education is under pressure to show productivity ("now") in order to justify itself to Congress and to obtain needed research funds.

Others are also influenced by "now" pressures. Researchers, for example, may underestimate project costs in order to land contracts and thus satisfy their own survival needs. As a result, their budgets may be inadequate to tackle the questions they want to answer. Similarly, difficult-to-research questions may be avoided. Superintendents have to evaluate teachers *today*; they can't take time to collect data to find out the effects of teaching. Clearly, we are tied to conflicts between distal and proximal goals at all levels. Historically, a good balance between proximal goals and distal goals has not been achieved. Coleman (1973) summarized the problem nicely: "As in the military, where long periods of inactivity and aimless, redundant makework are punctuated by intense bursts of frantic battle, the political battle forces in the federal government seem to alternate between enforced inactivity in which nothing seems possible because of conflicting interest, and bursts of last minute activity designing policy all at once as the legislative logjams break and anything is possible" (*Phi Delta Kappan,* Research Note, 1973, *54,* 490). If we are to move toward effectiveness, we must see to it that the accomplishment of distal goals is not always neglected in favor of immediate goals. To make the discussion more specific, we shall examine the day-to-day pressures that are exerted on the classroom teacher and see how the classroom teacher and a single school might achieve some balance between distal and proximal goals in the following section.

In this lengthy chapter introduction, we again have tied research and effective teaching together. If knowledge about teaching effectiveness is to be expanded, good research must be conducted which places appropriate focus on teachers, schools, and programs that make a difference. Below we will discuss general strategies that might be used by teachers to get usable information about their effects on students. Comments for researchers appeared in Chapter 3.

Awareness of Goals and Awareness of Behavior

Teachers are under constant day-to-day pressure. Lessons and tests must be prepared, parents must be reassured periodically, and there are systematic demands for self-improvement and participation in school related assignments such as pay schedules tied to graduate course work. Within such a framework, how can teachers realistically deal with collecting information that is related not only to immediate goals but also to distal goals? (In the case of the teacher, a distal goal might be thought of as information about students or oneself as a teacher that will help to design material later in the year or for next year's class.)

A good first step is to sort out school-defined goals that exert pressure in the classroom and personal teaching goals. In some school situations and classrooms there is but hazy, if any, understanding of target goals even when schools are in the midst of preparing for massive change! School staffs often cannot express particular dissatisfaction with an old procedure (for instance: What were students prevented from doing that they should be able to do?), nor define which desirable characteristics they seek in the new system.

Awareness of goals is the first step in planning school or classroom change. Without goals to direct and mobilize efforts and to evaluate effort (Where are we in comparison to where we wanted to be?), day-to-day activity will be dictated by pressing but mostly random events. That is, the educator is controlled by the present situation, and he responds to whatever "demands" his attention. Such a situation is very similar to the activities of some college students who spend their college careers responding to "present" demands (for three days all study time is used for the biology exam, then all time is used for the history test that follows).

That there are urgent demands in the classroom cannot be denied. Jackson (1968) has estimated that elementary school teachers engage in over 1,000 daily exchanges with students. Teachers must respond to "now" demands *if they are to be effective.* Responding to students who have difficulty with the curriculum, dealing with the class when it suddenly "goes wild," and other "now" demands are necessary preconditions for effectiveness, but we suspect that teachers who are "stimulus bound" (unduly controlled by immediate classroom demands) will never increase their present level of effectiveness. For the "born teacher" (and we believe there are some) who possesses excellent communicative skills, a flair for effective and low-key management, and an ability to establish instant camaraderie with students, the loss may not be major. But for most of us, failure to develop and augment our existing skills is a loss for us and our students.

Lack of Awareness

There is ample reason to believe that much of what goes on in classrooms is beyond the immediate recall of teachers. Teachers are especially likely to be unaware of *qualitative* aspects of their behavior toward individual students. For example, Good and Brophy (1974) found that teachers differed widely in the extent to which they stayed with students in failure situations (repeated or rephrased the question, asked a new question, and so on) or gave up on them (teacher gives answer or calls on someone else). Teachers largely were not aware of the extent to which they gave up or stayed with students in general, nor were they aware of which students they were more likely or less likely to stay with. Teachers were so preoccupied with running the classroom that awareness of this dimension of classroom life eluded them.

Other research also illustrates this problem. Indeed, even seemingly simple aspects of teacher–child interaction turn out to be complex perceptual problems. Martin and Keller (1974) note that teachers' awareness of the extent to which they call on boys or girls, the freqency with which students approach them, the number of times they initiate private contacts with students, and the amount of class time spent on procedural matters, were all inaccurately recalled.

Such lack of awareness has been found to interfere with teacher behavior in some research studies. Some teachers (but certainly not all) have been found to have more frequent and qualitatively better contacts with high achieving than low achieving students. Some of the qualitative ways in which teachers have expressed preferential treatment to high achieving students include: seating patterns (highs closer to teacher); more frequent praise after correct answers and less criticism after wrong responses than low achievement students receive; a longer time period to attempt a response before the teacher prods or calls on someone else; and more feedback (simple information about the adequacy or inappropriateness of their responses). For a full description of these variables and others, see Brophy and Good (1974).

It would seem that the classroom environment, at least in elementary schools, is so complex and busy that teachers, again, some more than others, are often subtly controlled by student behavior, such as calling on students who raise hands. The effect is that some students rarely receive teacher contact. The neglected pupil is more likely to be a low achiever than a high achiever, in part because low achievement students are less likely to initiate contacts with teachers. Teacher awareness is even related to student achievement. Jackson (1968) reports that teachers are much more accurate in their judgments about the attitudes of their high than low achievement students.

In summary, so much happens so quickly that it is impossible to see everything. If only fragments can be retained, teachers are likely to fall victim to the same forces that control the behavior of anyone working in a complex environment: bias and selective perception. Ambiguous cues from students (like furrowed brows) may be given meaning (they are confused versus they are thinking) on the basis of stereotypic impressions that are held toward the students. Thus, teaching behaviors may be based upon inappropriate but unchecked assumptions about students. Further, the complexity of certain classroom variables may prevent teachers from checking their assumptions even when they are motivated to do so. In such circumstances, teachers may need assistance in the collection and interpretation of information if they are to see more clearly.

We've strayed a bit from the major point of this subsection in order to show that teachers are unaware of much of their own classroom interaction. But this meandering has a purpose: Lack of information not only reduces the opportunity for modifying one's instructional behavior, but may also allow grossly inappropriate behavior to continue.

Does Awareness Make Any Difference?

We think that awareness of what transpires in a classroom can be very useful information. To begin with, teachers are concerned about the progress of students. When obvious instructional failures occur, such as certain students not being called on, it is usually because of lack of awareness rather than indifference. Awareness alone is not a sufficient condition for change, although it is a necessary prerequisite. For example, in one study teachers were supplied with information about differences in their classroom behavior toward different students with regard to how frequently they had contact with students and how frequently they stayed with them in failure situations. Teachers in general were surprised by the information, expressed interest in changing their behavior, especially the "stay with" behavior, and were successful in doing so. Also, there were indications that student behaviors were changing as a function of these new teacher behaviors (Good and Brophy, 1974).

However, there is ample evidence that feedback to teachers does not automatically change classroom behavior. Teachers may reject, often for good cause, either the source or type of information as irrelevant. But information about aspects of classroom life that teachers explicitly ask to be coded or that they find interesting will be useful for thinking about and perhaps reshaping classroom events.

Baselines

The first step in improving instructional effectiveness is to become *aware* of one's *goals* in the teaching situation. Goals mobilize behavior. Even general statements serve a directive function. For example, teachers or schools who want to influence creativity need to develop some hypotheses about the teacher behaviors and classroom arrangements that will increase creativity, become aware of how it is measured, and ultimately select an instrument to measure it. Similarly, the teacher who wants his students to acquire "minimum" respect and tolerance for individual differences can begin to direct his efforts accordingly. He also would need to select or devise appropriate attitude and behavioral measures to find out the extent to which students show respect for individual differences. Similarly, the teacher who wants the day-to-day work conditions to be perceived by students as acceptable will have to collect information about students' specific reactions to work arrangements. The second step is to become *aware* of present levels of student performance on the variables of interest. *Before* the design of classroom treatment studies, it is important to find out about student's present progress. The pattern of present performance, not the attractiveness of a program or idea, is the starting point in assessment and/or improvement programs. If students' performance on the creativity test (or whatever) is normal or acceptable, then teachers need not alter the present instructional program. If all but a few students are high on the measure, the teacher can begin to think about strategies for improving the performance of just these few students. On the other hand, if most students are low on the measure, the teacher can begin to consider more general strategies. In summary, teachers (or teacher teams) and the school unit (or grade level unit) need to be aware of their basic goals and collect baseline information to describe the existing situation. Despite the obvious utility of these steps, few schools or teachers possess such data. Schools' and teachers' goals are more likely to be accomplished if they are articulated, consistent (goals are not incompatible), and measured.

Focus on a Few Measures

When schools or teachers have too many goals, they become "responsible" for everything but specifically accountable or aware of very little. Amidst such complexity, "now" demands dominate while sharp awareness of performance related to particular goals (and the chance for *planned* change) suffers. Independent of the number of goals which teachers and schools must deal with, we suspect that they would make more progress by focusing on a few goals at a time.

Over a period of time, of course, a school could focus on a number of goals by progressively rotating its data collection. (See the rotating data collection schedule offered by The National Assessment Project in Chapter 6. During a given period of time (say two to four years), schools and teachers could collect data on three or four different types of dependent measures, plan and execute remedial programs on the basis of these data, and evaluate the success of planned intervention. The results at the end of the cycle would then direct subsequent activity. Poor results on a particular outcome variable would dictate the development and implementation of new strategies and raise questions about the ability of the school to influence the variable. Successful results would allow the school to concentrate on other goals.

This is not to suggest that schools mobilize efforts on only two or three goals. Schools have to carry out their day-to-day role responsibilities in the best way they can. We believe they should spend some proactive time (collecting records and so forth) in the *study* of a few specified goals. Unless extra attention is assigned to some specific goals, little progress is likely to be made. In most cases the extra attention can be achieved by using existing time in different ways. For example, rather than *random inservice meetings*, in which speakers are selected because of their ability to entertain or their availability, it would be possible to use inservice time in order to get consultant help in developing specific measures, interpreting data, and planning intervention strategies and methods of obtaining process and product measures to evaluate change.

Another example would include the use of supervisory personnel to collect information relevant to goals. Too often, supervisor's information has little impact upon subsequent teacher behavior because teachers and supervisors do not agree upon classroom goals. The establishment of specific goals could lead to the identification of process measures that eventually are useful in achieving baseline understanding about what takes place in classrooms (such as teacher behavior, room arrangement, student behavior, grouping patterns, and so on).

Teacher Goals

Teachers within schools can set up their own goals as well as help to collect information relevant to common school goals. Obviously, teachers can collect baseline data relevant to student progress on a few selected goals even if they teach in schools that do not set goals or collect data. Maximum advantage will probably come about in schools where at least some teachers cooperate on a few common goals, and also collect data relevant to one or two goals of special interest to them. The advantage for teachers working in a school that is interested in assessing its effects include:

1. Immediate stimulation and group support.
2. A system view that data are to be used to find out "where we are" and to plan change, rather than one where data are used to *evaluate* teachers. We suspect that teachers' willingness to keep certain types of records covaries with the "system's" use of such information.
3. Improved ability of the teacher to marshall resources—to control inservice activities and influence supervisor's data collection, and so on.

However, where teachers only collect information on common goals, two potential losses appear. First, teachers lose the opportunity to get information of major interest to them, and in time their interest and support may erode. (Let's do something! Why do we collect all these data?) The second problem is that the assessment system is likely to become set in its "values" and procedures such that, in time, the system becomes automatic, thoughtless, and ineffective. Teachers' questions and exuberance over the results of their own activities may lead to general renewal and new directions for the whole system.

Getting Started: Product Data

After specifying goals and determining how to measure those goals, teachers and schools are in position to collect relevant data. Beyond the advice to narrow the data collection to a few specific questions, one other general strategy appears to be useful when attitude measures are collected—namely, data should be collected at three or more points in the year to see if drops or rises in performance seem to be a function of situational factors (time or program changes, etc). It would be desirable, if possible, to collect data during the *first week of school*, sometime during the middle of the year, and toward the end of the year (but avoiding the bedlam associated with the last two or three weeks, especially in elementary schools). School could then organize the data by grade levels and be able to specify growth generally or for particular groups of students. One way to organize the data is illustrated in Table 10.1.

The classification suggested in Table 10.1 is, of course, arbitrary. It assumes that data on common goals (that include, for example, respect for individual differences, scores for verbal expressiveness) are collected in all classrooms. However, there are many situations where goals would be common only to a particular grade or organizational level. Also, the subdivision of data by sex and aptitude is done on the assumption that the performance of the students is likely to vary as a function of their sex and/or aptitude. However, on many measures this would be an inappropriate or irrelevant dis-

TABLE 10.1

Mean Performance of Students on "Measure A," Classified on the
Basis of Grade Level, Student Sex, and Student Aptitude

	Boys	Girls	High Aptitude	Middle Aptitude	Low Aptitude
Grade 1					
Grade 2					
Grade 3					
Grade 4					
Grade 5					
Grade 6					

tinction. In other cases, it would make more sense to distinguish student performance as a function of cognitive style or personality. This is especially likely to be true in cases where individualized programs are operative.

Collection and organization of product data describing student performance would yield baseline data that schools and/or teachers could use to see if they were satisfied with present student performance on three (or whatever) performance measures. But equally important, the data will provide a base to evaluate student performance in subsequent years. For example, it might be decided to attempt to raise performance on areas "A" and "B," but not "C." However, when evaluation data were collected, it would be possible to determine not only if progress had occurred on goals "A" and "B," but also to see if performance in "C" had been altered as a result of mobilizing school resources to the other two areas. Clearly, subsequent evaluation data could be used to evaluate differential progress in helping students who vary in such characteristics as aptitude, sex, cognitive style, personality, or combinations of these characteristics.

Process Baseline Data

Process data describing existing teacher–student interaction patterns, instructional groupings, and so on, are also necessary if "effects" (product data from students) data are to be interpreted meaningfully. If students in general or groups of students are relatively weak on measures of interest, it would seem sensible to know what has been happening in the learning environment. Process information provides us a base for forming hypotheses that suggest aspects of the environment that *may* be related to student gain. Here, too, the idea is to find out what is happening, not to prematurely prescribe good effects to any process.

A few examples of useful process questions will be presented later but, it is beyond the scope of this chapter to specify all the process measures that could or should be collected; to do so would call for another book. The essential point is that *goals* direct the type of process information needed. The organizational pattern of the classroom and available data on process-product relationships are other relevant criteria to use in selecting process measures.

What Process Information Is Coded?

Teachers who want to code classroom behavior or engage in some type of record keeping will ask, What information do I collect? There is no single answer to this question. One possible answer is to collect information relevant to important goals. Other ways to respond include: to study questions of special interest; to code behavior found to be promising on the basis of research evidence; to conduct general surveys of student atitudes or behavior; and to follow up anomolies that crop up in the process. The information will be useful to the extent that it applies to a specific question or goal that you really want to answer and that systematic records are kept so that answers can be obtained.

Countless questions can become the legitimate concern of anyone who teaches. Let's raise a few questions that could well become the target of study.

Do my low and high achievement students indicate that I have equal interest in them?

Do students report that I listen to them?

When I ask questions, what percent of the time do students respond with the correct answer? How does this figure compare with the "promising" rate suggested in Chapter 4?

How long do I *wait* for students to respond in the classroom if they do not respond immediately? Is this figure different for high and low achievement students?

What percent of my day is actually spent in instructional activities, as opposed to procedural, bookkeeping, etc.?

Are there some students who need help, but rarely seek me out to discuss academic material? Which students initiate contact with me and which one's don't? Why?

How much time do I spend with individual students in a given day?

How much time do I spend in math, social studies, language arts? Is this time emphasis reflected in student achievement gain?

How does the achievement level of my students at the end of the year compare with the achievement levels of other teachers or teams of teachers who teach similar types (SES, etc.) of children?

What percent of the time are students engaged (ostensibly) in their work during independent work (in math, social studies, etc.)?

How often do I get requests from students to tailor an assignment on the basis of their interest?

How much time do students in my class spend on their homework? More or less than I expected?

How much time do students in my class spend in study for my classroom tests?

How do they study for exams? In groups, individually, in pairs? Does it seem to make any difference?

What do they study (notes, text, supplementary handouts)?

How interesting do students rate various lesson or unit assignments? Does this interest fluctuate as a function of sex or achievement level? Does this interest relate to homework or unit test performance?

Which students never talk in their small group work?

The questions above are *not* intended to be a list of *critical* questions, but only representative of the types of initial questions that teachers might want to raise about their classroom. Answers to them would provide teachers with information about aspects of their classroom that they might want to change. That is, the results would lead to selected treatments and follow up evaluations. Teachers might ask questions such as:

1. Can I raise the average amount of time I spend with individual low achievers during mathematics from two minutes to five minutes a day? What impact, if any, does this have on their attitudes, achievement, and attention span (when they work independently)?

2. When I allow students to choose one of two homework assignments, do their study habits, performance levels, and/or attitudes change?

3. When I implement learning centers and peer tutoring activities, do I have more time to work with individual students? How do measures of work involvement (attention spans) collected on students in tutoring pairs and learning centers compare with measures collected on students working independently in previous years?

Using Process and Product Information

Let's consider an example to see how a teacher could use information to improve instructional effectiveness. Assume that sixth grade teacher Joe Bean's students do well[1] in all subjects but math. Their performance in math is not terrible, but it is noticeably lower than achievement in other subjects.

---

[1] *Obviously a teacher's concern could stem from many sources. For example, a simple comparison between student performance in different subjects that he teaches or a comparison of his teaching performance with other teachers teaching under similar conditions.*

Joe is puzzled by this. He enjoys teaching math and feels well qualified to do so. His concern about mathematics instruction is compounded by the fact that student attitude data collected earlier in the year is generally positive toward him and the instructional program. However, math drew the most criticism when students commented on specific subject areas.

Concerned about his students' low achievement and relatively disapproving attitudes towards math, Joe decides to obtain more information from students about the specific problems they encounter in math and about ways in which the program might be improved. He must go beyond general attitude data and ask a number of *specific* questions that might lead to changes in his instructional approach, so he collects anonymous data about how the math course might be improved.

However, he is discouraged to find that much of the information he has collected is contradictory (what some students prefer is disliked by others) or does not lead to suggestions for action (students do not feel that the math period is too long). One theme is evident in the comments of several students, though: "I often don't know what I'm supposed to do for my assignments in class"; "When we start a new unit in class I'm always lost"; "I don't understand my work until you explain it the next day."

Subsequently, Joe notices that students engage in more neutral or aimless activity when working on math assignments than at any other time during the day. Thus, Joe decides that his problem is failing to spend enough time explaining material and assignments (modeling how to do problems, explaining how the work relates to preceding work) before he actually gives the assignments. He realizes that the students need a clearer picture of what to and how to do it.

If students had expressed generally low interest, Joe might have considered peer tutoring or devising a mathematics learning center to add a degree of novelty and provide more time for him to work with individuals. But the students' self reports ("Often I'm confused, but after a period of time I catch on.") match his own observations that the problem was not motivational (boredom) but lack of direction. Thus Joe's plan is to increase his ratio of explanation and modeling to practice work, especially at the start of units, and to see if this will improve students' attitudes and achievement.

Remember, though, that Joe's plan is only a hypothesis, a hunch, about how to proceed. The only criterion to judge his plan is its effect on student performance. Too often plans become an "answer" independently of their effects on students. Thus, we stress that collecting information will suggest ways that instruction might be improved, but we do not claim that it will guarantee solutions.

Joe might find that some other factor (assignments too long, feedback inadequate) is related more directly to student achievement. However, by carefully measuring his attempts to alter classroom processes through the examination of student products (achievement, attitudes), he eventually will come up with a set of procedures that work *for him* in *this* class.

No solutions work for all or even most teachers in all situations. What works in a particular setting must be identified, ideally by the classroom teacher who uses process and product information in tandem.

In this example, we have seen that Joe chose to listen to students and that their feedback enabled him to identify a realistic starting point for change. We think that students (even primary students) usually can provide teachers with this kind of valuable feedback, if they are asked to do so. However, there are certain types of information that students may not be able to provide. In the next section, we will make the point that the type of information sought restricts the resources that a teacher can use to obtain feedback.

How Can Process Information Be Collected?

The nature of the question targets the type of information (achievement data, process information, student questionnaire, etc.), and the type of questions also influence the selection of the coder most likely able to collect the data. To illustrate this point, let's discuss three of the managerial concepts that Kounin's work has uncovered (see Chapter 4). One is accountability or the extent to which teachers hold students accountable for their work (call for show of papers that students were to work on while other students did board problems, call on students to comment upon the answers of other students, and so on). This variable and any concept that focuses upon specific teacher or student behaviors appears to be relatively simple for the teacher to monitor without outside assistance.

Another variable discussed by Kounin is smoothness (the extent to which the lesson is free of false starts, and so on). Although there are specific points that the classroom teacher could look for, it would seem that a fellow teacher coding in the room would be in a better position to monitor the overall ebb and tide of classroom proceedings.

The third concept we will discuss here is with-it-ness. With-it-ness is the teacher's ability to convince students that he is ahead of what's happening in the classroom ("has eyes in back of head"). Teachers do this through such behavior as correcting the "deviant" rather than an innocent bystander, or by *not* ignoring a major problem to deal with a minor problem. Although these behaviors are relatively specific and could be coded by observers, it would also be possible to collect this information directly from students via end-of-year questionnaires. (Does your teacher mean what he says?, and other similar questions.)

Thus, to some extent, the question one attempts to answer dictates both the type of information to be collected and who can collect it. But in some cases there are alternate ways of collecting the desired information, as we saw in the "with-it-ness" example. However, if classroom teachers limit their focus to only a few behaviors at any one time, they will be able to monitor their behavior, to some extent, on many meaningful aspects of classroom life. However, a "system" also can free resources to help teachers to get desirable information. Teachers' free time can be scheduled to allow for observing other teachers in the same grade, and other useful activities. Teachers or perhaps floating substitutes can occasionally be employed to code or to free other teachers for data collection.

Some assumptions are important to reiterate. (1) The purpose of observation data is to help the teacher to make decisions. (2) Thus, teachers should be getting information about behaviors that interest them. (3) The observation focus should be limited to a few but related sets of process measures that have implications for classroom practice. (4) Data often have to be collected over a long time period to assure an accurate description of what takes place in the classroom, that is, one must obtain an adequate description of what takes place *prior to* making intervention plans. (5) Information is collected and presented to the teacher through useful and nonthreatening procedures.

When the teacher begins to ask *complex* questions that demand the collection of process data that he cannot collect himself, efforts must be undertaken to get coding help. If a system of active inservice help and sharing does not exist in the school, the teacher may still be able to find a coding partner who is also interested in learning more about his or her behavior. That's all it takes to develop a system for getting reliable and useful process information.

Teachers Help Teachers

It is beyond the scope of this book to illustrate the variety of forms that can be used to tally behaviors that occur in the classroom or to show how such forms can be constructed. However, the *process* questions raised in this chapter all call for simple frequency or time measures that seem straightforward. Readers interested in seeing multiple examples of scales or in getting extended information about classroom coding can turn to other sources (Good and Brophy, 1973). Meanwhile, the following example is included to illustrate the power and value of these procedures.

Many of the ideas and variables that two of the authors (Good and Brophy, 1973) discussed about the benefits of teachers helping other teachers to become more aware of their classroom behavior have been incorporated in an extensive, three-year project sponsored by the Los Angeles County school office under the direction of Mary Martin and Sam Kerman (Martin, 1973).

Their project "Equal Opportunity in the Classroom" was an attempt to sensitize teachers to the possible damaging effects of their behavior toward low achieving students and to present teachers with a variety of skills to use with these students. The skills selected for the training program lent themselves to direct observation. Many of the dimensions were inspired by the Brophy-Good Dyadic System, but several new and useful dimensions were designed by the project team. The entire training program was designed and orchestrated by Martin and Kerman.

Space does not allow for a complete description of the project here, but one dimension of the program, "teachers help teachers," will be discussed because it is central to the present discussion. Teachers, in addition to being trained to perform certain behaviors, were also trained to code behavior associated with training goals and some of the teachers subsequently had the opportunity to be observed by fellow teachers.

Teachers' reports of the project underline the value of receiving feedback about their own behavior and the general stimulation from the opportunity to see life in other classrooms. Intensive observational records show that teacher behaviors were markedly changed as a function of the training. Also, the attitudes of experimental low expectancy students surpassed those of low expectancy control students. Furthermore, reading achievement scores of both low and high expectancy students surpassed those of their respective control groups.

Perhaps the gains occurred because teachers were participating in an experiment and their enthusiasm carried over into classroom preparations and/or presentations. The extent to which teacher behavior and student gains hold up in subsequent years will be examined in subsequent studies. The results from future data (much of it *already* collected) will help to clarify these issues.

The project demonstrates that teachers are interested in "seeing" more of classroom behavior and that many teachers are willing to accept the help of other teachers in collecting reliable information. Furthermore, it demonstrates that information *perceived to be relevant* by teachers can be used by them to change both their behavior and the performance of their students. To us, this type of behavior represents the degree of professionalism necessary if the quality of school life is to be systematically upgraded.

Summary

We have argued that teachers can and should become more aware of their own behavior, of student behavior, and of student performance levels on cognitive and affective measures of interest. Awareness of goals and of present performance levels will help to develop a "health" measure of a classroom at a particular moment in time. When gaps between aspiration and a performance goal are too wide, student attitude data and process measures relevant to that goal can be collected and assessed to identify possible changes in the classroom.

The classroom teacher can collect and interpret most types of product information with no or minimal support from others. Selected process measures can be monitored (by filtering information through concepts such as "Wait for students to respond") or recorded (wrist counter, or coding students as they work individually or in groups). However, support systems (of students, fellow teachers, and others) will be needed to collect other types of data.

But this assessment and subsequent prescription is only a hypothesis: The ultimate criterion is the effect on the performance level of students. Some problems may have to go through several cycles of hypothesis testing, and indeed some may be unsolvable with given resources.

Simply put, process measures in and of themselves cannot be used as direct predictors of classroom performance. The dangers of this simplified view have been pointed out elsewhere (Dunkin and Biddle, 1974). However, the careful collection and sensitive use of process and product information by classroom teachers will make them more aware of *what* does happen in the classroom, and increased awareness has the potential for upgrading many aspects of classroom life. Indeed, we feel that such behavior, coupled with the careful collection of classroom data of sensitive researchers, will help to unravel some of the factors that truly make a difference in the classroom.

Teachers teaching similar students have different effects on student performance. What is less clear is how teacher differences operate. Research in the last decade has started to provide clues. But the ending to this mystery cannot be provided here: It must be found in the classroom. We urge the reader to join us in the hunt.

References

Acland, H. The consistency of teachers' impact on pupil learning: Part 1. Cambridge: The Huron Institute, 1974 (mimeographed report).

Alexander, L., Elsom, B., Means, R., and Means, R. Achievement as a function of teacher initiated student–teacher personal interaction. Paper presented at the annual meeting of the Southwestern Psychological Association, 1971.

Alioto, R. and Jungherr, J. Using PPBS to overcome taxpayers' resistance. *Phi Delta Kappan,* 1969, *51,* 138–141.

Allen, D., and Fortune, J. An analysis of micro-teaching: New procedures in teacher education. In *Micro-teaching: A Description.* Stanford: Stanford University Press, 1966.

American Educational Research Association. Second report of Committee on the Criteria of Teacher Effectiveness. *Journal Educational Research,* 1953, *46,* 641–658.

Anderson, G., and Walberg, G. Learning environments. In H. Walberg (ed.), *Evaluating Educational Performance: A Sourcebook of Methods, Instruments, and Examples.* Berkeley, Calif.: McCutchan, 1974.

Anderson, R. Learning in discussions: A resume of the authoritarian–democratic studies. *Harvard Educational Review,* 1959, *29,* 201–215.

Aspy, D. A discussion of the relationship between selected student behavior and the teacher's use of interchangeable responses. Paper presented at the annual meeting of the American Educational Research Association, New Orleans, 1973.

Ausubel, D. *The Psychology of Meaningful Verbal Learning.* New York: Grune and Stratton, 1963.

Bargen, M. and Walberg, H. School performance. In H. J. Walberg (ed.), *Evaluating Educational Performance: A Sourcebook of Methods, Instruments, and Examples.* Berkeley, Calif.: McCutchan, 1974.

Barth, R. Open education: assumptions and rationale. Unpublished qualifying paper. Harvard University, 1969.

Barth, R. When children enjoy school: Some lessons from Great Britain. *Childhood Education,* 1970, *46,* 195–200.

Beers, J. and Campbell, P. *State Educational Assessment Programs 1973 Revision.* Princeton: Educational Testing Service, 1973.

Beller, E. Teacher education: Why, what, and how? *Peabody Journal of Education,* 1971, *48,* 125–139.

Beller, E. Research on organized programs of early education. In R. Travers (ed.), *Second Handbook of Research on Teaching.* Chicago: Rand McNally, 1973.

Bereiter, C. and Engelmann, S. *Teaching Disadvantaged Children in the Preschool.* Englewood Cliffs, N.J.: Prentice-Hall, 1966.

Berlyne, D. A theory of human curiosity. *British Journal of Psychology,* 1954, *45,* 180–191.

Berlyne, D. *Conflict Arousal and Curiosity.* New York: McGraw-Hill, 1960.

Biddle, B. The institutional context. In W. J. Campbell (ed.), *Scholars in Context: The Effects of Environments on Learning.* Sydney: Wiley, 1970.

Bissell, J. *Implementation of Planned Variation in Head Start.* Washington, D.C., Department of Health, Education and Welfare, Office of Child Development, 1971.

Blau, P. M. and Duncan, O. D. *American Occupation Structure.* New York: Wiley, 1967.

Block, J. (ed.). *Mastery Learning: Theory and Practice.* New York: Holt, Rinehart and Winston, 1971.

Bloom, B. Mastery Learning. In J. Block (ed.), *Mastery Learning: Theory and Practice.* New York: Holt, Rinehart and Winston, 1971.

Bloom, B. Innocence in education. *School Review.* 1972, *80,* 332–352.

Bloom, B. An introduction to mastery learning theory. Paper read at the annual meeting of the American Educational Research Association. New Orleans, 1973 (a).

Bloom, B. Mastery learning in varied cultural settings. Paper read at the annual meeting of the American Educational Research Association, New Orleans, 1973 (b).

Borg, W., Kelley, M., Langer, P., and Gall, M. *The MiniCourse: A Micro-Teaching Approach to Teacher Education.* Beverly Hills: MacMillan Educational Services, 1970.

Bowers, C. Accountability from a humanist point of view. *The Educational Forum,* 1971, *35,* 479–486.

Branan, J. Negative human interaction. *Journal of Counseling Psychology,* 1972, *19,* 81–82.

Brookover, W., Gigliotti, R., Henderson, R., and Schneider, J. Elementary school climates and school achievement. Paper presented at the annual meeting of the American Sociological Association, New York, 1973.

Brophy, J. Stability of teacher effectiveness. *American Educational Research Journal,* 1973, *10,* 245–252.

Brophy, J. Achievement correlates. In H. Walberg (ed.), *Evaluating Educational Performance: A Source Book of Methods, Instruments, and Examples.* Berkeley: McCutchan, 1974.

Brophy, J., Colosimo, J., and Carter, T. Applying a contingency management system to all students in each classroom in an entire elementary school. Research Report, The Research and Development Center for Teacher Education, The University of Texas at Austin, 1974.

Brophy, J. and Evertson, C. Low-inference observational coding measures and teacher effectiveness. *Catalog of Selected Documents in Psychology,* 1973 (a), *3,* 97.

Brophy, J. and Evertson, C. Appendix to first-year data of Texas Teacher Effectiveness Project: Complex relationships between teacher process variables and student outcome measures. *Catalog of Selected Documents in Psychology,* 1973 (b), *3,* 137.

Brophy, J., and Evertson, C. The Texas teacher effectiveness project. In T. Good (ed.), *Trends in the Study of the Classroom.* New York: APS Publications, 1974 (a).

Brophy, J. and Evertson, C. The Texas Teacher Effectiveness Project: Summary report. Research Report, The Research and Development Center for Teacher Education, The University of Texas at Austin, 1974 (b).

Brophy, J. and Evertson, C. The Texas Teacher Effectiveness Project: Presentation of nonlinear relationships and summary discussion. Research Report, The Research and Development Center for Teacher Education, The University of Texas at Austin, 1974 (c).

Brophy, J. and Good, T. *Teacher–Student Relationships: Causes and Consequences.* New York: Holt, Rinehart and Winston, 1974.

Brophy, J., Good, T., and Nedler, S. *Teaching in the Preschool.* New York: Harper & Row, 1975.

Broudy, H. Can research escape the dogma of behavioral objectives?, *School Review,* 1970, *79,* 43–56.

Burt, C. The genetic determination of differences in intelligence: A study of monozygotic twins reared together and apart. *British Journal of Psychology,* 1966, *57,* 137–153.

Bush, R. and Allen, D. Micro-teaching: Controlled practice in the training of teachers. Paper presented at the Santa Barbara Conference on Teacher Education, Ford Foundation, 1964.

Callahan, R. *Education and the Cult of Efficiency.* Chicago: The University of Chicago Press, 1962.

Carpenter, P. and Hall, G. *Case Studies in Educational Peformance Contracting.* Santa Monica, California: RAND Corporation, 1971.

Carroll, J. Problems of measurement related to the concept of learning for mastery. In J. Block (ed.), *Mastery Learning: Theory and Practice.* New York: Holt, Rinehart and Winston, 1971.

Case, D. A comparative study of fifth graders in a new middle school with fifth graders in elementary self-contained classrooms. *Dissertation Abstracts,* 1971, *32,* 86–A.

Cattell, R. Some theoretical issues in adult intelligence testing. *Psychological Bulletin,* 1941, *38,* 592.

Chall, J. *Learning to Read: The Great Debate.* New York: McGraw-Hill, 1967.

Chang, S. and Raths, J. The school's contribution to the cumulating deficit. *Journal of Educational Research,* 1971, *64,* 272–276.

Clark, B. *Educating the Expert Society.* San Francisco: Chandler, 1962.

Clifford, M. How learning and liking are related—a clue. *Journal of Educational Psychology,* 1973, *64,* 183–186.

Coleman, J. *The Adolescent Society.* Glencoe, Ill.: The Free Press, 1961.

Coleman, J. *et al. Equality of Educational Opportunity.* Washington, D.C.: Superintendent of Documents, U.S. Government Printing Office, 1966.

Coopersmith, S. *The Antecedents of Self-Esteem.* San Francisco: Freeman, 1967.

Coopersmith, S. and Feldman, R. Fostering a positive self-concept and high self-esteem in the classroom. In R. Coop and K. White (eds.), *Psychological Concepts in the Classroom.* New York: Harper & Row, 1974.

Corlis, C. and Weiss, J. Curiosity and openness: Emperical testing of a basic assumption. Paper presented at the annual meeting of the American Education Research Association, New Orleans, 1973.

Crier, R. and Carpenter, J. Experiences with a measure of self-concept in the Chicago schools. Paper read at the annual meeting of the American Education Research Association, New Orleans, 1973.

Cromack, T. Reinforcing and questioning behavior of teachers as a measure of teacher effects. Final Report. Project No. 2A 099, Grant No. OEG–1–71-0019(509). U.S. Department of Health, Education, and Welfare, Office of Education, 1973.

Davis, O. L., Jr. and Tinsley, D. Cognitive objectives revealed by classroom questions asked by social studies student teachers. *Peabody Journal of Education,* 1967, *45,* 21–26.

De Charms, R. *Personal Causation.* New York: Academic Press, 1968.

Deci, E. Work—who does not like it and why. *Psychology Today,* 1972, *6,* (No. 3), 57, 58, 92.

Della-Piana, G. and Endo, G. Reading research. In R. Travers (ed.), *Second Handbook of Research on Teaching.* Chicago: Rand McNally, 1973.

Dembo, M. and Jennings, L. Who is the "experienced" teacher? Paper presented at the annual meeting of the American Educational Research Association, New Orleans, 1973.

Dembo, M. and Wilson, D. Can poor readers read faster? *Phi Delta Kappan,* 1973, *54,* 626.

Duchastel, P. and Merrill, P. The effects of behavioral objectives on learning: A review of empirical studies. *Review of Educational Research,* 1973, *43,* 53–69.

Dunkin, M. and Biddle, B. *The Study of Teaching.* New York: Holt, Rinehart and Winston, 1974.

Dyer, H. Toward objective criteria of professional accountability in the schools of New York City. *Phi Delta Kappan,* 1970, *52,* 206–211.

Ebel, R. Criterion-referenced measurements: Limitations. *School Review,* 1971, *73,* 282–288.

Eisner, E. and Vallance, E. (eds.). *Conflicting Conceptions of Curriculum.* Berkeley: McCutchen, 1974.

Elam, S. The age of accountability dawns in Texarkana. *Phi Delta Kappan,* 1970, *51,* 509–514.

Ellison, A. The myth behind graded content. *Elementary School Journal,* 1972, *72,* 212–221.

Emmer, E., Good, T., and Oakland, T. Effects of feedback expectancy on choice of teaching styles. *Journal of Educational Psychology,* 1971, *62,* 451–455.

Emmerich, J. An experimental evaluation of new measures of cognitive and noncognitive performance for elementary school children. Paper read at the annual meeting of the American Education Research Association, New Orleans, 1973.

Evertson, C. and Brophy, J. High-inference behavioral ratings as correlates of teaching effectiveness. *Catalog of Selected Documents in Psychology,* 1973, *3,* 97.

Evertson, C. and Brophy, J. Texas teacher effectiveness project: Questionnaire and interview data. Research Report, The Research and Development Center for Teacher Education, The University of Texas at Austin, 1974.

Eysenck, H. *Race, Intelligence, and Education.* London: Temple Smith, 1971.

Featherstone, J. Measuring what schools achieve. *The New Republic.* December 15, 1973. Reprinted in *Phi Delta Kappan, 55,* 1974, 448–50.

Flanders, N. Teacher influence patterns and pupil achievement in the second, fourth, and sixth grade levels. ERIC, 1969, No. ED 051 123.

Flanders, N. *Analyzing Teacher Behavior.* Reading, Mass.: Addison-Wesley, 1970.

Fletcher, J. and Atkinson, R. Evaluation of the Stanford CAI program in initial reading. *Journal of Educational Psychology,* 1972, *63,* 597–602.

Fox, D. Expansion of the More Effective Schools program. New York: Center for Urban Education, 1967 (Evaluation of New York City Title I Educational Projects 1966–1967).

Franks, D., Wismer, S., Ritter, E., and Dillon, S. Peer labeling in Kansas City open schools. *Phi Delta Kappan, 1973, 55,* 75.

Fuller, F. and Manning, B. Self-confrontation review: A conceptualization for video playback in teacher education. *Review of Educational Research,* 1973, *43,* 469–528.

Gable, R. and Roberts, A. Affective and cognitive correlates of classroom achievement: Research for the counselor. Paper read at the annual meeting of the American Education Research Association, New Orleans, 1973.

Gage, N. Address appearing in Proceedings, *Research Résumé,* Burlingame, California: California Teachers Association, 1960, 16.

Gage, N. Paradigms of research on teaching. In N. Gage (ed.) *Handbook of Research on Teaching*. Chicago: Rand McNally, 1963.

Gage, N. *Teacher Effectiveness and Teacher Education: The Search for a Scientific Basis*. Palo Alto, Calif.: Pacific Books, 1972.

Gagné, R. Policy implications and future research: A response. In *Do Teachers Make a Difference?* Washington: U.S. Government Printing Office, Superintendent of Documents Catalog No. H E 5 258:58042, 1970.

Glass, G. Teacher effectiveness. In H. Walberg (ed.), *Evaluating Educational Performance: A Source Book of Methods, Instruments, and Examples*. Berkeley: McCutchan, 1974.

Good, T. and Brophy, J. *Looking in Classrooms*. New York: Harper & Row, 1973.

Good, T., and Brophy, J. Changing teacher and student behavior: An empirical investigation. *Journal of Educational Psychology,* 1974, *66,* 390–405.

Good, T., Coop, R., Dembo, M., Denton, J., and Limbacher, P. Teachers' view of accountability: an empirical survey. Technical Report No. 90, Center for Research in Social Behavior, University of Missouri, Columbia, 1974.

Good, T. and Grouws, D. Teacher rapport: Some stability data. Columbia, Missouri: Center for Research in Social Behavior, Technical Report No. 91, 1974.

Goodlad, J. The nongraded school. *National Elementary Principal,* 1970, *50,* 24–29.

Goodman, S. *The Assessment of Social Quality*. Albany: State Education Department of New York, 1959.

Gordon, C. *The Social System of the High School*. Glencoe, Ill.: The Free Press, 1957.

Gordon, I. and Jester, E. Techniques of observing teaching in early childhood. In R. Travers (ed.), *Second Handbook of Research on Teaching*. Chicago: Rand McNally, 1973.

Goslin, D. *The School in Contemporary Society*. Glenview, Ill.: Scott, Foresman, 1965.

Green, E. The business of education. *Nation's Schools,* 1970, *86,* 40–45.

Green, R., Hoffman, L., Morse, R., and Morgan, R. The educational status of children during the first year of school following four years of little or no schooling. East Lansing, Mich.: College of Education, Michigan State University, 1966.

Gronlund, N. *Preparing Criterion-Referenced Tests for Classroom Instruction*. New York: Macmillan, 1973.

Gubser, M. Accountability as a smoke screen for political indoctrination in Arizona. *Phi Delta Kappan,* 1973, *53,* 64–65.

Hamachek, D. Effects of early school failure on self-image development and implications for school counselors. Paper presented at the annual meeting of the American Educational Research Association, Chicago, 1972.

Harris, M. Modeling and flexible problem-solving. Paper presented at the annual meeting of the American Psychological Association, Montreal, 1973.

Hawthorne, P. Legislation by the states: Accountability and assessment in education. Madison, Wisconsin State Educational Accountability Repository, 1973.

Hess, R. Class and ethnic influences upon socialization. In P. Mussen (ed.), *Carmichael's Manual of Child Psychology*, 3d Ed., vol. 2. New York: Wiley, 1970.

Holt, J. *How Children Fail*. New York: Dell, 1964.

Homme, L. *How to Use Contingency Contracting in the Classroom*. Champaign, Ill.: Research Press, 1970.

Hoover, M., Politzer, R., and Brown, D. An experiment in teaching reading to bi-dialectical kindergarten children. Research and Development Memorandum No. 102, Stanford Center for Research and Development in Teaching, Stanford University, 1973.

Illich, I. *Deschooling Society*. New York: Harper and Row, 1970.

Jackson, P. *Life in Classrooms*. New York: Holt, 1968.

Jackson, P. After apple picking. *Harvard Educational Review*, 1973, *43*, 51–60.

Jackson, P. and Getzels, J. Psychological health and classroom functioning: A study of dissatisfaction in the school among adolescents. *Journal of Educational Psychology*, 1959, *50*, 295–300.

Janssen, P. Education vouchers. *American Education*, 1970, *6*, 9–11.

Jeffreys, J. An investigation of the effects of innovative educational practices on pupil centeredness of observed behaviors and on learner outcome variables. *Dissertation Abstracts*, 1971, 31, 5766-A.

Jencks, C. Education vouchers. In F. Sciara and R. Jantz (eds.), *Accountability in American Education*. Boston: Allyn and Bacon, 1972.

Jencks, C. et al. *Inequality: A Reassessment of the Effect of Family and Schooling in America*. New York: Basic Books, 1972.

Jensen, A. How much can we boost IQ and scholastic achievement? *Harvard Educational Review*, 1969, *39*, 1–123.

Jensen, A. *Educability and Group Differences*. New York: Harper & Row, 1973.

Karnes, M. Investigations of classroom and at-home interventions: Research and development program on preschool disadvantaged children. Final Report, Bureau No. 5–1181, Bureau of Research, Office of Education, U.S. Department of Health, Education and Welfare, 1969.

Katz, L. Developmental stages of preschool teachers. Urbana, Ill.: ERIC Clearinghouse on Early Childhood Education, 1972.

Kaufman, R. A system approach to accountability in education. In F. Sciara and R. Jantz (eds.), *Accountability in American Education*. Boston: Allyn and Bacon, 1972.

Keele, R. A comparison of the effectiveness of remediation of nonreaders by trained Mexican-American aides and certified teachers. Paper presented at the annual meeting of the American Educational Research Association, New Orleans, 1973.

Kifer, E. The effects of school achievement on the affective traits of the learner. A paper read at the annual meeting of the American Educational Research Association, New Orleans, 1973.

Klaus, R. and Gray, S. The early training project for disadvantaged children: A report after five years. *Monographs of the Society for Research in Child Development*, 1968, *33*, No. 4.

Klausmeier, H., Sorenson, J., and Ghatala, E. Individually guided motivation: developing self-direction and prosocial behaviors. *Elementary School Journal*, 1971, a *71*, 339–350.

Klausmeier, H., Sorenson, J., and Quilling, M. Instructional programming for the individual pupil in the multiunit elementary school. *Elementary School Journal*, 1971, b *72*, 88–101.

Kleinfeld, J. Instructional style and the intellectual performance of Indian and Eskimo students. Final Report, Project No. 1–J–027, Office of Education, U.S. Department of Health, Education, and Welfare, 1972.

Kohler, P. A comparison of open and traditional education: Conditions that promote self-concept. A paper read at the annual meeting of the American Educational Research Association, New Orleans, 1973.

Kounin, J. *Discipline and Group Management in Classrooms*. New York: Holt, Rinehart and Winston, 1970.

Kozol, J. *Death at an Early Age*. Boston: Houghton Mifflin, 1967.

Lawrence, G. Analysis of teacher-made tests in social studies according to the *Taxonomy of Educational Objectives*. *CLARMONTIANA* Collection, 1963.

Lipson, J. IPI Math—an example of what's right and wrong with individualized modular programs. *Learning*, March, 1974, 60–61.

Lucas, C. A teapot in the tempest. *Teachers College Record*, 1972, *73*, 577–583.

Lundgren, U. *Frame Factors and the Teaching Process: A Contribution to Curriculum Theory and Theory on Teaching*. Stockholm: Almqvist and Wiksell, 1972.

McAvoy, R., Kalin, M., and Franklin, T. An analysis of personality variables in individual modes of instruction. A paper read at the annual meeting of the American Educational Research Association, New Orleans, 1973.

McCall, R., Applebaum, M., and Hogarty, P. Developmental changes in mental performance. *Monographs of the Society for Research in Child Development,* No. 3 (Serial No. 150), 1973.

McCandless, B. and Evans, E. *Children and Youth: Psychosocial Development.* Hinsdale, Ill.: Dryden Press, 1973.

McDill, E., Meyers, E., and Rigsby, L. Institutional effects on the academic behavior of high school students. *Sociology of Education,* 1967, *40,* 181–199.

McLaughlin, W. Continuous pupil progress in the nongraded school: Hope or hoax? *Elementary School Journal,* 1970, *7,* 269–271.

Maeroff, G. The traditional school: keep it among the alternatives. *Phi Delta Kappan,* 1974, *54,* 473–475.

Mager, R. *Preparing Instructional Objectives.* Palo Alto, California: Fearon, 1962.

Malpuss, L. Some relationships between students' perception of school and their achievement. *Journal of Educational Psychology,* 1957, *44,* 475–482.

Marland, S. Accountability in education. *Teachers College Record,* 1972, *73,* 339–345.

Martin, M. Equal opportunity in the classroom ESEA, Title III: Session A Report. Los Angeles: County Superintendent of Schools, Division of Compensatory and Intergroup Programs, 1973.

Martin, R. and Keller, A. Teacher awareness of classroom dyadic interactions. A paper presented at the 1974 annual meeting of the American Educational Research Association, Chicago, 1974.

Mehrens, W. National assessment of educational progress. *Childhood Education,* 1970, *46,* 422–425.

Mehrens, W. and Lehmann, I. *Measurement and Evaluation in Education and Psychology.* New York: Holt, Rinehart and Winston, 1973.

Miles, M. *Innovation in Education.* New York: Teachers College, Columbia University, 1964.

Miller, J. Not performance contracting but the OEO experiment was a failure. *Phil Delta Kappan,* 1973, *54,* 394–396.

Moody, W. and Bausell, R. The effect of teacher experience on student achievement, transfer and retention. Paper presented at the annual meeting of the American Educational Research Association, New Orleans, 1971.

Moody, A. and Bausell, R. The effect of relevant teaching practice on the elicitation of student achievement. Paper presented at the annual meeting of the American Educational Research Association, New Orleans, 1973.

Morrison, A. and McIntyre, D. *Teachers and Teaching.* Baltimore: Penguin Books, 1969.

Mosteller, F. and Moynihan, D. *On Equality of Educational Opportunity.* New York: Random House, 1972.

Myers, R. A comparison of the perceptions of elementary school children in an open area and self-contained classrooms in British Columbia. *Journal of Research and Development in Education,* 1971, *4,* 100–106.

Nelson, R. An analysis of the relationships of the multiunit school organizational structure and individually guided education to the learning climate of pupils. Paper read at the annual meeting of the American Educational Research Association, New Orleans, 1973.

Nelson, R. The effect of different types of teaching methods and verbal feedback on the performance of beginning readers. Unpublished Ph.D. Dissertation, State University of New York at Stony Brook, 1973.

Newton, D. and Hall, P. A social psychological view of the open classroom. Paper read at the annual meeting of the Midwest Sociological Society. Omaha, Nebraska, 1974.

Owen, S., Froman, R., and Calchera, D. Effects of open education on selected cognitive and effective measures. Paper presented at the annual meeting of the American Educational Research Association, Chicago, 1974.

Pace, R. *College and University Environment Scales.* Technical Manual, New Jersey, Princeton, New Jersey Educational Testing Service, 1963.

Pavan, B. Good news: Research on the nongraded elementary school. *Elementary School Journal,* 1973, *73,* 333–342.

Peck, R. and Veldman, D. Personal characteristics associated with effective teaching. Paper presented at the annual meeting of the American Educational Research Association, New Orleans, 1973.

Pfeiffer, I. and Davis, O. L., Jr. Teacher-made examinations: What kinds of thinking do they demand? *Bulletin of the National Association of Secondary School Principals,* 1965, *49,* 1–10.

Pidgeon, D. *Expectation and Pupil Performance.* Slough, Great Britain: NFER, 1970.

Popham, W. Teaching skill under scrutiny. *Phi Delta Kappan,* 1971, *52,* 599–602.

Popham, W. Found: A practical procedure to appraise teacher achievement in the classroom. In A. Ornstein (ed.), *Accountability for Teachers and School Administrators.* Belmont, Calif.: Fearon Publishers, 1973.

Potter, D., Nalin, P., and Lewandowski, A. The relation of student achievement and student ratings of teachers. A paper read at the annual meeting of the American Educational Research Association, New Orleans, 1973.

Purkey, W., Groves, W., and Zellner, M. Self-perceptions of pupils in an experimental elementary school. *Elementary School Journal,* 1970, *71,* 166–171.

Quirk, T. The student in Project PLAN: A functioning program of individualized education. *Elementary School Journal,* 1971, *71,* 42–54.

Ragosta, M., Soar, R., Soar, R. and Stebbins, L. Sign vs. category: Two instruments for observing levels of thinking. Paper presented at the annual meeting of the American Educational Research Association, 1971.

Rickover, H. *American Education: A National Failure.* New York: Dutton, 1963.

Rist, R. Student social class and teacher expectations: The self-fulfilling prophecy in ghetto education. *Harvard Educational Review,* 1970, *40,* 411–451.

Rogers, V. and Davis, O. L., Jr. Varying the cognitive level of classroom questions: An analysis of student teachers' questions and pupil achievement in elementary social studies. Paper presented at the annual meeting of the American Educational Research Association, Minneapolis, 1970.

Rollins, H., McCandless, B., Thompson, M., and Brassell, W. Project success environment: An extended application of contingency management in inner-city schools. *Journal of Educational Psychology,* 1974, *66,* 167–178.

Rookey, T. IPI and the affective domain. In C. Burkett (ed.), *Research for Better Teaching,* Vol. IV. Philadelphia: Pennsylvania Association for Teacher Educators, 1973.

Rosenshine, B. *Teaching Behaviours and Student Achievement.* London: NFER, 1971.

Rosenshine, B. Teacher behavior and student attitudes revisited. *Journal of Educational Psychology,* 1973, *65,* 177–180.

Rosenshine, B. and Furst, N. The use of direct observation to study teaching. In R. Travers (ed.), *Second Handbook of Research on Teaching.* Chicago: Rand McNally, 1973.

Rothkopf, E. Some theoretical and experimental approaches to problems in written instruction. In J. D. Krumboltz (ed.), *Learning and the Educational Process.* Chicago: Rand McNally, 1965.

Rothkopf, E. and Bisbicos, E. Selective facilitative effects of interspersed questions on learning from written materials. *Journal of Educational Psychology,* 1967, *58,* 56–61.

Rowe, M. Wait-time and rewards as instructional variables: Their influence on language, logic and fate control. Paper presented at the annual meeting of the National Association for Research in Science Teaching, 1972.

Rubin, L. A study on teaching style. Paper presented at the annual meeting of the American Educational Research Association, 1971.

Sadker, D. Dimensions of the elementary school environment: A factor analysis study. *The Journal of Educational Research,* 1973, *66,* 441–442, 465.

Sadker, D., Sadker, M., and Cooper, J. Elementary school through children's eyes. *Elementary School Journal,* 1973, *73,* 289–295.

St. John, N. Thirty-six teachers: Their characteristics, and outcomes for black and white pupils. *American Educational Research Journal,* 1971, *8,* 635–648.

Sanders, J. Retention effects of adjunct questions in written and aural discourse. *Journal of Educational Psychology,* 1973, *65,* 181–186.

Scannell, D. and Steelwagon, W. Teaching and testing for degree of understanding. *California Journal of Instructional Improvement,* 1960, *3* (1).

Schmidt, W. Socioeconomic status, schooling, intelligence, and scholastic progress in a community in which education is not yet compulsory. *Paedogogica Europa,* 1966, *2,* 275–286.

Schockley, W. Models, mathematics, and the moral obligation to diagnose the origin of Negro IQ deficits. *Review of Educational Research,* 1971, *41,* 369–377.

Sciara, F. and Jantz, R. *Accountability in American Education.* Boston: Allyn and Bacon, 1972.

Sears, P., *et al.* Effective reinforcement for achievement behavior in disadvantaged children: The first year. Technical Report No. 30, Stanford Center for Research and Development in Teaching, Stanford University, 1972.

Sears, R. Relation of early socialization experiences to self concepts and gender role in middle childhood. *Child Development,* 1970, *41,* 267–290.

Shimron, J. Learning activities in individually prescribed instruction. Paper read at the annual meeting of the American Educational Research Association, New Orleans, 1973.

Silberman, C. *Crisis in the Classroom.* New York: Random House, 1970.

Simons, H. Behavioral objectives: A false hope for education. *The Elementary School Journal,* 1973, *73,* 173–181.

Soar, R. Teacher behavior related to pupil growth. *International Review of Education,* 1972, *18,* 508–526.

Soar, R. and Soar, R. Classroom behavior, pupil characteristics, and pupil growth for the school year and the summer. Research Report, Institute for Development of Human Resources, College of Education, University of Florida, 1973.

Soares, L., Soares, A., and Pumerantz, P. Self perception of middle school children. *Elementary School Journal,* 1973, *73,* 381–388.

Solomon, D. and Oberlander, M. Locus of control in the classroom. In R. Coop and K. White (eds.), *Psychological Concepts in the Classroom.* New York: Harper & Row, 1974.

Spaulding, R. The Durham education improvements programs. In D. Brison and J. Hill (eds.), *Psychology and early childhood education.* Toronto: The Ontario Institute for Studies in Education, Monograph Series No. 4, 1968.

Stake, R. Testing hazards in performance contracting. *Phi Delta Kappan,* 1971, *52,* 583–588.

Stallings, J. Differences in the classroom experience of Follow Through and non-Follow Through children in the relationship of educational processes to child outcomes on test scores. Paper presented at the annual meeting of the American Psychological Association, 1972.

Stephens, J. *The Process of Schooling.* New York: Holt, Rinehart and Winston, 1967.

Stucker, J. and Hall, G. *The Performance Contracting Concept in Education.* Report R–669/1–HEW prepared for the U.S. Department of Health, Education, and Welfare. Santa Monica, California: RAND, 1971.

Tenenbaum, S. Uncontrolled expressions of children's attitudes toward school. *Elementary School Journal,* 1940, *40,* 670–678.

Thompson, D. Evaluation of an individualized instructional program. *Elementary School Journal,* 1973, *73,* 213–221.

Thompson, M., Brassell, W., Persons, S., Tucker, R., and Rollins, H. Contingency management in the schools: How often and how well does it work? *American Educational Research Journal,* 1974, *11,* 19–28.

Torshen, K. The relationship of evaluation of students' cognitive performance to their self concept-assessment of mental health status. Paper read at the annual meeting of the American Education Research Association, New Orleans, 1973.

Traub, R., Weiss, J., Fisher, C., and Musella, D. Closure on openness in education. A symposium presented at the annual meeting of the American Research Association, New Orleans, 1973.

Travers, R. (ed.). *Second Handbook of Research on Teaching.* Chicago, Rand McNally, 1973.

Trent, J. and Cohen, A. Research on teaching in higher education. In R. Travers (ed.), *Second Handbook of Research on Teaching.* Chicago: Rand McNally, 1973.

Tschechtelin, M., Hipskind, M., and Remmers, H. Measuring the attitude of elementary school children toward their teachers. *Journal of Educational Psychology,* 1940, *31,* 195–203.

Tuckman, B., Cochran, D., and Travers, E. Evaluating the open classroom. Paper read at the annual meeting of the American Education Research Association, New Orleans, 1973.

Turner, R. and Thompson, R. Relationships between college student ratings of instructors and residual learning. Paper presented at the annual meeting of the American Educational Research Association, Chicago, 1974.

Tuta, K. and Baker, G. Self-concept of the disadvantaged child and its modification through compensatory nursery school experience. Paper presented at the annual meeting of the American Educational Research Association, New Orleans, 1973.

Veldman, D. and Brophy, J. Measuring teacher effects on pupil achievement. *Journal of Educational Psychology*, 1974, *66*, 319–324.

Vernon, P. *Intelligence and Cultural Environment*. London: Methuen, 1969.

Walberg, H. Optimization reconsidered. In H. Walberg (ed.), *Evaluating Educational Performance: A Source Book of Methods, Instruments, and Examples*. Berkeley: McCutchan, 1974.

Walker, A. The measurement of classroom environment. Final Report, Project No. O B034, Grant No. OEG–2–700030(509). U.S. Department of Education, Bureau of Research, 1971.

Walker, D. & Schaffarzick, J. Comparing curricula. *Review of Educational Research*, 1974, *44*, 83–111.

Warner, J. A comparison of students' and teachers' performances in an open area facility and in self-contained classrooms. *Dissertation Abstracts*, 1971, 31, 3851-A.

Wattenberg, W. and Clifford, C. Relation of self-concept to beginning achievement in reading. *Child Development*, 1964, *35*, 461–467.

Weikart, D. Relationship of curriculum, teaching, and learning in preschool education. Paper presented at the Hyman Blumberg Memorial Symposium on Research in Early Childhood Education, 1971.

Weiss, J. Openness and student outcomes: Some results. Paper presented at the annual meeting of the American Educational Research Association, New Orleans, 1973.

Welch, W. and Walberg, H. A national experiment in curriculum evaluation. *American Educational Research Journal*, 1972, *9*, 373–383.

Wiley, D. and Harnischfeger, A. Explosion of a myth: Quantity of schooling and exposure to instruction, major educational vehicles. *Educational Researcher*, 1974, *3*, 7–12.

Wilson, A. and Curtis, W. The states' mandate-performance-based teacher education. *Phi Delta Kappan*, 1973, *55*, 76–77.

Index

needed, 36–52
in open schools, 182–188
relating teacher behavior to student
outcome, 58–61
retrenchment of funds for, 3
teacher effectiveness, 12–14, 54–85
previous problems in, 28–53
on teaching, 8–9
Responses
interchangeable, 73
Rickover, H., 11, 253
Rigsby, L., 79, 251
Rist, R., 90, 253
Ritter, E., 247
Roberts, A., 199, 247
Rogers, C., 73
Rogers, V., 149, 253
Rollins, H., 71, 253, 255
Rookey, T., 69, 253
Rosenshine, B., 32, 58–61, 64, 67, 78,
79, 203, 253
Rothkopf, E., 148, 253
Rowe, M., 64, 253
Rubin, L., 50, 253

S

Sadker, D., 197, 213, 214, 253, 254
Sadker, M., 197, 213, 214, 254
St. John, N., 72, 253
Sampling
reliability and validity of, 49
teachers used in, 44–46
time, 50
units used for, 50–52
San Francisco School District, 9, 108
Sanders, J., 148, 254
Scannell, D., 149, 254
Schaffarzick, J., 67, 256
Schmidt, W., 65, 254
Schneider, J., 65, 244
Schockley, W., 16, 254
School Sentiment Index, 217
Scholastic Aptitude Tests, 100
Schools
criticism and, 11–27, 194, 220
decision-making in, 94–98

demands on, 87, 210
differences among, 2, 6–7
effectiveness of, 1–10, 19–25
goals of, 5
individualized, 157
influence on affective variables, 202
inhumaneness of, 196–198
open (see Open education)
pupil achievement and, 21–23
Sciara, F., 134, 137, 254
Scores, adjusted versus raw
as criteria for comparison in studies,
41–42
Sears, P., 70, 254
Sears, R., 201, 254
Secondary level studies, 79–80
Self-concept scores, 190–191, 200
Settings
naturalistic
need for in research, 37
Shimron, J., 181–182, 254
Silberman, C., 6, 254
Simons, H., 147, 254
Situational testing, 123–125
Skinner, B., 71
Soar, R., 74, 75, 253, 254
Soar, Robert, 48, 74, 75, 76, 77, 80,
203, 253, 254
Soares, A., 254
Soares, L., 254
Social reform
schools and, 94
Socialization
pupil
as school task, 88–89
Socioeconomic status
schools and, 4–5, 7
Solomon, D., 254
Sorenson, J., 250
Spaulding, R., 63, 254
Stake, R., 112, 255
Stallings, J., 29, 62, 255
Standardized tests, 143–146
State assessment, 125–140
Stebbins, L., 74, 253
Steelwagon, W., 149, 254
Steering groups, 61

About the Authors

Thomas L. Good was born in Owensboro, Kentucky in 1943. Educated at the University of Illinois (A.B. in Political Science) and Indiana University (Ph.D. in Educational Psychology), he is presently Professor of Education in the Department of Curriculum and Instruction and a Research Scientist at the Center for Research in Social Behavior at the University of Missouri-Columbia. Formerly, he was a faculty member in the Department of Educational Psychology at the University of Texas (Austin), a Research Scientist at the Research and Development Center for Teacher Education, and a Staff Development Coordinator for the Early Childhood Education Program at the Southwestern Educational Development Laboratory in Austin, Texas. His professional interests include the measurement of process behavior in educational settings, early learning research, and the general field of teacher behavior research and teacher education. He has co-authored a number of books concerned with education: *Problem Situations in Teaching* (Harper & Row, 1971); *Looking in Classrooms* (Harper & Row, 1973); *Student-Teacher Relationships: Causes and Consequences* (Holt, Rinehart and Winston, 1974); *Teaching in the Preschool* (Harper & Row, 1975); and has two books in preparation (an edited book of readings entitled *Classroom Observation* and an undergraduate Educational Psychology text for Holt). His personal interests include: travel; swimming; handball; tennis; and reading. Wisely, he married Suzi Fischer (his undergraduate sweetheart at the

269

University of Illinois) and they live happily with their two children, Heather and Jeff.

Bruce J. Biddle was born in 1928 and spent most of his childhood in Milwaukee. Educated at Antioch College (A.B. in mathematics), North Carolina, and Michigan (Ph.D. in social psychology), he is presently Professor of Psychology and of Sociology and Director of the Center for Research in Social Behavior at the University of Missouri-Columbia. He has a wide range of interests in life including music, electronics, tennis, standard poodles, flying, and Australia. He is married (to a sociologist) and is blessed with three, teen-age children. He is the co-author or co-editor of several other books concerned with education: *Contemporary Research on Teacher Effectiveness* (Holt, Rinehart and Winston, 1964); *The New Media: Their Impact on Education and Society* (Aldine, 1966); *Realities of Teaching: Explorations with Videotape* (Holt, Rinehart and Winston, 1970); and *The Study of Teaching* (Holt, Rinehart and Winston, 1974). He also publishes in the field of role theory: *Role Theory: Concepts and Research* (Wiley, 1966); *Role Theory: A Brief Introduction* (Dryden, 1975); *Roles: Expectations, Identities, and Behaviors* (Dryden, 1975). At present, his major time is spent in coping with the escalating burdens of administrative madness within his university, but when not so engaged he manages to teach an occasional course in social psychology, advise students, and conduct research on teaching, educational roles, role theory, and alcohol use among adolescents.

Dr. Jere E. Brophy is Associate Professor Educational Psychology at the University of Texas at Austin, as well as Principal Investigator of the Texas Teacher Effectiveness Project at the Research and Development Center for Teacher Education. He has co-authored *Looking in Classrooms* and *Teacher-Student Relationships: Causes and Consequences* with Dr. Good, and *Teaching in the Preschool* with Dr. Good and Dr. Shari E. Nedler of the University of Colorado at Denver. He also is preparing a child development textbook, an educational psychology textbook (co-authored with Dr. Good), and a book detailing the findings of his research on teacher effectiveness (co-authored with Dr. Carolyn M. Evertson).

Dr. Brophy's research interests focus on child development, especially the adult-child relationships involved in socialization, and on educational psychology, particularly teacher-child interaction in the classroom. In the past he has published research findings on such topics as the relationships between maternal socialization behavior and cognitive development in children, teacher expectations and the self-fulfilling prophecy effect, and the relationships among student individual differences, teacher expectations and attitudes, teacher-student interaction, and student outcomes. Presently he is conducting both large scale field observational studies as well as controlled experiments on effective teaching, attempting to identify teacher behavior which is effective in enabling teachers to accomplish both cognitive and affective goals for their students.